CHILDHOOD AND FOLKLORE:
A PSYCHOANALYTIC STUDY OF
APACHE PERSONALITY

by

L. Bryce Boyer, M.D.

The Library of Psychological Anthropology, *Publishers*

NEW YORK, NEW YORK, U.S.A.

CHILDHOOD AND FOLKLORE: A PSYCHOANALYTIC
STUDY OF APACHE PERSONALITY

Library of Congress Cataloging in Publication Data

Main entry under title:

Childhood and Folklore.

  Bibliography: p.
  Includes index.
  1. Apache Indians—Psychology. 2. Apache Indians—Legends. 3. Indians of North
America—New Mexico—Psychology. 4. Indians of North America—New
Mexico—Legends. 5. Psychoanalysis and folklore. 6. Folk-lore and children. I. Title.
E99.A6B83   301.2'1   79-15051

ISBN: 914434-09-8

To

My Wife and Colleague, Ruth M. Boyer,

and in Memory of

My Father

and My Friends

Dan Nicholas and Eric Tortilla

ACKNOWLEDGMENTS

It is with a deep sense of personal satisfaction that I can finally express publicly my heartfelt gratitude to some of the many people who have contributed to the experiences and personal development which have led to the writing of this book.

First I want to thank my Apache informants, living and dead, who have incalculably enriched my life. I regret that I can name only those who are now departed but I am pleased that I can belatedly recognize the contributions of my friends Willie Comanche, Sarah and Samuel Kenoi, Sr., Mary Noche, Dan Nicholas, John Tahnito, Bertha and Eric Tortilla and Anthony Treas. I wish to express my gratitude also to Stanley and Corinne McNatt, "Indian traders," and their sons James and Terry, who have provided invaluable information and contributed greatly to my enjoyment of field work.

I want to express my abiding appreciation to some of the colleagues who over the many years have collaborated with me in the field and sustained me emotionally. Primary among them is my wife, Ruth M. Boyer. Her personal support has been continual and her amazingly perceptive field observations and understandings of their meanings have supplied viewpoints without which my own considerations would have been relatively shallow. I am grateful also especially to Harry W. Basehart, Richard Day, George DeVos, Arthur E. Hippler and the late Bruno Klopfer for their having broadened my understanding of anthropological and psychological theories and techniques and widened my capacity to synthesize cross-cultural theories and trans-disciplinary data and speculations, enabling me to resolve some apparent paradoxes and rectifying methodological and theoretical errors.

Additionally, I want to thank the members of the Research Committee of the San Francisco Psychoanalytic Society which I co-chaired during the years 1967-1973, the participants of the ongoing American

Psychoanalytic Association Colloquium on Psychoanalytic Questions and Methods in Anthropological Fieldwork which has met annually since 1966 and which I have had the honor to chair since 1970, co-members of the Asociación Psicoanalítica Mexicana who have reviewed the research data critically since the inception of my field work and lastly a private discussion group with whom I have met for a shorter time. I want to name from those groups especially Edward C. Adams, Gene Borowitz, Jean L. Briggs, Fernando Cesarman, Fernando Díaz Infante, Daniel M. A. Freeman, Michael Harner, Robert F. Holter, Joseph M. Lubart, Werner Muensterberger, Robert F. Murphy, Paul Parin, José Remus Araico, Charles Sarnoff and Earl J. Simburg. I am indebted to other friends and colleagues as well, particularly George Devereux, Dieter Eicke and Angel Garma.

Finally, Alan Dundes has meticulously reviewed not only various of my earlier faltering contributions to folklore and taught me much of what I know about folkloristics but carefully edited a first draft of this book, supplying new information and correcting methodological mistakes. Obviously, however, its remaining flaws are my own responsibility.

Foreword

Among folklorists, it is a commonplace that psychiatrists, especially psychoanalysts, who write about folklore invariably suffer from two fatal flaws. The first is that they know little or nothing about the formal discipline of Folkloristics. Typically, they analyze (or *re*-analyze) a classical Greek myth (Oedipus is a particular favorite!), a narrative from the Bible, or a well-known European folktale, e.g., from the Grimm canon, with little or no reference to the massive comparative data and scholarship which has already been devoted to such materials. The second 'flaw' is the failure to carry out their own fieldwork. The folklore they analyze is almost always from written or literary sources. That is, the data examined has been gathered by others. Since the study of folklore is more or less only an intellectual hobby for such psychiatrists, it is, of course, understandable that they are disinclined to spend the long months in the field necessary for eliciting folklore in cultural context.

Bryce Boyer is an exception. He is a psychoanalyst who has taken great pains to familiarize himself with the field of folklore and who even more impressively has spent approximately twenty years in ongoing albeit intermittent fieldwork among the Mescalero Apache, greatly helped by his equally knowledgeable wife, anthropologist Ruth M. Boyer. Frankly, I know of few professional anthropologists or folklorists who have spent as much time in the field as have the Boyers. The fascinating data gathered and the psychoanalytic treatment of that data are probably unique in the annals of anthropological research. One can, to be sure, point to a few precursors. Geza Roheim who was originally trained as a folklorist in Hungary eventually turned to psychoanalysis and undertook considerable anthropological fieldwork in aboriginal Australia (Dadoun 1972). Melville Jacobs, a student of Franz Boas, utilized psychoanalytic theory in his important studies of Clackamas Chinook narratives (1959). But the extensive field experience of the Boyers, coupled with their psychoanalytic sophistication, could not easily be matched among contemporary anthropologists and folklorists.

Childhood and Folklore will surely have an impact upon both folkloristics and psychiatry. It should help demonstrate to folklorists that there is more to folklore than merely transcribing tales and noting parallel narratives among neighboring peoples. The subtle but crucial relationship between the personality of the raconteur and the content of the tale he tells must be better understood if the field of folkloristics is ever to advance. In this respect, Bryce Boyer's discussion of relationship of Better to See You's life story to the version she tells of "The Man Who Turned Into a Snake" is remarkable. It is one thing to assert that folklore presents a screen upon which individual anxieties may be played out and quite another to document it—especially in a nonEuropean-American setting.

The effect of *Childhood and Folklore* upon psychiatrists might be to encourage others to engage in similar investigations among other nonEuro-American cultures. Freudian theory (as opposed to Jungian theory) can indeed be reconciled with cultural relativism. It is the potential isomorphic relationship between infantile situations in a given culture and the adult projective systems (including folklore) in that same culture which may be found crossculturally rather than specifices of content. "The Man Who Turned Into a Snake" is not a narrative related in the Indo-European and Semitic world just as the evil eye, so common in the Indo-European and Semitic world is not found in aboriginal North and South America, subSaharan Africa, Oceania, etc. I know of no single item of folklore absent from subSaharan Africa. But that does not reduce the potential utility of applying culturally relativized psychoanalytic theory to folklore materials all over the world. To the extent that folklore is projective in nature (Dundes 1976), it is perfectly appropriate—in fact, it is essential that psychoanalytic theory be employed to illuminate and elucidate the unconscious content of folklore. But we need more intensive investigations of the sort carried out by Bryce Boyer.

If one examines the fourteen hefty volumes of Grinstein's enormously valuable *Index of Psychoanalytic Writings* (1956-1975), one can easily see that American Indian myths and folktales have not received much critical attention from psychoanalysts. General overviews of folklore and psychoanalysis (La Barre 1948; Carvalho-Neto 1972) as well as specific psychoanalytic studies of Saint Nicholas (de Groot 1965), Euro-American dirty jokes (Legman 1968, 1975), or the hero pattern and the life of Jesus (Dundes 1978) continue the longstanding traditional emphasis on the materials of Western cultures. In contrast, Bryce Boyer's *Childhood and Folklore* represents a signficant piece of research, the culmination of many years of fieldwork and thought, which departs from the Euro-American arena to explore in depth the psychological world of the Apache. It is an exciting book, full of rich data and keen insights. No doubt the majority of folklorists, threatened as they are by the application of psychoanalytic theory, will remain skeptical of some of the interpretations offered by Bryce Boyer. Sometimes the discussions of symbolism in Apache folklore do not appear to be culturally relative so much as possible ethnocentric extensions of Euro-American symbolic formulas. For example, is the symbolic significance of stone as reported from clinical material from Euro-American patients really analogous to the symbolic significance of stone in Chiricahua Apache culture? But even skeptics cannot fail to be impressed by the detailed documentation provided in terms of both texts and informants. Bryce Boyer's goal throughout the book consists of trying to better understand Apache culture—in this case through the mirror of Apache folklore. The reader may judge for him or herself as to how well this laudable goal has been achieved.

Alan Dundes
University of California, Berkeley

Carvalho-Neto, Paulo de
    1972 *Folklore and Psychoanalysis.* Coral Gables: University of Miami Press.
Dadoun, Roger
    1972 *Geza Roheim.* Paris: Payot.
Dundes, Alan
    1976 Projection in Folklore: A Plea for Psychoanalytic Semiotics. *Modern Language Notes* 91:1500-1533.
    1978 The Hero Pattern and the life of Jesus. *Essays in Folkloristics.* New Delhi: Manohar Book Service. Pp. 223-270.
Grinstein, Alexander
    1956-1975 *The Index of Psychoanalytic Writings.* 14 vols. New York: International Universities Press.
Groot, Adriaan D. de
    1965 *Saint Nicholas:* A Psychoanalytic Study of his History and Myth. The Hague: Mouton.
Jacobs, Melville
    1959 *The Content and Style of an Oral Literature.* Chicago: University of Chicago Press.
La Barre, Weston
    1948 Folklore and Psychology. *Journal of American Folklore* 61:382-390.
Legman, G.
    1968 *Rationale of the Dirty Joke:* An Analysis of Sexual Humor. New York: Grove Press.
    1975 *No Laughing Matter:* Rationale of the Dirty Joke, 2nd Series. New York: Breaking Point, Inc.

*

page viii, lines 16 and 17 should read: "I know of no single item of folklore which is universal—even the widespread myth of the flood appears to be largely absent from subSaharan Africa."

TABLE OF CONTENTS

MESCALERO MAIDEN DANCING IN THE BIG TEPEE
DURING THE PUBERTY CEREMONY
July 1961
(Courtesy Barbara Funkhouser, El Paso, Texas)

I

Introduction

People have always been fascinated by folklore. In Western cultures, children delight in fairy tales and imaginative stories, while adolescents and adults are particularly intrigued by legends and myths and their extensions into rites and religions. In other cultures, especially those that are or were aboriginally nonliterate, the distinctions among the many varieties of folklore are often less clear and much of the oral literature appeals to and is known by individuals of every age. Until recently, the reasons for the intense interest people have in folklore remained largely conjectural. Today we know that from the standpoint of society, folklore assists children and youths in their quest to become, and adults to remain, acceptable and useful group members. From that of the individual, folklore helps alleviate unresolved psychological conflicts which, in very large part, have their roots in childhood, and it may play a significant role in character development. It has become obvious that the influence of folklore on and its uses by groups and individuals is greater among nonliterate peoples, where enculturation depends more on oral communications from adults to children than is true in literate societies.

Knowledge concerning the social and individual functions of folklore and the psychological messages it conveys symbolically did not come from studies of traditional folklorists. Those folklorists were and in the main continue to be interested in linguistic and historical roots of oral literature and in the collection and comparison of the manifest contents of the folklore of all cultures and subcultures. Rather, the knowledge has resulted from the complementary investigations of cultural anthropologists and psychologists, predominantly psychoanalysts. Anthropologists have been principally interested in determining the group functions of folk literature, while psychologists have been concerned in the main with its uses by individuals.

Recently, the psychoanalyst Bettelheim (1976) wrote extensively of the meaning and importance of one variety of folklore, the fairy tale, to the children of Western cultures. He demonstrated how fairy tales help children to make coherent sense out of their confusing feelings and often contradictory self-centered and group-oriented wishes, and thereby find sufficient meaning in life that they can achieve psychological health and become useful and creative members of society. He also showed, largely implicitly, how fairy tales help adults in dealing with their asocial and antisocial urges while remaining good citizens. No study exists which systematically illustrates the ways in which folklore similarly assists the members of a non-Western society in dealing with the intrapsychic problems entailed in becoming and remaining useful citizens. The present book consists of such a study of the Chiricahua and Mescalero Apaches of the Mescalero Indian Reservation of south central New Mexico, people who were nonliterate until they were seriously influenced by contact with white people, beginning in the late nineteenth century.

The data that make possible this elucidation have been amassed during an ongoing study, which has lasted thus far twenty one years, by collaborating anthropologists and the author, a Freudian psychoanalyst. The investigation has involved a thorough, traditional ethnological study, done predominantly by Dr. Harry W. Basehart, now Professor Emeritus of the University of New Mexico, and the author's wife, now Professor of Humanities and Science at the California College of Arts and Crafts, and a highly sophisticated, extensive and intensive investigation of child-rearing practices by Professor Boyer. The author's initial research method was to serve as a psychiatrist for these Apaches, conducting psychoanalytically oriented psychotherapeutic interviews, studying resistances and transference reactions and their implications. The longest continuous period during which he worked in this manner lasted some fifteen months.[1]

From the earliest days of our study, it became startlingly evident that much of what these Apaches told us included overt or veiled references to folklore material. We soon learned that the child-rearing practices regularly included patent and implicit lessons which stemmed from traditional oral literature, and that the lessons were reacted to in emotionally significant ways by the children.

We had not orginally intended to make a particular study of folklore. In part, this was because prestigious anthropologists had recorded the vast majority of the folk literature of these Apaches during the 1930's. More importantly, we were unaware of the commonness of folklore in the everyday communications of Apaches of all ages, and, while we had an intellectual grasp of the functions of traditional oral literature which have been mentioned above, we were initially unaware of the entent of their importance. As a psychoanalyst, the author had been impressed by the significance and uses of folklore varieties, largely fairy tales, by a few patients, but his practice had included analysands from cultures which had long been literate and whose socialization experiences had not been so imbued with folkloristic lessons and communications as we soon found to be the case with the Apaches.

Eventually we learned that in order to comprehend more fully the child-rearing practices and the personality development of these Apaches, it would be mandatory to acquaint ourselves thoroughly with as much of the folklore as we could. In consequence, the Boyers learned all of the remaining folklore which was accessible. Their learning did not result from a formal, traditional collection of folk literature and its extensions into religion, but rather from pursuing leads given by informants and patients. The body of knowledge concerning folklore and child-rearing practices that we have accumulated provides, so far as we know, a unique opportunity to study the interrelationships among folklore, socialization experiences and personality development. Before that body of knowledge is exploited, information will be presented which deals with the history of psychoanalytic involvement in the study of folklore and the manner in which psychoanalysts use knowledge acquired during the treatment of patients to understand the latent meanings of traditional oral literature.

Almost from the inception of psychoanalysis, its practitioners have been vitally interested in the study of folklore. Reflecting the major interests of the professional folklorists of the late nineteenth and early twentieth centuries, psychoanalysts initially sought to understand the origins and meanings of great Classical and Judaeo-Christian myths and the reflection of their themes in religion. However, their approach was radically different from that of the folklorists, who endeavored to establish non-psychological origins and meanings for folklore, and even tried to explain the irrationalities in oral literature on historical and linguistic bases. Psychoanalysts, to the contrary, soon discovered that the irrationalities in folklore could be deciphered, as could the dreams of patients, by application of knowledge they had acquired concerning the attributes of unconscious mentation. The spontaneous productions of their patients also forced psychoanalysts to study from early times the meanings and uses of fairy tales. It was not until later, after cultural anthropologists had begun to interest themselves in the social uses of folklore by nonliterate groups, that psychoanalysts became involved in seeking to understand the meanings of such oral literature and the uses to which it was put by individuals.

Once psychoanalysts had discerned that when the manifest contents of oral literature had been analyzed through application of the attributes of the thinking of the unconscious mind, they found that its dominant themes were the same as those which were expressed in their patients' dreams, fantasies and reveries. Those themes regularly pertained to childhood conflicts which had been repressed. Subsequently, psychoanalysts concluded that folklore itself could be viewed functionally as a group-supported means of seeking to resolve those repressed conflicts and to allow their expression in manners which were relatively free from anxiety and guilt.

As is commonly known, psychoanalysis is a scientific discipline which was begun by Freud and remains indissolubly associated with his name (Brenner 1974). From the outset, Freud sought to establish fundamental hypotheses for his new discipline. He soon concluded that two basic hypotheses were those of psychic determinism or causality and the proposition that consciousness is an exceptional rather than a regular attribute of mental functioning. At the same time, Freud tried to conceptualize models of the psychic apparatus. He held it to be mandatory that an acceptable theory of mental functioning must offer a satisfactory explanation of intrapsychic conflict.

Freud's first model of the psychic apparatus appeared in *The Interpretation of Dreams* (1900). There he distinguished three psychic systems, based on the accessibility of mental contents to consciousness. Those contents which were immediately accessible to consciousness he placed in the system Cs. (from "conscious"); those which were relatively inaccessible were assigned to the system Pcs. (from "preconscious"); and those which were inaccessible without gross distortion were designated as being in the system Ucs. (from "unconscious"). In his view at that time, neurotic anxiety results when the repressive force of the preconscious fails to keep forbidden sexual wishes in the unconscious. However, he found that he could not account for two clinical phenomena with the topographical theory: (1) in neurotic conflicts the forces in the mind which oppose the sexual wishes in question are not always accessible to consciousness and (2) a need for punishment is often found to be inaccessible to consciousness. Stated otherwise, he found that one of the deficiencies in the topographical theory is that it does not take the importance of aggressive-drive derivatives into adequate account.

Accordingly, in *The Ego and the Id* (1923), Freud presented a second model of the psychic apparatus, the structural theory.[2] There he divided the mind into two major parts, the id and the ego.

The id consists of unconscious mental representations of the erotic (or libidinous) and aggressive drives. The erotic- and aggressive-drive derivatives are always fused. No matter how loving a fantasy or action might be, some element of aggressive energy will be discharged in it and, however cruel or destructive a fantasy or action might be, analysis will show some degree of erotic gratification as well. The energic investments (cathexes) of the id are mobile and press for immediate discharge. This mobility of cathexis influences the type of thinking which is characteristic of unconscious mentation, known as primary-process thinking, as paleologic and by a number of other like terms. Such cathectic mobility produces instantaneous displacement of one idea for another or condensation of two or more ideas. There are no negation, no doubt, and no degrees of uncertainty, and there is no acknowledgment of time. In Freud's (1915:187) summary words, "(There are) exemption from mutual contradiction, primary process (mobility of cathexes), timelessness, and replacement of external by psychical reality."

In Freud's original thinking, the ego developed out of the id, being influenced simultaneously by constitutional factors as they interacted with the baby's earliest socialization experiences. There are some advantages to viewing, as did Hartmann (1950), the id and the ego as evolved from an undifferentiated matrix, but they need not be discussed here. The ego is more coherent and more organized than the id. It regulates or opposes the drives, mediating between them and the demands of the external world. It can be seen as a psychological stimulus barrier against excessive stimuli from both the inside and the outside, replacing the inborn physiological stimulus barrier which Freud found to be inadequate to defend the baby from internal stimuli (Boyer 1956). A separate division of the ego is called the superego; its functions are the moral ones, which may be highly contradictory, dealing with both the internalized thou-shalts and the thou-shalt-nots of the individual's culture, as mediated through his family.

Both the ego and the superego have conscious and unconscious elements. The type of thinking used to deal with conscious elements is logical, Aristotelian, and that which deals with elements which have been repressed into the unconscious ego are dominated by the primary process. The energy which motivates the activities of the ego stems from both erotic and aggressive drives; the self-punitive trends, which in large part led Freud to develop the structural hypothesis, are especially motivated by the aggressive drive.

In the topographical theory, conflict was between repressed erotic wishes and the repressing force of the system Pcs. In the structural hypothesis, conflict need not be unconscious and may be between id and ego or between various drive derivatives of the ego or of the superego. Any attempt to list ego functions would have to include consciousness, sense perception, the perception and expression of affect, thought, control of motor action, memory, language, defense mechanisms which serve to keep unacceptable wishes repressed or to permit them expression in modified form, control, regulation and binding of instinctual energy, the integrating and harmonizing function, reality testing and the capacity to inhibit or suspend the operation of any of these functions and to regress to a primitive level of functioning.[2]

Psychoanalysts have learned that at each stage of bio-socio-psychological development, the growing individual experiences anxiety- or guilt-producing conflicts which are more or less specific to that stage. The conflicts, conscious or unconscious, may be the product of the contradictory strivings of id and ego aims, personal wishes and external demands (A. Freud 1936), or the need to reconcile divergent goals of the ego (Hartmann 1951, 1953). The presence of too high a degree of anxiety will hamper further psychological growth and interfere with the person's task of becoming a useful and acceptable member of his society. The cultural group affords institutional supports which supplement the individual's personal defensive mechanisms and efforts toward adaptational development (Hartmann 1939).

As has been noted above, one defensive mechanism employed by the ego is a kind of "forgetting" whereby unresolved anxiety- or guilt-producing conflicts are repressed into the unconscious part of the ego or superego; repressed infantile conflicts, those pertaining to problems of childhood, continually seek access to consciousness. Other functions of the ego seek to disguise unconscious conflicts so that they can reach consciousness in forms which permit their discharge without producing incapacitating anxiety and guilt. The dream is a major form of mental activity which seeks to accomplish this aim. (Altman 1969; Freud 1900).

Every dream owes its contents to contemporary and past conflicts. The dream cannot exist without the impetus of an instinctual-drive derivative which, although infantile in origin, retains an appetite for gratification throughout life. As infantile wishes make their way upward into preconscious or conscious mentation, perhaps decades after their onset, they are accompanied by an apparatus of inhibitions and prohibitions which are just as primitive in nature. Current experiences, emotions, hopes, disappointments and fantasies also contribute to the dream. However, the day residue itself is insufficient to produce the dream. A dream is formed only when the present event makes contact with an unresolved infantile wish. A contemporary experience may be so evocative of a repressed earlier one that it pulls into preconscious or conscious mentation an infantile urge which otherwise might have remained latent. On the other hand, a remote event, because of its persisting importance, may invest a recent experience with a meaning it would not have in its own right.

As has been noted earlier, psychoanalysts conceptualize the quality of mental events according to their relation to consciousness. The content of the dream belongs to qualitatively different states of consciousness as well as to different periods of life.

The manifest content of the dream represents its latent content in a form which has been masked by the dream work. The manifest dream is a cryptic message which requires deciphering to permit the investigator to uncover the preconscious and unconscious conflictual ideas and feelings which have let to its formation.

Anthropologists and folklorists have complained about the seemingly arbitrary interpretations by psychoanalysts of symbols to be found in dreams and folklore. Their concern is matched by that of psychoanalysts. Freud (1916) resignedly remarked that "in contrast to the multiplicity of representations in the dream, the interpretations of the symbols are very monotonous, and this displeases everyone who hears of it; but what is there we can do about it?" The psychoanalytic position with regard to symbology will be dicussed in Chapter IV.

Psychoanalysis as a therapeutic method developed initially from the treatment of people who suffered from the hysterical neuroses (Breuer and Freud 1895; L. Freeman 1972; Freud 1908). Freud's work at Charcot's clinic in Paris in 1883 had shown him the power of the unconscious in patients who under hypnosis knew what troubled them, although the knowledge was unavailable to them when they were awake (Jones 1953). Freud was discouraged with the effects of hypnosis as a cure for the hysterias and developed the "free association" method which eventually led to later psychoanalytic developments.

It was soon discovered that a major causative factor in the etiology of the hysterias was a failure of resolution of conflicts that small children have regarding sexual wishes for the parent of the opposite sex. Boys were found to wish to get rid of their fathers and take their mothers for themselves as sexual objects, and girls were found to wish to replace their mothers in their fathers' beds. One of the problems confronting the boy in his attempt to achieve his goal pertained to his fear of castration. One way the boy had of defending himself against his wish to slay his father, and, thereby of retaining his father as a needed comforter and protector, was to wish instead to remove his father's genitals, which the boy perceived to be agents by means of which the father had controlling access to the mother. His wish to castrate his father was then projected onto the father, who, in the son's thinking, conceptualized the boy as a serious sexual rival and wanted to castrate *him*. It was found that some children defended themselves against the anxieties resulting from Oedipal problems by renouncing heterosexual wishes and striving instead to become the sexual object of the parent of the same sex.

Psychoanalytic patients were found to include in their so-called "free" associations references to themes and characters from all varieties of folklore. They treated the manifest content of folklore as they did that of their dreams. Sometimes psychoanalysts were hard put to decide whether a patient's presentation of a folklore element was the recitation of a dream. Patients used both folklore and dreams in an effort to express and transiently resolve their intrapsychic conflicts. While the folklore included latent themes pertaining to an infinite variety of conflicts, a problem with which patients regularly sought to deal through using folklore material consisted of unresolved Oedipal wishes. This was found to be especially obvious in their use of *Märchen,* loosely translated into English as "fairy tales."

In almost every fairy tale, a young hero or heroine defeats or kills a wicked, villainous adult, also either male or female, marries a beautiful, usually royal, lad or damsel, becomes elevated in status and lives happily ever after. In fairy stories the protagonist is always good and often mistreated, and the rival or rivals are inevitably despicable and richly deserve their ultimate misfortune: the triumphant protagonist with whom the child identifies has no reason to feel guilty for his or her implicitly cruel or otherwise forbidden behavior. Every fairy tale has many variations and each variation has special appeal to some child. Two examples of particularly popular fairy tales will suffice as illustrations. Each is very old and has been changed over time to disguise its themes so that they are less obvious and potentially disturbing. The alterations resemble the secondary revision to which dreams are subjected on recall, for more adequate disguise. They make the stories more suitable for the expression through them of troublesome conflicts with diminished guilt and anxiety.

Using terms taken from Freud's analyses of Greek myths, psychoanalysts named the problems which resulted from the boy's forbidden wishes the Oedipus complex, and those which ensued because of those of girls, the Electra complex. In common parlance, such problems of both boys and girls have come to be subsumed under the rubric "Oedipus complex." Problems entailed in the resolution of the Oedipus complex continue to be considered as of central importance in the etiology of the psychoneuroses; some psychoanalysts consider them to be important also in the genesis of psychosis.

The Cinderella story is perhaps the best-known and best-liked fairy tale of all. It has been traced to ninth-century Chinese origins, which no doubt explains the presence in it of tiny feet, since in the first-known version the feet of the protagonist were bound (Waley 1947). "Cinderella" has undergone many modifications over time. While in today's most popular rendition Cinderella is abused by and defeats a stepmother and stepsisters, in some versions her rivals have been her actual mother and sisters. The many idiosyncratic uses that psychoanalytic patients have made of "Cinderella" to help them resolve problems remaining from childhood have been elucidated in a voluminous literature; those uses have been detailed by Bettelheim (1976:236-277) in a lengthy exposition.[3]

Cinderella's defeat of her degrading and abusive mother- and sister-surrogates involves two major themes, the most obvious one a happy resolution of problems pertaining to sibling rivalry. For that reason, the Cinderella story is especially appealing to younger children, particularly girls. The Oedipal theme is also patent; it is Cinderella who marries the handsome prince, the father surrogate, and lives subsequently in eternal bliss.

"Jack and the Beanstalk" or "Jack the Giant Killer" has special attraction for boys. While in the modern, most popular version of "Cinderella" the aspects of the Oedipal situation which are stressed have to do with love and marriage, in "Jack" parricide and castration are emphasized. It is of interest that in an earlier version of "Cinderella" the castration theme was symbolically redirected, since the feet of Cinderella's sisters were mutilated (Grimm 1884). When the first daughter tried on the gold slipper, it was far too small. Following her mother's behest, she cut off her big toe and the slipper fit. As she and the prince rode away on horseback toward the palace where they would consummate their marriage, blood poured out of the shoe and the deception was detected. The second daughter followed her mother's instruction to cut off her heel, with the same result. Finally, Cinderella's foot was small enough. At that time, a tiny foot was commonly equated with a tiny, virginal vagina in Europe (Rudofsky 1974). The nonvirginal state of the older sisters had been exposed. It is a common fantasy of children that all are born with penises and that girls lose theirs as the result of some actual or fantasized sin. It would seem that the castration of the older sisters was the penalty paid for their premarital intercourse, symbolized in the fairy tale by the horseback riding. It was not until the latter part of the nineteenth century that the slipper was said to be made of aseptic glass, probably as a means of disguising the commercial aspects of the implied whoredom in earlier versions in which the slipper was gold.[4]

The earliest recorded version of "Jack" is "Jack and His Bargains," of English origin (K. Briggs 1970). There, Jack is sent by his father to sell a cow but instead trades the cow for a wondrous stick. All its owner has to say is "Up stick and at it"and the stick will beat all enemies senseless, symbolically killing them. Jack's father, expecting money for the cow, is enraged and gets a stick with which to beat his son. In self-defense, the wronged Jack calls on *his* magical stick and beats his father until he cries for mercy. The symbology here of phallic competition is obvious. Without disguise, the message is that the son's phallus makes the father's impotent, or the son castrates the father. Only later in "Jack and His Bargains" is the remainder of the Oedipal theme elucidated. Jack is then sent by his father to sell two other cows; for one he gets a bee that sings beautiful songs and for the other a fiddle that plays marvelous music unassisted. The king of that part of the country has a daughter who can't smile; he has promised her in marriage to the suitor who can please her. Many rich and noble men vie for her hand, but none of them can make her smile. But Jack, in his ragged clothes, delights her with the bee and the fiddle and he beats off all his rivals with the stick, thereby winning her as his bride and becoming himself royalty. The other suitors are barely disguised Oedipal rivals.

Over time, "Jack and His Bargains" was altered into today's popular version, which is too well known to warrant recapitulation here. In the modern version, the Oedipal conflict within the boy is externalized onto the ogre and his wife, who live somewhere in the sky. The magical stick has become the bean which miraculously sprouts during the night into a huge, upright stick substitute. It is well known that children view the change which occurs when the relatively little penis becomes erect to be the result of a miracle. The giant whom Jack robs of his valuable and magical possessions is not his father, but a beastly cannibal who would devour Jack if the mother surrogate, the ogre's wife, didn't prefer Jack to her vile husband and protect and assist him. The very small child seeks to express its hostility in oral-sadistic manners. In "Jack," the oral sadism is projected onto the giant. After Jack descends the beanstalk with the ogre's valuables, now having the wherewithal to properly "take care of" his real mother, he chops down the beanstalk, and his doing so results not just in the symbolic castration but also in the actual death of the giant. The ogre's valuables are regularly equated in patients' associations with his genitals, and sometimes with feces as well. Children often equate the fecal stick with a magical erection. In some versions of the story, the ogre had previously killed Jack's father and stolen *his* valuables, so Jack is a guilt-free, pious avenger, not a parricide, and his newly acquired magical possessions had orginally been his father's. It is not he but the ogre who slays the father and takes his powerful genitals. In the happy ending of the story, Jack has without guilt and anxiety acquired his father's valuables and has his mother for himself.

The foregoing material illustrates to some degree how psychoanalytic patients have been found to use folklore as a group-supported means of expressing and transiently resolving unresolved, repressed infantile conflicts, as a complement to the defensive and adaptive functions of individual dreams,, fantasies and daydreams. The manners by which the Chiricahua and Mescalero Apaches use their folklore for similar purposes will be illustrated in this book. We shall demonstrate also how the traditional lore of these Indians projectively reflects their personality configurations and socialization experiences. Further, we show how a thorough knowledge of the oral literature of a group can enhance the investigator's understanding of the verbal and nonverbal communications of its members. This, combined with awareness of the sometimes apparent meanings of certain behaviors, stories and projective systems, can alert the field worker to certain psychodynamics which might then be eventually verified over a long period of rapport, inquiry and collecting of relevant data, such as child-rearing experiences. Finally, the book will demonstrate how an intimate knowledge of the folklore of a group can assist a psychiatrist to understand patients who have cultural backgrounds radically different from his own.

But this book is concerned not only with data which were accumulated in the field and an understanding of them through applied psychoanalysis, but it also explores facets of the development of the thinking of three disciplines as well as the difficulties that anthropologists, folklorists and psychoanalysts have experienced in their attempts to use information provided by one another. Accordingly, we now seek to synthesize some of that material. While parts of the following data will be redundant for scholars in each of the three disciplines, it is anticipated that other parts will be new.

II

Interaction Among Folklorists, Anthropologists and Psychoanalysts

Men have studied folklore since at least as long ago as the fourth century B.C., when the Sicilian philosopher Euhemeris suggested that myths are based on historical traditions, that myth heroes are real people and that man made gods in his own image, and thus anticipated a psychoanalytic idea (Brunvand 1968:85). The modern systematic study of folklore and folkloristics was begun by the brothers Grimm in 1812 (Dorson 1963; Manheim 1977), who sought to answer questions pertaining to the origins, meanings and modes of transmission of the folktale (Thompson 1946:368). Following the ideas of Deslongchamps (1838), the Grimms (W. Grimm 1856) theorized that folktales were broken-down myths which had originated among prehistoric Indo-European tribes and had been disseminated during their migrations throughout Europe. Kuhn (1843, 1845, 1859) found the folklore of the Indo-Germanic literature to contain recurrent themes, and traced the figures of various gods and heroes back to Vedic sources. Müller (1885, 1888, 1897, 1909) and Steinthal (1856, 1860, 1862, 1871) supported Kuhn's work and extended it from the linguistic standpoint. Thoms introduced the term "folklore" in 1846 to replace the previously used terms "popular antiquities" and "popular literature" (Emrich 1946; Merton 1846).

There is no commonly accepted definition of folklore. Not only do folklorists in different countries hold varying concepts of folklore, but those in a single nation have varying ideas concerning its nature. *The*

Standard Dictionary of Folklore, Mythology and Legend (M. Leach 1949-1950) presents twenty-one concise definitions. Incompletely successful attempts have been made to delineate folklore from the standpoint of the means of its transmission and through defining the folk (Dundes 1965). For the purposes of this book, folklore will be said to *be* or to be *in* oral tradition and, as became apparent in the introductory chapter, it is used synonymously with oral or folk literature.

While the laity customarily separate mythology from other forms of oral literature, folklorists include it among the major genres, along with other varieties, such as legends, folktales and fairy tales, proverbs and superstitions. Each of these major divisions of folk literature requires a lengthy definition (Brunvand 1968; Rôheim 1941; Thompson 1946; Utley 1961). Dundes (1965) lists numerous minor genres.

Even if there were general agreement as to what constitutes folklore, discord would remain concerning its origins. The history of folkloristics is perfused with the remains of elaborate theories explaining how folklore arose.

The now-discarded theory of solar mythology was introduced by the philologist Müller through his study of comparative mythology (Rose 1928; Thompson 1946:371-383). He postulated a "mythopoeic age" in which truly noble conceptions of the Aryan gods first arose. The age began not at the beginning of civilization but at stage so early that language could not carry abstract notions. Müller compared the names and details in various mythologies with those of heavenly bodies in Sanskrit, and concluded that all of the principal gods' names had originally stood for solar phenomena. His followers extended celestial explanations of myths, applying them to texts around the world. Similar research also produced a now equally debunked "zoological" interpretation that read animal symbolism into myths (DeGubernatis 1872).

Two of the characteristics that most of the theories pertaining to the origins of folklore have sought to elucidate are irrationality and multiple existence.

IRRATIONALITY IN AND THE MULTIPLE EXISTENCE OF FOLKLORE

Prior to the advent of psychoanalysis, anthropologists and folklorists generally considered the irrationality found in folklore to consist of primitive thinking which had persisted from prehistoric times. When Freud delineated the rules of logic used in unconscious thinking and the dream, it was possible to see the influence of those laws in oral literature. Now it is agreed by members of all three disciplines that the most satisfactory explanation for the irrationality of traditional literature is

that its formal structure fails to obey the laws of Aristotelian logic. Instead it follows the rules of reasoning which have been described various-
ly as those involved in schizophrenia and other autistic conditions (Arieti
1948), used by the young child who cannot distinguish between a symbol
and the object it symbolizes (Vigotsky 1939), those of primary-process
logic (Freud 1915), and those of the Von Domarus principle of paleologic
which, paraphrased, states that, whereas the person who employs
Aristotelian logic accepts identity only upon the basis of identical subjects, the paleologician accepts identity on the basis of predicates (Von
Domarus 1944). While non-Aristotelian logic is used in folklore and
religious statements, those metaphorical and allegorical cultural expressions are not to be designated as schizophrenic (Richardson 1976). In the
words of Meissner (1976:86), "the schizophrenic is not schizophrenic
because of his language, but because of the *intent* of his
language that expresses a concrete identification based on
pathogenic introjects, which promote his conviction not of his similarity
to past religious figures, but his *delusional identity* with them."

It has long since been observed that the manifest content of oral
literature contains themes which are found in the folklore of many parts
of the world. Two principal explanations have been offered to explain
multiple existence: polygenesis, on the one hand, and monogenesis and
diffusion, on the other.

According to the theory of polygenesis, which is associated with the
concept of psychic unity in man, the same item might have originated independently many times. Advocates of this idea hold that man is
everywhere fundamentally the same psychologically and that his mental
products, including folklore, could be and apparently are manifestly
very similar.

According to one scheme of polygenesis, which was strongly supported by the English Anthropological School of Comparative
Mythologists whose foremost spokesperson was Andrew Lang (1901), all
men evolved in one evolutionary path through three identical stages of
savagery, barbarism and civilization (Brunvand 1968:84-85; Dundes
1965:53-54). Savagery was thought to be exemplified by aboriginal
Australian and American Indian cultures, and civilization by Victorian
England. It was believed that the ancestors of nineteenth-century English
people must have been savages exactly like aborigines. This supposition
was crucial for folklore theory since it was also postulated that folklore
arose during the stage of savagery, and that, as man evolved, he left his
folklore behind him. With evolution, only fragments of folklore, called
survivals, remained in civilized times. The urban Victorian English were
thought to be too logical to express themselves in the manner used in the
manifest contents of oral literature. Since the survivals were so fragmentary, they could not be understood without speculative historical

reconstruction, a favorite scholarly pastime which was allied to Romanticism and the worship of the past. The task of historical reconstruction was thought to be facilitated by the study of oral literature of modern "savages," which was believed to hold the precursors of European folkore. This theory purportedly explained why folklore in Europe was thought to exist especially among the peasants, who were equated with barbarians.

Few modern anthropologists subscribe to the theory of polygenesis as it pertains to folklore, although they agree that practical tools and appliances, such as the loom, were invented simultaneously in many areas. In a recent review of the cult of the serpent, Mundkur (1976:429) noted that "man's reverential fear of this animal is extraordinarily primordial." Yet he and his numerous discussants limited their comments to the avenues of diffusion; none ventured to suggest that the cults could have arisen independently. Dundes (1965:53-56) opined that anthropologists refuse to consider seriously the polygenetic hypothesis as it pertains to folklore because of its inclusion of the concept of psychic unity. Rooth held that the majority of folklorists continue to agree with Lang's view that "motifs and beliefs of a similar kind could arise spontaneously under similar external conditions" and believe that "a historical view could no longer be accepted [as] sensible" (Rooth 1962:11). At the same time, she used the distribution of the creation myths of North American Indians to support the ideas of monogenesis and diffusion, in an effort to rebut the attempt of some folklorists to regard the resemblances among myths as the product of Jungian archetypes in the ancestral memory (Rooth 1957).

The Freudian psychoanalytic viewpoint is that neither polygenesis nor monogenesis and diffusion is understandable without including a concept of psychic unity.

PSYCHIC UNITY AND FOLKLORE

Psychic unity has come to be conceptualized in three ways, each of which differs from the viewpoint of the ninetenth-century British anthropologists. Freud, Jung and Lévi-Strauss agree that the determining force in man's production of myth is to be found in his unconscious mind. In contrast to the view of the majority of early anthropologists, they conceptualize the symbols and motifs of folklore as consisting of projected symbols of intrapsychic conflicts. Their idea, of course, is by no means new. It was implicit in the ideas of Euhemeris and explicit in the writings of Brinton (1896, 1899).

For Jung (1916, 1935), the creative power is ascribed to the impetus afforded by racially inherited archetypes in the "collective unconscious," as distinguished from the repressed conflicts in the "personal un-conscious," which consists of the remnants of individual life ex-periences. The archetypes are viewed as omnipresent, unchanging and universal and as having been present from time immemorial. There is an apparent continuity between Jung's thinking and that of the nineteenth-century anthropologists, whose ideas reflected Darwinian evolution transposed invalidatably into the psychological sphere. Jung considered his archetypes to determine aspects of the dreams of normal and neurotic people, the hallucinations of psychotics, and certain images in the great myths and art forms of all mankind. Some followers of Melanie Klein ex-tend Jung's ideas to include the notion that actual ideational content is inherited (Rascovsky et al. 1971).

In the opinion of E. Leach (1970), the writings of the prolific struc-turalist Lévi-Strauss (1949, 1958, 1962, 1964, 1967) are obscure and con-tain many inherent contradictions. The view of Lévi-Strauss that only the study of the "mythology" of "people without history," such as the South American Indians, is relevant to the study of folklore seems to be a continuation of the survival theory. While he has done much field work among nonliterate peoples, Lévi-Strauss spent little time with any one group and never learned an indigenous language. Leach judged "the fun-damental properties of the physical and psychical universe" which Lévi-Strauss (1955:60) found in Amazonian groups to be the result of Lévi-Strauss' seeing only affirmation of his preconceived ideas, themselves based on untestable extrapolating "from geologic notions into the psychical." Let me hasten to add that Leach (1958:147) had strong opi-nions about psychoanalysis as well. He wrote: "Logically considered, almost the whole of psychoanalytic theory rests on the most glaring fallacies; yet somehow or other it often proves illuminating."

For Lévi-Strauss, the unconscious is empty of content but endowed with an innate structuring faculty which brings a logical order to sensory perceptions. The unconscious is reduced to a specifically human function and its structuring function determines the content of folklore, which is invented to symbolically establish categorical order into natural phenomena. How the actual content of the folklore results is explained only vaguely.

Nevertheless, Burridge (1967) and Ducey (1977) find that, in terms of myth analysis, the combination of psychoanalytic interpretation and Lévi-Strauss' structural interpretation offers more explanatory poten-tial than can be offered by either alone.

As will be elucidated later, Freud's early application of psychoanalysis to folklore was strikingly similar to Jung's. However, whereas Jung's stand remained essentially static, Freud continually revised his theoretical position, so that the views of modern psychoanalysts have come to be in consonance with those of today's ethologists, paleontologists and psychologically minded anthropologists.

The current position of Freudian psychoanalysts is that the roots of folklore are to be found in repressed conflicts pertaining to actual individual life experiences.

Human beings have a species-specific genetic inheritance which, because the unfolding of innate potential traits depends upon time-appropriate interactions with nurturing caretakers, is essentially biosocial. The psychological developmental level at birth has been designated as the undifferentiated phase from which id and ego emerge (Hartmann 1952). The character of the human psyche is particularly dependent on the nature of interactions with nurturing figures, initially most significantly the mother (Brody and Axelrad 1970; Erikson 1966; Mahler et al. 1975). Prolonged socialization is required to enable the child to become an acceptable member of his social group. Human beings have like biological and psychological needs and are subject to like frustrations and intrapsychic conflicts. The vicissitudes of their innate drive derivatives are shaped by cultural requirements, reflected in child-rearing methods.

Children have wishes which they consider to be unacceptable to their parents. When those parents express similar desires or do not disapprove of the revealed wish of the child, the child feels less apprehension. The adult remains to some extent a child and requires external approval and reinforcement of individual psychological defensive maneuvers. Influential societal members, secular or religious, are used as parent surrogates. Religious superiors are more useful as models for reduction of anxiety regarding the arcane: the public expression of their dreams and fantasies is further disguised by secondary revision into items of folklore, and they are thus altered in manners which make them culturally acceptable. The visions of prophets provide the contents of religious systems (Arlow 1951; Campbell 1959; Lantenari 1960, 1975) and the power dreams of shamans give rise to folklore items, as will be demonstrated anew in Chapter VII. Thus, because of this community of intrapsychic conflicts and primitive meanings of symbols and the limited number of techniques available to the ego, all of which are reflected in dream motifs, identical or similar folklore items can arise anywhere at any time.

When anthropologists speak of folklore diffusion, they refer to the inclusion into the oral literature of one group the manifest folklore themes and symbols of another. The literature is replete with studies which trace avenues of such diffusion (Utley 1974).

SOME FUNCTIONS OF FOLKLORE

Folklore serves both group and individual functions. In order for an item of the folklore body of one group to be suitable for incorporation into that of another, it must contain properties which make it useful for either or both of those functions. Once included into the oral literature of the second group, it may serve substitutive or supplementary purposes. If it is to serve substitutive functions, its presentation of latent themes may be better disguised or its overt themes may be more striking. On the other hand, its inclusion into the folkore stock of the second group may result from social conditions such as those which obtain when a more powerful society imposes its traditional literature onto a weaker one. Again, the members of one group, envious of those of another, may emulate them through assumption of various of their cultural traits, as is known to have occurred in the cargo cults (LaBarre 1970). Whatever the reason may be that elements of the folklore of one group are accepted into that of another, its latent themes and symbols must present alternate means of presenting group-cohesive lessons and of supporting individual defensive and adaptive techniques. The manifest content of the folklore will change, but it will serve to disguise the same intrapsychic conflicts which are common to the majority of the members of the social group and those which are idiosyncratic for the individual.

According to Freudian psychoanalytic thinking, were it not for the existence of psychic unity, the dreams and fantasies of an individual could not be incorporated into the folklore of his group, nor could the traditional literature of one society be embodied in that of another. Each transmission and inclusion can be viewed as a variety of diffusions.

In general, anthropologists and folklorists who are well acquainted with modern ideas pertaining to ego psychology hold that the polygenetic hypothesis is tenable. Campbell, who demonstrates that the major civilizations of the world share a significant body of mythological beliefs, makes a convincing case for the origin of these beliefs in the simultaneous resonance of the personal physical and fantastic experience, the immediate interpersonal experience and the perceived mathematical order of the earth and the celestial bodies (Campbell and Abadie 1975). His data suggest an origin of ideas in the early Bronze Age in the Near East and their transmission by diffusion to other civilizations. Dundes (personal communication) also holds that groups would have to develop idiosyncratic folklore to defend against the guilts and anxieties attendant upon intrapsychic conflicts resultant from socialization experiences, were oral literature unavailable to them via diffusion.

The study of folklore has been widely employed by anthropologists, who have found in oral, artistic, religious and gestural expressions of tradition many clues for the understanding of social structure, socialization processes and aspects of the mental functioning of groups under investigation (Bascom 1953; Eliade 1951; Fischer 1963; Fox 1967; Lowie 1924; Radin 1927). The study of the complex relationships between the materials of folklore and those of literature have widened the understanding and utility of both subjects (Jacobs 1959, 1960; Radin 1915, 1954-1956; Taylor 1948).

Bascom (1954) discussed the social context of folklore, the relationships of folklore to culture and the functions of folklore. Concerning the last, he elaborated the amusement factors of folklore, its role in validating culture, its educational utility and its part in maintaining conformity to the accepted patterns of culture. He considered it to be the duty of the non-anthropologist to delineate in depth the means by which the psychological functions of folklore operate. Psychoanalysts, who are in full accord with the notion of the group functions of folklore, have long sought to meet Bascom's challenge.

PSYCHOANALYTIC APPROACHES TO FOLKLORE

Early applied psychoanalysis dealt almost exclusively with attempts to understand aspects of folklore and religion through the use of Freud's new insights concerning the unconscious mind. It was met with disapproval from most social scientists of other disciplines. Their objections were by no means solely the product of psychological resistance. Some few anthropologists an folklorists, following Abraham's (1909, 1912) expositions, accepted the idea that psychological aspects of folklore and religion could be understood in terms of the language of the dream. However, even those who granted that there *were* psychological aspects to expressive culture were affronted by a prevalent circular reasoning (Arlow 1961). When their thinking was dominated by id psychology or the topographical hypothesis, many analysts used the study of folklore to demonstrate the validity of their recently acquired knowledge concerning unconscious mechanisms and particularly symbolism. They sought simultaneously to interpret folklore from its manifest contents and then to use the same concepts they had employed in their interpretations to support those concepts (Maeder 1909; Rank 1909, 1912, 1922; Riklin 1908; Silberer 1910; Storfer 1912; Wilke 1914). Other social scientists also objected to psychoanalytical assumptions of psychic unity in all mankind, believing that there were peoples, presumably the so-called "primitive" peoples and the European peasantry, whose psyches had not developed sufficiently for them to distinguish between Aristotelian and non-Aristotelian, or secondary process and primary-process logic. They also objected strenuously, as many do today, to psychoanalysts' studying the traditional literature of cultural groups without investigating the social structure and child-rearing processes of those groups.

Two of Freud's early works have greatly influenced the attitudes of anthropologists and folklorists toward applied psychoanalysis.

Freud's (1900) analysis of the Oedipus Rex myth is the best-known example of psychoanalytic involvement in folklore. Analysis of the myth and investigation of the complex which was named from the myth have been the principal foci of hundreds of books and articles written by members of various social disciplines. Mullahy (1948) used the myth and complex as the hub for his comparison of the psychoanalytic orientations of Freud, Jung, Adler, Sullivan, Horney and Fromm. Lessa (1961) collected tales from Oceania and reviewed folklore literature from around the world. He concluded that diffusion rather than polygenesis explained the distribution of the Oedipus myth. With Malinowski (1927, 1929), he judged the Oedipal situation to be culturally determined and not to be universal, "for there are many social systems not conducive to its development" (Lessa 1956:71).

Parsons (1964) sapiently reviewed the well-known Malinowski-Jones debate about the applicability of the Oedipus complex to non-patrilineal cultures. She noted that the question of the Oedipus complex has two sides to it, the first related to instinct and fantasy and the second to identification and object choice, which perforce are dependent on social structure and social norms. While she agreed that defensive displacement might result in the use of another family member as substitute for the father, she held that, in some groups, the Oedipal situation scarcely could be considered to have arisen, and that the members of these groups remained essentially pre-Oedipal in their level of psychological development. In an unacknowledged agreement with Singer (1961), Parsons (1964:326) concluded that "the original question as to whether the Oedipus complex is universal or not is no longer very meaningful in that form and that more important contemporary questions would be: what is the possible range within which culture can utilize and elaborate the instinctually given human potentialities, and what are the psychologically given limits of this range?" She continued, "Or in slightly different terms: what more can we learn about what Claude Lévi-Strauss (1949) has characterized as the 'transition from nature to culture?' To answer fully questions such as these will require the equal and collaborative efforts of psychoanalysis and anthropology." E. Leach (1958:151) did not fully share her optimism: "Freud's assumption that ethnographic materials have significance for psycho-analytic theory is, I believe, largely fallacious. But the converse is less clear. It may well be that psycho-analytic materials have significance for anthropological theory."

Stephens (1962) studied aspects of the Oedipus complex cross-culturally, testing the hypothesis that "young boys — at least under optimal conditions — become sexually attracted to their mothers. This generates lasting sexual fears and avoidance. These fears are at least in one instance mediated by unconscious fantasies" (p.17). He concluded that cross-cultural evidence gives "massive, impressive support to the hypothesis'' (p.48).

Fortes' (1959) comparisons of the myths of Oedipus and Job with aspects of the religion of an ancestor-worshipping tribe of West Africa is a remarkable example of the elision of multideterminism. Seeking to understand the myths and rituals solely in terms of British social structure, Fortes ignored the castration symbology of Orestes' biting off his own finger after slaying his mother, of Zipporah's having circumcized her son to avoid his being killed by Yahweh, of Oedipus' blinding himself and of ritual circumcision in initiation rites (Bettelheim 1954). Many anthropologists have contented themselves with explaining myths, rituals and religious concepts solely in terms of their social functions (Middleton 1967, 1967a, 1967b).

DeVos (1975) has limned cogently both the possibilities and serious limitations of the work of those anthropologists who hold that social-structural changes proceed without the contribution of input from individuals of the culture in question and who believe that even expressive culture can be understood in solely social-functional terms.

Reider (1960) and Reik (1923) found many medieval legends about Judas to be understandable in terms of the Oedipus myth. The Rascovskys (1970) found the filicidal behavior of Oedipus' parents to be responsible for Oedipus' "acting out and psychopathic behavior." Grunberger (1962) wrote of Oedipal elements in anti-semitism.

Freud's (1913) *Totem and Taboo* has probably influenced anthropologists' attitudes toward applied psychoanalysis more than any other single factor, aside from stubborn resistance against recognition of the strength of unconscious thinking.

The principal thesis of *Totem and Taboo* is that, at some point in paleohistory, both totem and taboo had their origins in a hominid horde in which the strongest, jealous and tyrannical male dominated the females and, as his sons approached maturity, drove them off. His dispossessed offspring, one day united, killed and ate their father, and took their mothers and sisters for themselves. At this point, as guilt and remorse led the brothers to renounce the ill-gotten females as well as any future partaking of a father-symbolizing totem animal, both totem and taboo arose. Freud linked totemism with exogamy and his concern with totemism was secondary to his concern with incest.

Freud based his retrospective hypothesis on three elements: (1) the totemic fantasies of three boys, Little Hans (Freud 1909), Little Arpad (Ferenczi 1913) and a patient of Wulff (1912); (2) Savage's and Wyman's (1847) and Darwin's (1901) notions about the primal horde, combined with Atkinson's (1903) conjectural concept of the original Cyclopean form of the family; and (3) Robertson-Smith's (1914) observations on the totemic meal (Derek Freeman 1967). Freud's second element was even then considered highly suspect, and subsequently has been dismissed by ethological studies of highly developed nonhuman bipedal groups (Schaller 1963). Clearly Freud's ideas were and remain untestable. Implicit in his argument was the notion that the consequences of that imagined event have had a persisting effect on the brain and behavior of the human animal by some process of inheritance — a Lamarckian cast of thought which has been refuted by geneticists (Dobzhansky 1962; Etkin 1964).

Beginning from the invalidatability of this part of Freud's hypothesis, Whiting (1959) used the cross-cultural method to test Freud's interpretations of totemism. Robertson-Smith had supposed the sacramental killing and communal eating of the totemic animal to be an important feature of totemic religion, but Frazer (1910) found only two examples of such a totemic sacrament. Additionally, in his theory that the animals which the boys feared symbolized only the Oedipal father, Freud failed to take into account the fact that Little Arpad had said he wanted to eat "a dish of potted mother." Whiting found cannibalistic desires directed much more commonly toward the mother than the father and suggested that totemism is a culturally provided defense against the child's repressed hostile wishes toward her. He indicated that while the Oedipal elements were valid, they were incomplete. Hippler et al. (1975) found in their study of the northern Athabaskan potlatch ceremony support for Whiting's view but learned that such cannibalistic desires are aimed also at re-establishing a fantasized symbiotic union or intrauterine bliss.

Early anthropological critics of *Totem and Taboo* ignored Freud's quiet statement in that book that his position was conjectural and that it could be interpreted as a just-so statement. Kroeber (1920, 1939) and Mead (1930, 1963) were initially adversely critical, but later came to see psychological value in Freud's thesis. So, too, has Fox (1967), who concluded that some of the reasons for the genesis, change and persistence of even kinship systems might be affectual. In doing so he might have partially vindicated Jones (1924), who, in a rebuttal to Malinowski, had postulated that matrilineal social organization can itself be seen as a defense against the father-son ambivalence characteristic of the Oedipal situation.

It must be underscored that Freud's 1913 thinking had similarities to to the invalidatable position of Jung and, as some interpret her, of Melanie Klein pertaining to the inheritance not only of a species-specific genetic inheritance but of thought content itself.

Freud's early adherence to such notions was so offensive to social scientists that until recently the vast majority acquainted themselves solely with Freud's libido or topographic theory and ceased reading psychoanalytic literature written after the teens of this century; many continue to reject as out-of-hand applied psychoanalysis in general (Boyer 1976). The attitudes of two eminent folklorists are illustrative.

Thompson (1946) dismissed applied psychology as "unrealistic." Dorson found the "Freudian psychoanalytical school of interpretation" to be "most abhorrent to orthodox folklorists." His "Theories of Myths and the Folklorist" (1960) and his review article entitled "Current Folklore Theories" (1963) reveal a startling ignorance of psychoanalytical theoretical ideas subsequent to the introduction of the structural hypothesis. Dorson (1963:105) equated psychoanalytic ideas with solar mythology, writing: "Psychoanalytical readings of myths and folktales substitute a sexual symbolism for the nineteenth century symbolism of heavenly phenomena."

Sadly, some current articles written by psychoanalysts who seek to understand folklore continue to deny the need to understand the traditional literature within its cultural context. Kernberg (1972) and Zetzel (1956) have noted that some modern psychoanalysts even confuse symbols with that which is symbolized. Unfortunately, too, some social scientists have a tendency to throw the baby out with the bath water. Thus, because the psychoanalytical orientations of Róheim (1941a, 1945, 1951, 1953) and Carvalho-Neto (1956, 1957, 1961) were id psychology oriented, their contributions to anthropology and folklore in general have been derogated by some specialists in those disciplines.

The early use of folklore by psychoanalysts prevailed as long as the topographical theory of personality organization constituted the most mature effort at establishing a general framework within which to understand human psychology. However, Freud gradually revised his thinking. By 1915 he had clearly found his topographical theory to be wanting in its explanatory power and by 1923 he had formulated the structural theory, which provided the basis for the development of ego psychology. Hartmann's (1939) plea for an extension of the psychoanalytic theory of ego development into the field of adaptational influences upon ego maturation and his concept of the conflict-free ego sphere became the groundwork for a solid frame of psychoanalytic and sociologic knowledge encompassing adaptational factors. Longitudinal developmental studies of children (A. Freud 1965; Mahler et al. 1975; Ritvo and Solnit 1958; Spitz 1959) focused on the influences of environment on ego and superego development.

Since the introduction of the structural theory and the greater emphasis on ego psychology, anthropologists' objections to psychoanalysts having approached the study of mythology from the topographical viewpoint have become less meaningful (Arlow 1961). This point has been demonstrated implicitly in the work of social scientists who have set out to validate various psychoanalytic hypotheses, for example, Whiting and Child's (1953:356) proposition that personality is "an intervening hypothetical variable determined by child rearing which is determined by maintenance systems and which is finally reflected in projective systems." Some researchers have concluded that social structure has a determinative influence upon socialization processes, which, in turn, have a predictable and causative effect on expressive cultural phenomena and even crime rates (Spiro and D'Andrade 1958; B. Whiting 1963). Kluckhohn (1944) and LaBarre (1958) complained about the quality of anthropological studies which seek to investigate the effects of folklore on alleviating individual conflicts and the role of folklore in shaping personality, and they attributed the deficiency in those studies to the researchers' lack of psychoanalytic sophistication.

Recent works of some social scientists attest to the growing acceptance of modern psychoanalytic investigations of various elements of expressive culture and myths. Slater (1968), who stressed the roles of multiple determinism, found that argumentation as to which of several interpretations of a myth or its components is the *best* elucidation constitutes an "academic luxury." He deemed Fromm's (1951) attempts to repudiate Freud's interpretation of the Oedipus myth and to substitute a nonsexual one to be a "gratuitous waste of a not inconsiderable talent," as did Torres (1960). Ekeh (1976) found both Freud's and Fromm's understandings of the Oedipal myth to be inadequate, offering an alternate hypothesis of social survival. He (Ekeh 1976:65) compared the Oedipus myths of the city-state civilizations of classical Greece and of Benin to "shed light on the functioning of elementary city-state civilizations and to generalize from the elementary forms of civilization to the dynamics of more modern, complex forms of civilization." Dundes (1962) suggested that myths can be interpreted both with and without knowledge of the culture which uses them to the extent that there are human universals, and he considered it reasonable to analyze a myth as if it were intrinsic to all cultures within which it appears. Muensterberger (1950) illustrated how the social scientist can use psychoanalytic knowledge for the enhancement of anthropological understanding and, reciprocally, how analysts come to know about universal problems of mankind through *sophisticated* study of valid data produced by social scientists.

Various anthropologists and folklorists have made psychological interpretations of prose narrative. Such interpretations have been based on psychoanalytic models and have provided results which the investigators have deemed to have assisted them in their understanding not only of native individuals, but also of aspects of socialization and social structure (Barnouw 1949, 1955; Davidson and Day 1974; Dundes 1962; Jacobs 1952, 1960; Lantis 1953; Posinski 1954, 1956, 1957; Róheim 1925; Skeels 1954; Valory 1972). Dundes (1967), citing Boyer (1964) and Kaplan (1962), thinks the most important psychological studies of American folklore have been made by psychologists and psychiatrists who go into the field themselves.

Psychoanalysts have found few socialization studies to afford sufficient data, particularly pertaining to early stages of development, to enable them to draw valid conclusions about the personality development of cultures other than our own. They deem the vast majority of the studies used by Whiting and Child (1953) to be too superficial to be dependable. They believe that studies must be done by anthropologists who are well grounded in psychoanalytic theory and who know what to look for and that the investigating teams must include a woman. Anthropologists, too, have recognized these needs (B. Whiting 1963). Devereux and LaBarre (1961) suggested that the psychoanalytically oriented culture and personality studies of expressive culture will become one of the most effective means for the study of man in society.

THE PSYCHOLOGICAL FUNCTIONS OF FOLKLORE: A MODERN VIEW

We turn now to a systematic account of modern psychoanalytic ideas pertaining to the psychological functions of folklore which supplement its group functions. They were formulated especially by Arlow (1961).

The myth is a special form of shared fantasy which serves to bring the individual into relationship with members of his cultural group on the basis of common psychological needs. It can be studied from the point of view of its roles in psychic and social integration; not only does it assist in alleviating individual guilt and anxiety, but it constitutes a form of adaptation to reality; as a form of community illusion, it adds to the cohesion of the social group. Thus it influences the development of a sense of reality and the superego.

Freud (1915) demonstrated that the type of mental activity known as unconscious fantasy is peculiarly inchoate. Drive derivatives seek immediate discharge and their dynamic force activates the mental apparatus to reproduce sensory impressions which mime previously perceived, highly gratifying impressions. A function of the ego is to delay the discharge of instinctual drive derivatives and to facilitate their expression in an adaptive, integrated manner, and thus to avoid intrapsychic conflict and clash with the world of reality. Depending on the nature of the data of perception, the level of cathectic potential and the state of ego functioning, different forms of mental products emerge; out of this martrix of ego activity are created dreams, symptoms, fantasies and expressive culture. Important external events become integrated into existent organizations of unconsciously fantasized wishes, and reality is experienced in terms of internal need.

The hierarchy in the fantasy life of each individual reflects the vicissitudes of individual experience as well as the influence of psychic differentiation and ego development. Unconscious fantasies have a systematic relationship to each other and are grouped around instinctual wishes and drive derivatives. The groups are composed of varying editions of attempts to resolve intrapsychic conflicts concerning the wishes, and each version corresponds to a different psychic movement in the history of the individual's development. At different times and under varying circumstances, one of the organized images may be brought into focus. The defensive needs of the ego may be so strong as to endow each successive set of images with such vividness that the fantasies are experienced as realities from the past.

Myths and related phenomena are group-accepted images which serve as further screening devices in the defensive and adaptive functions of the ego. They reinforce the suppression and repression of individual fantasies and personal myths (Eggan 1955; Kris 1956). A shared daydream is a step toward group formation and solidarity and leads to a sense of mutual identification on the basis of common needs. Myth makers serve the community alongside poets and prophets, presenting communally acceptable versions of wishes which theretofore were expressed in guilt-laden, private fantasy (Freud 1911, 1911a; Sachs 1942). Arlow (1951) showed that the same motivations operate in the realm of the ecstatic religious revelation and the prophetic calling. Idiosyncratic personal dreams are made to be forgotten. Shared daydreams are instruments of socialization and thereby character formation. The myth must be remembered and repeated. The externalization of the impulses which give rise to fantasy makes possible the process of sharing and potentiates the containment of fright and guilt through the means of art and symbolism. Folklore, art and religion are institutionalized instruments which bolster the social adaptation ordinarily made possible by the nightly abrogation of instinctual renunciation in the dream. In the genesis of myth, for both individual and group, only a kernel of realistic experience is needed. The revision or falsification of the past and its heroes by the group serves the purpose of defense, adaptation and instinctual gratification for the group and its individual constituents; it also serves in character-building.

In following chapters of this book, Western nosological statements will be used to delineate traits which are common to the Chiricahua and Mescalero Apaches. The use of such statements affronts some anthropologists and folklorists, who misinterpret such diagnostic comments and psychoanalytic definitve terminology to be pejorative. To the contrary, we use them because they are *accepted terms* that have specific meanings which are understood to psychologists in general, and we use the psychoanalytic frame of reference because we consider it to provide the most comprehensive and explanatory psychological system in existence. *No* negative connotations toward Indians are suggested. A growing number of anthropologists have come to agree, after unsuccessful attempts to use the thinking of other psychological schools to understand the mental operations and personality development of peoples of non-Western cultures (LaBarre 1958; Spiro 1974).

The use of some psychoanalytic language and Western nosological terms may give some readers the erroneous impression that the author's view of these Apaches is unduly ethnocentric. Such an understanding would be based on an incomplete comprehension of that language and those terms. A possible second source of such a false impression is that the book seeks only to illustrate how *expressive culture* deals with conscious and unconscious conflicts, and expressive culture emphasizes conflicts which are generally kept out of awareness. it is beyond the purview of this book to illustrate other manners in which these Apaches deal with the deep-seated and intense conflicts which are the product of their once-adaptive social structure and socialization processes and the devastating effects of deculturation and acculturation. One might get the mistaken notion from the material presented here that there is an implication that such conflicts are greater among the Apaches than among the vast majority of cultures in the processes of deculturation and acculturation. It is generally acknowledged that hunting and gathering societies have particularly severe problems of adjusting to Westernization. It is our impression that these Apaches have adapted themselves better than most nomadic groups who have been subjected to like pressures. Yet a third potential source of the erroneous impression stems from the fact that our aim was to study predominantly the typical Apaches, and they are those who have neither totally failed to meet the challenges of the need to become Westernized while yet retaining Indian identification, nor been unusually successful. While the number of Apaches who have been able to adapt themselves with singular success to the process of deculturation and acculturation was small at the beginning of our project, it is growing steadily and the general outlook for the future of the Apaches in terms of achieving successful acculturation has become brighter.

The functions of folklore among the Chiricahua and Mescalero Apaches can be understood only on the basis of an understanding of their aboriginal and modern group and individual problems. Accordingly, Chapters III and IV present data pertaining to Apache history, social structure and child-rearing practices and to the role of these factors in shaping the elements of personality organization which are common to these Indians.

III

Chiricahua and Mescalero Apache History and Social Structure

HISTORICAL ORIGINS

Perhaps a millennium ago, groups of hunting, gathering and raiding Indians who came to speak the language stock known as Southern Athabaskan (Hoijer 1938) migrated southward from northwestern Canada and finally settled in the Great Southwest and in northern Mexico (Boas 1911; Hall 1944; Huscher and Huscher 1942; Schroeder 1974; Worcester 1942). During the ensuing 700 or so years they divided; one portion was influenced heavily by the resident Pueblo Indians and became known as the Navahos, while the other continued its earlier nomadic life and was designated Apache (Shepardson 1961).

The Apaches were a ferocious, proud people of whom Cremony (1868:203) wrote: "In point of intellect, in cunning and duplicity, in tenacity of purpose and wondrous powers of endurance, (they) have no equals among the Indians existing in North America." Schwatka (1887) and Chittenden were awed by the ability of the Apaches to humiliate the governments of Mexico and the United States; the latter wrote (1902:882): "In their whole career of more than two centuries, the Spanish and Republican governments ... seem to have existed only by their sufferance."

Eventually the groups which remained nomadic became the Chiricahua, Jicarilla, Kiowa, Lipan, Mescalero and Western Apaches.

All but the Kiowa Apaches, who remained behind in the Great Plains (Mails 1974:11), claimed large, overlapping areas of land in what is now Arizona, New Mexico and northern Mexico for their migratory subsistence pursuits. Of them, the Chiricahuas and Mescaleros were the most closely related peoples, both culturally and linguistically (Basehart 1959, 1960; Opler 1933). They were normally at peace and there was frequent intermarriage. They had a common genetic background and their social structures and child-rearing patterns appear to have been very similar. We assume that their aboriginal personality organizations were also very much alike. They have had a practically common folklore in recorded times.

The Mescaleros had sporadic hostile contacts with the Spanish explorers and settlers from the early 1500s, but they and the Chiricahuas began to be influenced heavily by white pressures in the early middle of the nineteenth century. Following their defeat by the armies of the United States and Mexico, a reservation was established in 1873 for the Mescaleros in south central New Mexico, in the heartland of their prior subsistence activities.

The reservation occupies some 461,000 acres ranging from 4,500 to 12,000 feet in elevation. West of the reservation lies a dazzlingly white sink of gypsum on which a major experimental missile range now exists. Separating White Sands National Monument from the pine-forested slopes and mountain meadows that characterize the Indians' land is a narrow strip of desert, seemingly infertile but abounding in plants and animals once prized in Apache subsistence, and even now precious in terms of emotional usages. Here we find mesquite bushes, sources of a favorite bean. The yucca, so spectacular when in blossom, supplies tender shoots and flowers which are combined with Indian bananas, gooshgunnéh, to make tasty, sweet desserts. The root of the yucca is still used as shampoo by the elderly and during rites. The century plant, used for the baked mescal, is less prevalent than formerly but still may be found in areas just off the reservation, especially to the south. Cacti supply the tuna, a tasty, red fruit, the Apache name for which appropriately closely resembles their word for the red ant. Rabbits and deer are still to be found, as are gophers and other rodents, formerly among the favorite sources of protein.

In the valleys of the streams wending westward from the mountain heights are now to be found apple orchards which produce high-quality fruit. Formerly, berries of many kinds made their seasonal appearance. Tules are to be found and are used as they were before, for ceremonial purposes.

In the higher elevations, deer and pronghorns continue to be plentiful, as once again are elk, recently reintroduced from Yellowstone National Park. The forests and meadows now support the two major tribal industries, lumbering and cattle raising.

On the reservation, the Mescaleros were subjected to gradual deculturative and acculturative processes by relatively noninterfering Bureau of Indian Affairs practices. The pressures to which the Chiricahuas were subjected were quite different. Following the ultimate capitulation of Geronimo in 1886, they were taken as prisoners of war, transported to military camps, first in Florida, then Alabama, and finally Oklahoma, and ultimately freed in 1913 when a majority chose to join the Mescaleros and become an official part of their tribe. However, middle-aged and older members of the two groups even now retain their ethnic identity. The acculturative and deculturative changes in the lives of the Chiricahuas were precipitous.

Ticho (1971) has described culture shock as a result of a sudden change from what Hartmann (1939) called an average expectable environment, and Garza-Guerrero (1974) has noted that such culture shock results in reactive mourning and identity confusion. The Chiricahuas defended themselves against depression and partly resolved their identity confusion by using the mechanism called identification with the aggressor (A. Freud 1936), becoming in some ways like their soldier-captors and thereby developing some of the characteristics of lower-economic-class whites (Boyer and Boyer 1967). While the Mescaleros retained more obvious features of aboriginal personality organization (Boyer, Boyer et al. 1964), both they and the Chiricahuas retained a common modal personality (Kardiner 1939; Kardiner et al. 1945) or cultural personality (Hippler, Boyer and Boyer 1976) and their similar if not identical prelatency socialization practices seem to have remained essentially unchanged. Those practices and their effects on the personality development of these Apaches will be detailed in Chapter IV.

KINSHIP, SOCIOPOLITICAL ORGANIZATION,
ECONOMICS AND RESIDENCE PATTERNS

The northern Athabascan progenitors of these Apaches had matrilineal clans and reckoned their lineage solely from the maternal side. While the kinship system of the Apaches was formally bilateral, it tended to be functionally matrilineal. Formerly, the significant kinship unit was composed of the matrilocal extended family. Sociopolitical organization was influenced strongly by the necessity for mobility, stemming from subsistence practices. The largest solidary group conceptualized was the tribe. The greatest concrete political unit was centered about a particular male leader; he and his followers constituted a "band." A kinship group of the leader formed the nucleus of the band and the proportion of relatives in a band was a function of the size of the group. The distribu-

FORT PICKENS, FLORIDA
Cell block where Chiricahua men were imprisoned
(Courtesy Arizona Pioneers' Historical Society, Tucson, Arizona)

tion of resources and variations of climate favored regular seasonal movements. The subsistence pattern represented a balance between hunting and gathering, but the more consistent contribution was provided by the collecting activities of the women. The hunting and raiding men were at times gone for weeks or months, leaving old people, women and children in their camps.

At the same time, no Apache was committed to permanent affiliation with a specific group; he could become a member of another leader's group as he chose. The Apaches placed a high value on movement as such.

The leaders, while respected, had no definite or constant authority over members of the band. Their tenure depended on their ability to sense the wishes of the majority, on their effectiveness and on the degree of supernatural power ascribed to them.

The band, when camped together, was an important economic group. For some bison hunts, groups from several bands would at times collaborate. Subsistence products circulated throughout the band. Various family units became linked through a network of economic and social obligations.

While depicting the anomie of the Sioux, Erikson (1945, 1959:21) indicated that their historical group identity as romantic bison hunters stood counterposed to the occupational and class identity of the American civil-service employee. The historical group identity of the Apache male, still retained by persons of the older two or three generations, is that of the hunter, warrior, raider and horseman. In present reservation life, this identity is counterproductive.

While there is a pronounced trend toward neolocality based on the arrangements of new housing units, matrilocality remains the preferred pattern for most of the Indians. This kind of residence, involving the proximity of two or more generations of female kin, combined with the frequently physically absent father, resulted in the closest emotional ties occurring between mothers and daughters and between sisters. Today many fathers tend to be psychologically absent and the closeness of female ties continues to be prevalent.

The women of the tribes also tend to be emotionally more secure and to have clearer sexual identity on both conscious and unconscious levels (R. Boyer 1964). The men remain less integrated into family structure than is usual in groups with neolocal residence patterns.

Although they have been confined to reservation life for a century, these Apaches retain a clear tendency toward the roaming patterns typical of hunting and gathering societies. From time to time they like to camp, and many prefer to live for some period of the year near the site of their earliest home. They like to change residence and they find minor excuses to move from expensive new housing units and return, often, to less convenient, more familiar quarters; they like to attend ceremonies and pow-wows of other tribes and to visit relatives on other reservations. It may be that the psychological effects of perpetuation of movement constitute one of the most important elements which permit the Apaches to continue to identify themselves as a solidary group. The persistent Apache tendency to roam and return to meaningful childhood locations reminded Dr. E. C. Adams (personal communication) of the young child who attempts to master being left by the mother (Freud 1920; Mahler *et al.* 1975).

As is true among the Athabascans of Alaska (Hippler and Conn 1972), the native legal system functioned in terms of the degree of guilt and commitment to repentance manifested by the transgressor. There were seven types of delicts: those meriting the most serious punishment — capital punishment or exile — were the practice of witchcraft or incest (MacLachlan 1962).

The earlier custom of sharing goods functions sporadically today. Thus, when a person receives a financial windfall, he is apt to spend it immediately in a fashion which Anglo observers judge pejoratively as "squandering," since thousands of dollars may be devoted to partying or buying poor-quality material goods which within a few months may be in a state of disrepair. At the time this socialization study was undertaken, although the *average* income of the Apache family was adequate to provide a comfortable livelihood, there were very well-off and very poor Apaches and the majority tended to live a hand-to-mouth existence. In sharp contrast to the past, little respect was accorded the aged, who were largely expected to fend for themselves. As an example, whereas previously the old people were automatically fed and housed on a level equal to the younger, today it is customary for middle-aged and younger progeny to charge their parents for rides to the grocery store.

The definition of masculine and feminine roles will be discussed in Chapter IV.

THE ROLE OF ALCOHOL

Formerly, these Apaches made a beverage with low alcohol content, *tulapai,* or *tiswin,* which they drank on partying and ceremonial occasions. When intoxicated while partying, they sometimes gave vent to accumulated hostilities, and family feuds resulted in injuries and deaths; at times, there was a diminution of sexual morality. Today, drunkenness is almost a way of life for many Apaches. Most crimes are associated with intoxication and in general are committed against family members. The incidence of Apache crime is much higher than the national average (Boyer 1964a; Kunstadter 1960).

The majority of deaths among adolescents and adults can be related to alcohol intake. Chiricahuas and Mescaleros take little or no personal responsibility for their drinking; they frequently blame whites for providing liquor to be bought. When sober, these Apaches are in general gentle, humorous, inhibited, courteous and considerate. Drunk, they can become lewd and brutal to a startling degree and their sexual and aggressive behavior is not concealed from children of any age. Two examples will suffice.

Two men had been lifelong best friends and were clearly brother-surrogates. One of them, perhaps unwittingly, offended the other, who gave no overt behavioral evidence of resentment. Then one evening they drank together and camped out in an area which was surrounded by houses in which there were children of all ages. When the offender had become besotted, his friend dragged him to the campfire and charred one of his forearms so severely that amputation was required. According to rumor, this occurrence was reported by an observing child.

A rather promiscuous woman and her drunken companion had intercourse in broad daylight in a shallow arroyo while children watched. The woman's intoxicated husband happened by and beat his wife with a club. He was soon joined by her sexual partner in the attack on his wife. Eventually, one of the two shoved a sharp stick up the woman's vagina. She eventually died of peritonitis.

Summarily, then, in earlier times these Apaches were self-sufficient, independent, hardy people who had stable but internally flexible social structures and clearly defined roles for men and women. Currently, dwelling on the reservation as a tribal member constitutes a "protected" existence. The inconsistently administered governmental policies, although called paternalistic, have coincided in fact with what Apaches expect from maternal figures, and supported dependency and lack of personal responsibility are widespread. Apache immaturity has been and is fostered by tribe, state and nation. The diluted and attenuated aspects of reservation life which were demonstrated by Mead (1932:64-75) hold for these Apaches.

RELIGIOMEDICAL PHILOSOPHIES AND PRACTICES

From the beginning of my contacts with the Apaches of the Mescalero Indian Reservation, I was known as a psychiatrist, which term, translated into native thinking, is equated with medicine-man or shaman, "someone who deals with things of the mind," in contrast to Western medical doctors in general. I was never asked to prescribe medicines.

For reasons which will be delineated later, the Chiricahuas and Mescaleros simultaneously suspect their shamans of being witches and view them with the ambivalence which is so prevalent toward all parental and sibling surrogates. Initially, I was the object of this customary ambivalence. While one group adopted a "wait-and-see" attitude to judge whether I would use my ascribed supernatural powers for moral or evil purposes, another assumed that my intentions were solely good. A third group was sure that my ends were bad and rationalized its view in an interesting way. My having learned to speak and understand some of the Apache language before I arrived on the reservation and continuing to take formal lessons once there pleased some people, but others were suspicious of my motives. They recalled that during World War II Athabascans and other Indians were used by the military to transmit messages that could not be decoded; they were certain that the United States and Russia would soon be at war and decided that I was a Soviet spy who had been sent to learn the Athabascan language.

After I had been on the reservation for six months or so, my intentions were generally assumed to be good. By then, not only supernatural power but also omniscience was ascribed to me, and some Apaches had asked me to serve as their family shaman. Eventually, several of the native shamans requested that I assume the responsibilities of the tentative new position of chief tribal shaman, including being the repository of their erstwhile secret lore, owning their ceremonies and even the songs and rituals of the Mountain God dancers and the puberty ceremony for girls, and "bringing up future generations of real Apaches." Although I could not accede, some people assumed that I had done so and material was provided that has supplemented the monumental data previously obtained by others, notably Harry Hoijer and Morris E. Opler, to whom we are indebted for dependable information about aspects of the aboriginal lore of the Eastern Apaches.

RELIGION, MEDICAL PRACTICE, WITCHCRAFT AND SHAMANISM

According to Brinton (1868), "there was no class of persons who so widely and deeply influenced the culture and shaped the destiny of the Indian tribes as their priests." Although the influence of the aboriginal religion upon the lives of the Apaches is ebbing, it can yet be perceived in every aspect of their thinking and actions.

There is no way of determining to what degree Western European contact has modified the Apaches' mythology and philosophies (Opler 1935). The basic concept of Apache religion is that of vague, undefined, diffuse supernatural power. "This force floods the universe and renders even inanimate objects potentially animate" (Opler 1947:1).

Features of the aboriginal concept of power are presented in the following quotations:

> Power has no definite attribute of good or evil; its virtue is its
> potency. An Apache who could control some of this power might
> accomplish things close to his heart, it is felt. In contrast to the
> might of the supernatural stands the human individual. Alone he is
> a pitiable object, a prey to sickness, to enemies, to want, to the
> machinations of evil men. And so he hopes for supernatural help ...
> (Opler 1936:144-5).

> However, in order to become effective, power must "work through"
> mankind. Its method is to utilize the animals, plants, natural
> forces, and inanimate objects familiar to the Chiricahua, as chan-
> nels by means of which to get in contact with men. After this con-
> tact has been made, the power appears in a personified guise and
> offers a ceremony or supernatural aid to the person approach
> (Opler 1947:1).

> ... the Apache, usually at a time of mental or physical stress, lies
> down and believes himself to be approached and addressed by one
> of the agents to which reference has been made above ... (he)
> recognizes it as a vision experience. Whatever has come to this
> Apache speaks to him of his weakness, of his need for something
> which will warn him of danger, which will be ever at his call, which
> will help him cure the illnesses of his children, relatives and friends.
> The power offers him a ceremony, and, if he accepts it, the songs
> and prayers which establish the rapport between the power and the
> practitioner are revealed; the details of the ceremony, the uses to
> which it can be put, and the evils against which it will prove ef-
> ficacious are all explained. If it is a bear that has approached this
> particular Apache, for instance, those who are cognizant of his en-
> counter with the animal will say that their friend "knows" bear, or
> that bear "works through" him. Thereafter anyone who becomes
> sick from bear may come up to this man to have a curative
> ceremony performed (Opler 1936:145).

Opler (1947) has written that, in the earlier Apache conceptualization,
supernatural power could be obtained by dream, hallucination, gift or
purchase. The modern Apache notion is that power makes itself
available to an individual only through "power dreams" or hallucinations. Ceremonies can be learned from an "owner," and they retain
some degree of power despite the transfer. But some Apaches now
believe that ceremonies alone have no more power than prayers. Opler
(1935) called the Apaches "a nation of shamans," reasoning that any

person who owned a ceremony possessed supernatural power. Yet Bourke (1892) indicated that "small villages" had no more than one or two of "their doctors," and, in 1960, when the population numbered approximately 1200 individuals, only thirteen reservation Apaches were accepted as shamans. By 1974 the number had been reduced to three, although there were then some 2000 tribal members. In 1976, with the pan-Indian upsurge of interest in re-establishment of "the old ways" and "Indian power," a few more people were tentatively accorded the shamanistic status. In recent years, almost all adults and some Apaches as young as six years old have been thought to possess ceremonies. "It seems to be in their families." In accordance with current Apache conceptualizations of shamanism, the shaman can be defined as an individual who is considered to possess supernatural powers which support and are supported by the common values of his culture.

Opler (1941:200) wrote: "In the great enterprise of traffic with the supernatural there is no hierarchy of religious leadership." It is not clear whether he referred to a hierarchy of supernatural powers or of shamans. Since he indicated that power conferred by a single source—like lightning—may be stronger or weaker depending on the shaman who uses it, he may have meant that the power source is not intrinsically important and that "sun power," for instance, is *in itself* no more potent than "mescal power."

Currently, there is no doubt that some shamans are considered to be "stronger" than others; even if two individuals are thought to have acquired supernatural power from the same source, it may prove to be more effective when used by one of them. Most Apaches agree that a power obtained from a celestial source (sun, moon, star, lightning, cloud, wind and so forth) can be used to rectify a variety of ills, to ward off divers dangers, to forecast the future, to determine whether an object has been lost or stolen and ensure its recovery, et cetera. A power from a terrestrial source (yucca, lizard, bear, waterbug and the like), however, can be used only to counteract sicknesses or misfortunes resulting from an affront to the "boss," *diyin* (spirit) or *nant?a* (leader) of that source. Yet there is at least one area of confusion, for the *diyin* of the snake is considered the same as that of the lightning.

In addition, there are celestial and terrestrial classes of power of varying strengths. According to some Mescalero shamans of the 1960's, one who is entitled to call upon the "little whirlwind" or "little star" has "little power"; one who can summon the strength of the *diyin* of the sun or moon has "medium power"; one who can invoke the *nant?a* of the lightning, wind, or large hail has "big power." As far as we have been able to learn from the literature, the concept of the hierachy of bosses has not been described, although there is an allusion to it in Henry's (N.D.) study of the cult of Silas John. The concept is ill-defined, and in-

MOUNTAIN SPIRIT DANCER AND SACRED CLOWN
(Sculptural models made by Amos Gaines)

formants' statements are contradictory about detail. Mescalero, Chiricahua and Lipan shamans, as well as other informants, however, all state that each natural phenomenon has a boss of its own.

The hierarchy of powers resembles a military chain of command. He-Who-Created-Us, *Yusn,* God, is the "commander-in-chief." Three powerful *diyi*^{n}, "angels," control events in the heavens, the earth and the water. Lesser *nant?a* concern themselves with individual celestial and terrestrial phenomena. For example, Thunderman, Thunderlady, Thunderboy and Thundergirl have poorly defined roles related to the behavior and effects of lightning, thunder, rain and snow. There is a boss in charge of land animals, another of land plants. A *diyi*^{n} governs water animals; another, water plants. Lower-order bosses control faunal and floral families and, in addition, each living species has a *diyi*^{n} of its own. Large geographical features and stones of varying sizes, shapes and colors are thought to have individual *nant?a.* The *diyi*^{n} of sacred places may have more power than those of inanimate objects.

There is no evidence that aboriginal Apaches believed that there was a hierarchical arrangement of bosses. Such a notion is, however, consistent with Christian beliefs. Effective contact with Christianity has existed for both Chiricahuas and Mescaleros since prior to the establishment of this reservation. Additionally, a large number of these Apaches have become acquainted with hierarchical concepts during more than a century of service in the United States military forces.

The Mountain Spirits (*ga*^{n}*heh, jajadeh)* have been a most important element in the ceremonial aspects of Chiricahua and Mescalero religion (Bourke 1892; Goddard 1916; Harrington 1912; Hoijer 1938a; Opler 1941, 1946). According to Opler (Hoijer 1938a:143-144):

> The Mountain Spirits are a race of supernaturals who dwell within the interiors of many mountains. ... There they are said to live and conduct their affairs much as the Apaches used to do in aboriginal times. The Mountain Spirits conduct a dance and ceremony in which some of their men are masked and appear with their bodies painted in various patterns. Occasionally an Apache is fortunate enough to have a supernatural experience with the Mountain Spirits of a particular mountain, to witness the performance of these masked supernaturals, and to be influenced in the songs, designs, and prayers which belong to the rite.

Such an experience, according to our informants, always involves an ordeal (see Chapter V). Opler (Hoijer 1938a:144) continues:

> After this Apache returns to the world outside, and to his own people, he masks and paints Apache men in imitation of the super-

naturals he has seen, and sends them out to dance at times of widespread sickness or impending disaster. This procedure or rite is expected to establish rapport between the shaman and the aboriginal supernaturals from whom he has obtained his power. ...the real Mountain Spirits sometimes come out upon this world in person to punish those who have profaned their rite or to succor Apaches in need of their assistance. Now it is said that only those appear who are "made" or dressed in imitation of the true Mountain Spirits.

The "made" dancers, however, carry the same name as did the masked supernaturals. The Mountain Spirit teams consist of four dancers and one or occasionally two clowns. Opler was given to understand that all the "made" dancers, or at least their leaders and clowns, were shamans. During the years of our work, only one team leader was accorded the status of shaman as an individual. The other leaders, the dancers and the clowns, were simply men who were selected, trained and hired to perform the ceremonies.

The clown of the Mountain Spirits is clearly a figure which personifies for the Chiricahuas and the Mescaleros Coyote of the Coyote Legend Cycle (Boyer and Boyer 1978). The Mountain Spirits became figures of the Apache religio-medical tradition through diffusion from the Pueblo Indians, with whom they have had recorded intimate contact since at least as early as the sixteenth century.

The function of the shaman is limited to the cure of an individual, but the role of the Mountain Spirits is to ensure "good luck" for the entire society. They dance at all important tribal functions which involve attempts to ward off epidemics, droughts, floods, fires or disasters of any nature. A team of ga^nheh customarily has been hired to dance for each girl during her puberty ceremony. (In 1976, however, when only two teams were available and four girls "came out," each group of ga^nheh danced for two girls.) While in the puberty ceremony the ga^nheh are to ensure the maiden a long, happy and moral life, their ultimate purpose is to help her to become a good wife and mother and rear children who will function in the service of the tribe, and ensure intragroup tranquility.

In 1974 and 1975 the tribe erected a palatial inn for tourists. In the building process, to obtain water for a large reservoir to be used for recreational purposes, they diverted water from a stream which had been used for hundreds of years to irrigate the crops of Anglo and Spanish American farmers and orchardmen who lived in a large valley below. These agriculturalists belatedly took the matter to court. Recently, Mountain Spirits were hired to dance, in hopes that their ceremony would influence a ruling in favor of the Apaches. Again, it is said that before a national election took place a few years ago, *jajadeh* danced in an (unsuccessful) effort to achieve the election of a man who was thought to be particularly friendly to the Indians.

While power itself is considered to be neutral, the prevailing attitude toward individual supernatural powers has been that they are hostile, just as parental surrogates are suspected of being intrinsically malevolent. Although the belief is waning, formerly, whenever an Apache wished to use an animal, plant or inanimate object for his sustenance or shelter, he was expected to make obeisance to its *diyin*.

The shaman seeks to protect offending human beings from the anger of affronted *diyin*. He may mollify those who are merely annoyed, but the rage of the seriously insulted boss must be deflected onto some person other than the miscreant. Additionally, any person who owns supernatural power may use it as he chooses or his personality dictates, for good (collectivity-oriented) or evil (witchcraft or sorcery) purposes. To own power is considered to be hazardous. A shaman who saves a life must at some future time atone by ceding his own or that of someone dear to him, usually a relative. According to the opinion of thoughtful informants, in the final analysis the death of that person is implicitly ascribed to the shaman's having practiced witchcraft or passively permitted a death that had been demanded by one of the *nant?a*.

Opler (1941:229-237, 1946, 1947) found that old-time Apaches attributed almost all misfortune and disease to the actions of insulted *diyin,* witches or ghosts. Today, with influences traceable to acculturation, credence is increasingly placed in the existence of fortuitous mishaps and white concepts of the genesis of disease. Nevertheless, the great majority of today's Apaches of all ages remain involved to varying degrees with aboriginal beliefs. It is our judgment that the concepts are in the main ego-syntonically integrated into the world-view of the large majority of those who are fifty years of age or older, while they may be compartmentalized or loosely joined in the majority of younger Apaches.

As already indicated, earlier conceptualizations of means for acquiring shamanistic powers have changed. The current prevalent notion is that a person must experience a power dream or hallucination to gain supernatural power. Yet confusion remains. Opler inferred that sorcery could be practiced only by those who possessed supernatural power, but in the 1960s charges of witchcraft practice were leveled at people who were not thought to own such power. Also, although all shamans were thought to be capable of practicing witchcraft, only about half of them were accused of doing so.

WITCHCRAFT

Aboriginally, various procedures could be employed to determine the identity of a witch. A shaman could have a patient look into a reflecting surface and command him to see a picture; the patient sometimes identified the person who had "witched" him. Indians who were sexually aberrant and those who committed incest were assumed to have been bewitched or to be witches. Ideal collectivity-oriented behavior demanded an absence of intragroup trouble-making. No person was supposed to have possessions greatly in excess of those of his neighbors. The chronic braggart, trouble-maker and miser were thought to be sorcerers. A person accused of being a witch could undergo tests to prove his innocence. Examples of these tests include the suspect's eating elk meat (a witch would vomit the meat, which was relished by the ordinary person) and the suspect's being hung by his thumbs over a fire (if a confession did not result within a certain period, the individual was freed). Confession constituted complete evidence of guilt, and the witch was burned to death. (It was possible, too, that a person found not guilty by the suspension test might still be killed by relatives of his supposed victims [Opler 1941:248-253].)

Schwatka (1887) observed a variant test of witchcraft guilt. A woman was stripped to the waist and suspended by her thumbs so that only her toes touched the ground. Everyone in the group was at liberty to "flay" her with sharp switches. The woman confessed before her tormentors tired and was beaten and stoned to death.

Today, a person is diagnosed as a witch principally through his actions and personality. As a rule, he or she will be more than sixty years old. At least until very recently, a person was suspect if one or more of his ancestors had been thought to be a powerful witch. If a person pointed at people with a finger rather than his lips, was afraid to sleep indoors with others, ate solely his own cooking, danced naked in the woods, was unusually paranoid, a braggart or a miser or, above all, "talked mean," he was suspected of being a witch. On two occasions I heard that a woman was turned into a witch because she refused to have sexual intercourse with a man who was thought to possess supernatural power. Capital punishment for witchcraft has disappeared. There are no punishments beyond gossip and some degree of ostracism, which encourage further intragroup tensions.

Witches have three principal methods of operating: using magical words and gestures, calling upon their supernatural powers, and controlling the actions of ghosts.

Sorcerers can use silent or spoken curses to harm individuals or entire tribes. The current general drunkenness and decrease of water supply on the reservation have been attributed to witchcraft practiced by sorcerers of other Indian tribes or Mexican enemies. Should the witch choose to bring "bad luck" to a person, he can cause that individual to be penetrated by a "witch's arrow." In past times, such "arrows" were usually made of portions of cadavers or objects that had touched them. The witch found a dead body and used its bones and/or hair to make a tiny or invisible bow and arrow, which could be tipped with a piece of dried corpse flesh, a fragment of clothing, feathers, a spider, horsehair, a needle or any other object that had touched the corpse. The bow had magical powers and could shoot the arrow into a given person at any distance. Today, a favorite practice of a witch is to obtain hair, feces, urine, sputum or menstrual blood from the intended victim and shoot it into him or her. Cursed herbs or a decoction of excreta from the individual to be bewitched may be put into his or her food or drink.

GHOSTS

Witches have traffic with ghosts of dead human beings. They can change such spirits or living persons into any animate or inanimate object. The sorcerer can cause the disguised ghost or human being to contact any person and cause him misfortune. Every ghost is potentially dangerous. The spirits of individuals who have died after "a full life" are feared less than those of people who have died "before their time," violently, or who were "mean" or witches. Ghosts of the satisfied dead are thought to go to some nebulous "happy hunting ground" (or, since Christianization, heaven). They must be very few. Others hover about in the darkness, waiting to frighten or inconvenience the living, ultimately to drive them crazy to the point of committing suicide or foolishly losing their lives. In some cases, ghosts are thought to desire the deaths of loved ones, so that the spirits of the latter will join the ghosts and relieve their loneliness. Or the ghosts are said to seek vengeance, to make others die before their time, so that they, too, will be unhappy. Ghosts can become re-embodied voluntarily into various animals and birds.

The Apache attitude toward ghosts reflects their concept that small children are not yet truly human (see Chapter IV). While ghost-chasing ceremonies are considered to be mandatory to avert the effects of the departed spirit of the adult and often that of the adolescent, when a pre-teenager dies such a ceremony is practiced only rarely, and the rite is deemed unnecessary when a younger child dies. At the same time, some Apaches now forego the customary ritual and have only Christian funerals for their dead.

Although any animal, bird or plant can be used for the purposes of the witch, owls, and canines are particularly feared as agents of sorcerers and are sometimes called witches. If they are inhabited by ghosts, either through the choice of the spirit or the machinations of the sorcerer, they have the power of speech, which all animals are presumed to have had "in the beginning." Owls, dogs, coyote and foxes have oracular powers. To foretell the death of an individual or relative, they speak his name and say, "I am going to drink your blood."

Witchcraft, then, can cause an individual or a group to suffer any kind of disaster. Ghosts affect people with great fear and create a psychic disturbance, known as "ghost sickness."

ITSEH

A third class of disorders results from Apache negligence of bosses. This group of conditions is specifically referred to as *itseh* (it makes sickness) or *nitseh* (it makes you sick). In the old days, before any living or inanimate object could be used safely by an Indian, it was necessary that he perform a ceremony to appease its *diyi^n*. If mescal were to be gathered, the woman who did the collecting had to pray to its *nant?a,* expressing thanks, promising that the food would be used for collective purposes and requesting a good crop the next year. If she failed to conduct the little rite, the mescal *diyi^n* caused the plant she gathered to spoil, cook improperly or fail to nourish her and her family, and/or the next year's growth was diminished. Ultimately, group starvation would threaten. If the boss of the deer, antelope, yucca or any other food source were similarly affronted, like results were to be expected. If trees were cut or rocks collected for building purposes and their *nant?a* were affronted by negligence, erection of the proposed dwelling was made impossible or the dwelling fell down once built. Herbs, other medicines and sacred materials that were improperly collected did not perform their appointed tasks, and their collectors were punished in various manners. If the *nant?a* of any object were seriously insulted, he turned the offender into an animal, a plant or a stone, or afflicted him with a fatal disease or mishap.

Certain *diyi^n*, when affronted, cause specific disease syndromes, all of which involve manifestations of acute anxiety. If an Apache steps on a spider and fails to apologize properly to its boss, he will soon suffer from "spider sickness." The symptoms consist of cracks (or sensations as though there were cracks) in the skin, that resemble the spider's web. If the *nant?a* of the arachnid is not appeased by a shaman who has either a celestially derived power or spider power, soon the weblike cracks will invade the heart and kill the victim. "Snake sickness" results from touching a snake or a place a snake has recently inhabited. It is a disease in which some or all of the skin peels off like the skin of the reptile when it is being shed. In addition, aches, pains and crawling sensations occur on the surface of the body. If no shaman with lightning or snake power treats the victim, the crawling will reach the offender's heart and he will surely die. (It is noteworthy that today, when no shamans own spider or bear power, spider and bear sicknesses no longer appear as diagnoses.) If an owl flies near camp and an Apache does not properly salute its *diyi^n*, he will suffer from tremulousness, sweating, great fear, contractions and arrhythmias of the heart, muscle spasms, insanity and ultimately death from committing suicide or "acting foolishly." The similarities of these various conditions to anxiety-neurosis are apparent.

Each syndrome caused by an affronted boss has its own name. Theoretically, according to one recently deceased shaman, there are 60,000 such illnesses, many of which are named; but few are evident today. Ceremonies consecrated to *diyi^n* of specific objects to be hunted or gathered are rapidly disappearing. Still, the majority of Indians in their thirties or older pray cursorily to God, Jesus or the Virgin before they hunt or gather. It is our impression that most elderly Apaches still regularly invoke the *nant?a* of traditional ceremonial foodstuffs before such items are gathered or hunted , and that they continue to pray to the spirits of plants which are to be used for ceremonial purposes. They feel anxious when younger people omit such ritual behavior; their worry is manifested by their scolding the miscreants.

ETHNO-CURATIVE PRACTICES

It is clear from the foregoing that any disease syndrome or disaster may have three different sources. The diagnosis of *goobinitseh* (snake-his-power-it-makes-you-sick), if the symptoms are classic, is not difficult to make. But the shaman may be hard put to determine whether the sickness resulted from the actions of *goobidiyi^n* (snake-his-boss), a witch or a ghost. In early times, there was a crucial need to differentiate among the three potential causes. If the sickness were the result of the actions of a ghost who had entered the reptile and then, as a snake, touched the intended victim, the work of the shaman was defined: to "chase the ghost." If the illness were determined to have been caused by witchcraft, the healer's job was to battle the specific sorcerer who had been hired or otherwise chosen to harm the sufferer. If the sickness were inflicted by the affronted *goobidiyi^n*, only the shaman with snake or lightning power was capable of influencing the boss of the snake to permit the offending Indian to live.

Of the treatment afforded by Apache shamans in the early 1930's, Opler (1936a:1372) wrote:

> The Apache shaman is not a credulous dupe of his own super-
> naturalistic claims and boastings, who undertakes to cure any ail-
> ment, no matter how hopeless. The shaman was a shrewd and
> wary person who recognized and as a rule refused to accept respon-
> sibility for the cure of serious organic disturbance. Sometimes he

resorted to legerdemain to demonstrate that his treatment would be ineffective. The shaman was quick to treat less serious indispositions, however, and to solidify his reputation by rendering prompt relief.

He was "often interrupted by his 'power' while in the midst of his ceremonial songs and directed to dose his patient with some common laxative or emetic" (p. 1373). To be sure, the decoction was administered ritualistically.

Although the shaman usually refused to treat serious organic disorders, he did sometimes accept such cases. There were, of course, built-in safeguards. If he were convinced of failure in advance of or at some point during the treatment, he could claim his diagnosis had been erroneous because his client had given him faulty information, or he could state that his power had told him the Apache whom he was treating had too flagrantly insulted a boss. The curer insisted that a patient who sought his help have absolute confidence in the efficacy of the ceremony to be performed and the integrity of the practitioner. An Apache and his relatives had to humble themselves before the shaman from whom they sought assistance. After he had magnanimously acceded to their pleas, the shaman would demand four ceremonial gifts for his "power":

A representative set of such gifts would be a pouch of pollen, an umblemished buckskin, a downy eagle feather and a piece of turquoise. Even after these have been presented, he has other orders to give. A special structure for the rite, with the door facing the east, is often demanded, and the close relatives of the patient are expected to furnish all the labor involved. By such requirements the Apache shaman takes pains to eliminate half-heartedness at the outset, and he proceeds on the assumption that for best results confidence in the technique he is to use, his ceremony and his "power" must be instilled. Accordingly, when all is in readiness and the ceremony is about to begin, the shaman's first act is to validate his ceremony, and to impress the patient and the assembled relatives with its potency and its source. He describes the supernatural encounter which led to the acquisition of the ceremony; he relates how he was led into the "holy home" of the "power" and there tested in every conceivable way, how the ceremony and its uses were unfolded before him, and how, through his ceremony, he has since been able to enlist the aid of his "power" in the curing of those who come to him in the proper fashion (Opler 1936a:1375-1376).

If the patient remained apathetic toward the shaman and the

ceremony, the healer would sometimes terminate proceedings and blame his failure on the client. Also, it was usual for the shaman to invoke small taboos on the behavior of relatives and clients; for example, he might forbid them to scratch lice bites with their fingernails during the ceremony. Breaches of conduct could then be blamed for failure.

The Chiricahuas and Mescaleros are highly suggestible and subject easily to altered ego states, a fact of considerable import in ethnomedical practices. Children, for example, often enter trance-like states during which they hallucinate, and Apache mothers while taking care of infants can enter a dreamy condition in which they are oblivious to the noisy activities of others in crowded rooms. Quite aside from the active practice of hypnosis by shamans during curing ceremonies, trances were formerly induced in the person being treated and many observers. Then, for endless hours during four consecutive nights the patient and his family and close friends were crowded together inside a specially built small structure in the center of which was a fire; the room became hotter as the night progressed and all became sleepier. Monotonous drumming was accompanied by repetitive chanting and both the patient and the audience experienced hypnogogic alterations and hallucinations. The shaman also frequently knew the technique of autohypnosis and later claimed that, while he was in the resultant altered ego state, his soul went into the world of spirits, where it battled mightily with hostile powers.

Curing ceremonies have changed considerably, though trance-like states are still elicited. Present curing ceremonies usually last for only one or two nights and do not include drumming in the home of the patient. Those which I was permitted to attend were solemn and involved monotonous chanting and repetitious gesturing. Everyone present, including me, became relaxed and dreamy, and the audience as well as the patient reached a state in which they would have been unable to detect trick maneuvers on the part of the shaman. I did not observe the removal of a witch's arrow.

Formerly, during curing rites shamans resorted at times to prestidigitation. As trick photography is used to create a pleasing illusion, "the Apache ceremony is designed to inculcate belief in the shaman's powers" (Opler 1936a:1377). After the initial ritual, the shaman, who had much factual knowledge of the client's life beforehand, made a great display of enumerating significant events of the patient's past and present. He warned the sufferer that facts must not be withheld. Subjected to strong suggestion techniques, when the client's memory was jogged with data he had suppressed or repressed he would sometimes respond associatively, and the actual event or trauma that had crystallized the tic or seizure was often abreacted; in the course of such associations the symptoms at times did disappear.

After the shaman had exposed the symbol of the patient's distress (bear, snake, lightning and so forth), he attempted to determine *why* the embodiment of evil "bothered" his patient.

> For the answer to this question he invokes his "power." He sings his ceremonial songs and recites his prayers in an effort to com- municate with his "power," to obtain its aid in tracing down the forces which have made his patient ill and to gain its support in op- posing those forces. The effort to enlist the co-operation of the "power" in this work is often a stirring spectacle ... In the end, he announces, of course, his "power's" complete interest in the case and its determination to prosecute it to a successful conclusion (Opler 1936a:1379).

Then followed the dramatic battle between the shaman and his power(s) and the opposing evil machinations of witch or ghost. In the event that witchcraft was diagnosed, a witch's arrow was ultimately "sucked" or "grabbed" from the sufferer. Factually, the "arrow" had been secreted in the shaman's mouth or palmed. During the past century, a cartridge has sometimes been removed from the victim, rather than an arrow. The cartridge, like the arrow, is a penetrating instrument.

> At the conclusion of the ceremony the shaman makes a final gesture which may in some cases have decided therapeutic value. He imposes upon the patient some restriction or taboo. It may be an injunction to eat no meat from the head of the animal, to eat no entrails, to refrain from picking up some object which has been dropped, etc. It offers, in place of a tic or compulsive symptom, a clever substitute. When it has served its purpose and becomes irksome, a short ceremony at the hands of the one who pronounced the taboo makes its continuance unnecessary (Opler 1936a:1383).

Today, the majority of physical illnesses are treated by the United States Public Health Service physicians. These doctors are, however, considered completely unable to deal with disorders that the Apaches prediagnose as psychogenic. For these types of disorders, the shaman re- mains indispensable. I was able to obtain stated records of the incidence of employment of ten shamans during a period of one year. A Lipan man, who did not divulge the source of his powers, chased a ghost from a house in which death had occurred and performed two ceremonies to relieve sufferers of alcoholic hallucinosis thought to be caused by ghosts. A Mescalero woman, who said she received her powers from the "spirits of the long-ago dead," was hired fifteen times to chase ghosts, once from a child who had "doll sickness" (R. Boyer 1962) and the other times from houses in which people had died and from sufferers of alcoholic hallucinosis. A Mescalero man, who claimed powers from numerous celestial sources in addition to the bear, snake and horse, said he was hired on "several occasions" to practice witchcraft and, alternatively, to remove witches' arrows, to make women fertile or sterile, to make a man potent, to perform love magic and to determine whether objects which had disappeared had been lost or stolen.

My own services were directly solicited on a number of occasions. Once a singer at the girls' puberty ceremony asked me to kill by witchcraft a shaman who was generally thought to be evil. I was noncommittal, a manner consonant with customary Apache behavior. We were outdoors on a totally calm and cloudless day. Some years previously I had given this singer a Roschach test; now I asked him to produce another protocol. He hesitated to respond to one of the cards. At that moment, a blast of wind sudenly filled the air with dust and blew the cards aside. Severely frightened, he looked pleadingly at me and said, "You didn't have to do that; I would have told you." That night he was killed in a head-on collision caused by another driver's crossing the middle of the highway. No one ever referred to the incident. It is not known whether those to whom he had revealed his intent merely assumed that I had collectivity-oriented reasons to cause *his* death by witchcraft rather than to kill the evil shaman.

On another occasion, one of the few people on the reservation who were generally considered to be witches asked me, after a splendid dinner and in the presence of various relatives, to be the family shaman. Again, I was noncommittal. My first assignments were to cure her husband, who had a terminal disease, to alleviate her suffering from a chronic gerontological disorder and, much more importantly, to kill a man by witchcraft.

Today, the four gifts required for advance payment always include "smoke" (tobacco to be used in rolling cigarettes, which are to be smoked ritually during shamanistic ceremonies) and a black-handled knife, and, usually, dress materials if the shaman is female or a gun if the curer is male, and money. Sometimes a shaman will ask for a piece of turquoise. Black is the color most efficacious in ghost-chasing. Ashes and pollen are always used to ensure the successful outcome of any ceremony. Fire and its products are prophylactic against witches and ghosts. No special structures are used in contemporary ceremonies, which, do, however, sometimes remain dramatic in character. Peyote is rarely used to help the shaman or the patient hallucinate the source of the difficulty (Boyer *et al.* 1973). Hypnosis is sometimes used.

The interpretation and use of dreams have occupied man's thoughts from earliest times (Campbell 1959; Oppenheim 1956). They have been part and parcel of the religion and therapy of numerous nonliterate peoples (Eggan 1961; Firth 1934; Hallowell 1936, 1941; Herskovitz 1934;

Honigmann 1961; Kilborne 1974; Kracke 1976; LaBarre 1947; Lantenari 1957; Lincoln 1935; M.K. Opler 1959; Reay; Róheim 1947, 1953; Wallace 1958). Aside from their own interpretations of "power dreams," which have been mentioned before, most Apaches believe that all other dreams foretell the future, in terms of good and bad luck (Boyer 1962; Opler 1941:190-193). Certain manifest contents forecast illness or misfortune. Fire, floods, falling teeth, the return of a dead person, a pig, the colors red or black, being chased by a wild animal and, especially, any of the usual cultural bogeys — all tell the dreamer something "bad" will happen if he does not take preventive measures. Any dream that frightens an individual has the same general connotation, regardless of its content. However, the Apache believes that a dream in which some action directly affects the dreamer prophesies the opposite.

"If you dream you are going to be sick, that means you are going to stay well. If you dream that a snake bites you, that's good. It won't happen. If you dream that you die, it means you will live a long time. If you dream that your father, mother, brother or sister dies, it doesn't mean that one. It means that someone outside the family is going to die" (Opler 1941:190).

Other dream contents indicate the future occurrence of something good: "If you dream about summer, about everything green, about things growing and fruits and pollen, everything is all right." Opler (1941:190). Deer, horses, mules and burros are good-luck symbols.

If a person dreams of fire, he can prevent potential misfortune by building an outdoor fire. To prevent dreams about ghosts, one should not put clothing at the head of one's bed, especially in contact with one's pillow. Should one be frightened by a dream and know no countermeasure, a shaman might be consulted for a ghost-chasing ceremony or instructions. Not all shamans in the past claimed interpretive powers for dreams.

Among the Apaches of today, no shaman inquires about his clients' dreams. If a patient spontaneously relates a vision, the curer interprets its occurrence or its symbology as has been outlined. At least one shaman occasionally hypnotized a client, with or without the aid of peyote, in order to make an hallucination occur. The reverie is supposed to reveal the identity of the witch or disclose the conflict about which the patient feels guilt. If it does not, the experience is used to impress the client further with the shaman's and the ceremony's powers and to forecast in general terms the outcome of the curative rite. Several shamans said that they examined their own dreams closely in order to determine whether or not they were in danger of being subjected to witchcraft practiced by rivals. They were particularly attentive to dreams and hallucinations that occurred before and during curing ceremonies.

For many years I sought to obtain arcane information from a devout and revered shaman, who, while she liked me very much, was afraid that if she divulged private information her powers would punish her. Finally, a mutual friend accompanied me and successfully reassured her that knowledge provided me would not be used improperly. She fearfully revealed a few mundane facts. Recently she informed me in the presence of her husband that after that occasion she had been terrified and had kept to her bed in constant anxiety for two weeks, during which she had had repeated "visitations" which informed her that before she saw me again either she or our mutual friend would have been killed by her power. She implied that she believed that my supernatural power was stronger than hers and would protect me from harm. In fact, our friend died unexpectedly within a few months.

COMMENT

Formerly, families gathered around campfires every night, and lessons pertaining to Apache lore were transmitted to children by knowledgeable raconteurs, usually maternal grandmothers or great-grandmothers or their surrogates, although at times old men were favorite narrators. On rainy nights, children in bed were lulled to sleep by tales. The storytelling was enjoyed by all, particularly when the myriad antics of Coyote were recounted. The lore was related through historical accounts and "stories," legends and myths. Each growing child was thoroughly steeped in factual and fantasized folkloric information, which relayed to it Apache beliefs and behavioral expectations. Later chapters will provide illustrations.

Today, such enjoyable family occasions are diminishing and inconsistent, while television and Hollywood movies supply other kinds of implicit lessons. Similarly, as will be detailed in the next chapter, the many ceremonial observances which previously accompanied almost every step of the child's development have waned drastically. Nevertheless, in the child-rearing practices themselves, aboriginal beliefs and values continue to be transmitted. While the Apache child and youth of today do not know the details of the traditional stories, legends and myths, their educational and mystical qualities continue to be transmitted and the role of folklore continues to be of great importance in socialization. Observation of human behavior itself now substitutes for traditional lore, the contradictory messages inherent in which are epitomized by the implications of the variant actions of, for example, Coyote.

Following the explication of puericultural practices which constitutes the next chapter will be a discussion of the interactions of Apache modal personality structure with shamanism and witchcraft.

IV

Child Rearing and
Personality Organization

The two most striking characteristics which typify today's Apache parental attitudes toward and treatment of their children are ambivalence and inconsistency. While most parents consciously have strongly positive feelings toward their young, their behavior reveals intense preconscious and unconscious hostility toward them. We infer that those characteristics prevailed aboriginally as well, although perhaps less obviously than is true now, on several bases: (1) information obtained from aged informants, (2) reading between the lines of Opler's (1941) idealized account of earlier puericultural patterns, (3) a careful study of all of the data which are available concerning socialization practices of both northern and southern Athabascan-speaking Indians (Hippler and Wood 1974), and (4) field work done with two northern Athabascan groups, one of which as had meaningful contact with whites only since the second World War (Hippler *et al.* N.D., N.D.a).

When the Apaches were nomads, they lived in a hostile environment beset by human and nonhuman enemies. That some of those enemies were imaginary has been illustrated in the preceding chapter. The relative unreliability of subsistence products required the maintenance of optimal numbers of band members for group survival. An average of perhaps forty members in a band was needed to obtain the necessary means for living. Resources which might support more people were not regularly available. The dangerous life pattern of the Apaches necessitated the development of hardy people who could tolerate privation and adversity without serious psychological effects.

Although no reliable statistics exist for aboriginal times, it is certain that infant mortality was high and life was tenuous for all. So far as can be determined, the incidence of infant death was the same for boys and girls, from which we can deduce that children of both sexes were equally prized (deMause 1976). This is consistent with the fact that males and females were equally important in procuring subsistence products, although the amount of plant food collected by the women was somewhat more dependable than the amount of game provided by the hunting men. Additionally, of course, the men were warriors and raiders and were responsible for capturing women and children to replenish band members.

Over time, Apaches evolved child-rearing practices that produced people with personality configurations which were adaptive to their aboriginal life-style. Those configurations included a high degree of aggressivity and stoicism, independence, suspiciousness, suggestibility and the capacity to withstand the loss of kin and kith through death or desertion without debilitating depressive reactions.[1]

Perhaps because of the high rate of infant mortality, the Apaches developed over time a degree of emotional detachment from their young and unconscious hostility toward them. Evidence for this detachment and hostility is found in practices and attitudes which persist. As remains generally true, the baby was not considered to be "really human," "a real person," until it reached a year and a half or two years of age, that is, until its parents might have some confidence that it would survive. This attitude resulted in death practices having to do with the prevention of ghost sickness, as was discussed in Chapter III. Startling evidence for unconscious hostility toward babies is especially clear in the aboriginal practice of killing one of twins. The birth of twins was attributed to the practice of witchcraft, infidelity or "too much sex." One of the twins was customarily placed on an ant hill in the blazing sun to die while being bitten. Sometimes the eyes of the newborn infant were smeared with honey or some other sweet substance. This method of extermination was otherwise reserved for some enemies in battle. Old people state that the parents of the child who was killed in this manner did not feel guilty, and present-day informants, questioned about the practice, shrug and say, in effect, "That's just how it was." The last known time this custom was practiced was about seventy years ago. On that occasion, a childless woman rescued the baby girl who had been placed on the ant hill and reared her; her biological parents refused to have later contact with her. People who were questioned concerning their feelings about the practice were satisfied with the explanation that a mother did not have enough milk for two babies and saw no contradiction between this datum and the fact that wet-nursing was common for other babies whose mothers were unable to feed their young.

A highly significant common denominator is to be found in the socialization practices which prevail with every step of the child's maturation: these practices fostered, and continue to foster, strong aggressive tendencies that have to be channelized so that they can be used without guilt against actual enemies and also projected onto and discharged against culturally provided actual and imagined objects, to preserve family and group solidarity and maintain personal pride and relative intrapsychic comfort.

Let us now examine the aboriginal and current childhood practices that have produced Apaches with the aforementioned personality configurations, that were formerly adaptive but are much less so today.

ATTITUDES TOWARD AND PRACTICES
RELATED TO PREGNANCY

According to Opler (1941:5-10), in aboriginal times the birth of a baby was uniformly consciously welcomed; taboos concerning pregnancy, childbirth and infant care were regularly obeyed; and numerous protective ceremonies were routinely performed. Then, sexual abstinence was ideally practiced from the time pregnancy was recognized, to avoid possible damage to the fetus by intercourse, ultimately by the phallus. Interviews with modern Apaches indicate that this act of kindness toward the unborn baby constituted in part a reaction formation against aggressive wishes stemming from intense sibling rivalry, which resulted from practices to be described below. Information obtained in the psychoanalytically oriented psychotherapeutic interviews which constituted the principal research tool of the author revealed that Apaches, like white analysands, unconsciously equate baby and phallus, and that the fantasy that the erect penis would kill or damage the fetus stemmed from the man's commonly viewing his wife as a mother surrogate.

Aboriginally, sexual abstinence was supposed to continue throughout the two- or three-year nursing period. Such abstinence was facilitated for the man by his often having two or more wives, either in the same band or, frequently, in separate geographical areas. (R. M. Boyer and Gayton N.D.). Sororal polygyny was not uncommon, but sometimes the other wife or wives might be captives. Our aged female informants scoffed at the idea that women regularly tolerated sexual abstinence, saying that the rule was frequently breached. Occasionally a woman appeared to be totally surprised by her giving birth to a child. It may be that then, as is sometimes true today, the woman's lack of awareness of her pregnancy resulted from unconscious denial, based in part on her wish to continue to have sexual relations without cultural disapprobation.

The unconscious hostile wishes which lay behind some restrictions imposed on the pregnant woman aboriginally are too obvious to detail. She was not to eat an Apache delicacy, intestines, lest the umbilical cord strangle the fetus. She was not to ride a horse because "shaking is not good for a pregnant woman." Many of today's gynecologists hold that physical activity, including horseback riding, should continue during the first two trimesters of pregnancy and that, should miscarriage ensue, it is "nature's way to get rid of an abnormal fetus." The sexual symbology of shaking while horseback riding, bouncing on the phallic symbol, is patent.

The woman was not to attend ceremonies where masked dancers participated, because seeing the hooded figures might cause the baby to be born with a caul, and smother. Even her husband could not observe the performance of the masked dancer, for the same reason. When the time for the delivery drew near, the husband left the home. He could not be present at the childbirth. When a modern man was asked why the husband could not be present, he responded with a joke about a man who accidentally killed a child. Other men were not only allowed to attend childbirth but their presence was solicited at times, even though they might not be shamans. However, men usually shunned deliveries, saying they did so because of their equation of the birth discharges with menstrual blood, which was thought by males and females alike to be dangerous to men and even to frighten game away.

Following the child's delivery, the afterbirth was not to be burned or buried. Were it buried, animals might dig it up and consume it and the infant be magically harmed. We can view this idea as expressing in a rationalized, disguised form the projected oral aggression of the parents toward their young. The placenta and umbilical cord were to be tied by the midwife or some other good woman to a fruit-bearing tree such as the piñon, "because the tree comes to life every year and they want life in this child to be renewed like the life in the tree." The tree was to be in a secret place, to hide the afterbirth from hostile people who might wish to destroy it and thereby damage the baby or deprive the new parents of their child. Such people might be enemies of the parents or their family or they might be envious sterile women. The destruction of the afterbirth would most likely be accomplished through hired witchcraft services. Later in its life, "bad luck" would ensue if people referred to the child's beauty or other good qualities. This behavior is reminiscent of evil-eye beliefs and practices elsewhere, which have been demonstrated to involve projected hostility (Róheim 1952). The child itself will be treated later in an inconsistent manner, being praised for some accomplishments but at the same time being told it is intrinsically "no good." The effects of this experience will be discussed later.

We can but speculate as to why the afterbirth was not to be burned. No modern informant offered any cogent reason. In Chapter VII is to be found evidence for the idea that burned human parts can be used for witchcraft.

The typical modern Apache woman reveals her latent or conscious hostility toward her pregnancy and the fetus by her lack of preparation for childbirth and the future baby's care. Although there is a fairly modern hospital on the reservation and widely advertised prenatal services are available, many Apache mothers-to-be have, at least until very recently, eschewed attendance at the prenatal clinic, and most who have attended have done so only sporadically. Frequently no layette is prepared and the construction of the cradleboard in which the child ideally continues to be placed when four days old is delayed until after childbirth.

CRADLE DAYS

The construction of the cradle or cradleboard remains essentially the same as in the old days (R. M. Boyer 1962:216-226; Mason 1889:192-193; Opler 1941:10-12). It consists of an elliptical frame across which are laid wooden laths. At the top a rounded hood or canopy extends to guard the baby's head. At the bottom projects a narrow board on which the baby's feet may rest or against which it may kick, which may be lowered to lengthen the cradle as the child grows. The top of the hood and the side extensions of the cradle were formerly made solely of buckskin but today are sometimes constructed of canvas; the same material, whichever it is, is used for lacing the child inside the cradle. The lacing is in two sections: the legs may be left free and the upper half of the body restrained, or the arms may be free and the legs restrained. Formerly grasses lined the cradle, providing softness for the baby's comfort and to absorb excreta. The canopy is decorated with amulets and toys, some of which hang from thongs. At the rear of the cradle is a strap which may be brought across the mother's chest while she carries the baby on her back, and it used to be hung over the saddle horn during travels on horseback. A scarf is thrown over the hood to protect the baby's face from sun or flies. The baby's head moves freely within the cradle. The legs are held straight. As the child grows, more freedom is allowed the arms, in part so that it can reach for hanging amulets or toys.

The infant is in the cradle all day, except when it is being fed or bathed. The cradle is upright most of the time and the canopy serves as needed protection, especially against the accidental or willed actions of older, jealous siblings. At night the infant sleeps with its parents, usually in

DISMANTLED CRADLEBOARD FOUND IN REMOTE AREA OF
THE RESERVATION
(Photograph by the author)

close bodily contact with its mother.

The cradle soon becomes a source of much comfort for the baby, who cries to be replaced within it. The hostility ascribed to children toward the restrictions imposed by the cradle by many observers (Benedict 1949; Dennis and Dennis 1940; Leighton and Kluckhohn 1948:18-26; Mead 1954:395-409) is not seen among these Apaches. Certain actions of drunken Apaches are interesting in this regard. Their walk is characteristic in that their arms are held in the same position as is observed during late infancy when they are in the cradleboard, and, if they have "passed out," they usually lie on their backs with their legs held straight. Other peoples who are unconscious from too much drink are apt to lie on their sides, often in a fetal position.

One of the amulets which was formerly hung regularly from the canopy, and which is seen at times today, consists of the strong, stiff black bristles which hang five or six inches from the turkey gobbler's neck. Its purpose is to avert the child's being struck by lightning. Such projecting objects are at least preconsciously understood to be phallic symbols by some Apaches, who quite consciously equate the forked flash of lightning with the undulations of the moving snake. As was discussed previously, lightning and snake power are the strongest in the operational hierarchy of supernatural powers and are conceptualized as phallic in nature. The use of the bristles as a protective amulet can be understood to involve the well-known body-phallus equation, which we know to hold for the Apaches, and the projection of unconscious parental hostility toward the baby onto the snake and lightning. Again, an occasional Apache child revealed in play therapy the unconscious wish that the father's phallus would kill a presumed intrauterine rival (see Chapter V).

EARLY CHILDHOOD

Previously, "little" protective ceremonies accompanied every step of the child's development (Opler 1941:15-24). The rearing of children and childhood were two of the adults' most serious preoccupations. Ceremonies regularly invoked the assistance of supernatural powers to protect the child from the ascribed baneful wishes of other people, "powers" or witches. Today one no longer sees the "Putting on Moccasins" ceremony which formerly accompanied the child's first steps, and one very rarely observes the "Hair-cutting Ceremony."

Chiricahua and Mescalero mothers are usually very tender and considerate in their physical relationships with their infants. During the symbiotic phase (Mahler *et al.* 1975) there is much bodily contact, especially at night, and the bathing and anointing of a baby, during which the mother's rapt attention is totally directed toward her child, might take hours. During this procedure, the mother sometimes enters a dreamlike ego state and clearly deems the nursling to be an extension of herself.

The same mother who has given such devoted attention to her infant in the morning, however, might desert it later in the day when she impulsively pursues selfish wishes. Formerly her mother or sister would have been available to care for the child, but today she might leave it for hours or even days to the care of siblings as young as four years old. In one extreme instance we observed, the family dwelling was burned down three times as a result of a mother's behaving so. Another mother passively neglected one twin to the extent that it died.

A regularly observed practice which was startling to us and that has been determined to date from aboriginal times reveals with particular clarity the unconscious hostility of Apache parents toward their young. The vast majority of Chiricahua and Mescalero parents have deserted one or more of their children or given them away, and without conscious guilt. The Apache words for this practice translate literally as "throwing the child away." Obtaining accurate genealogical records was complicated by this practice. Parents of every generation had "forgotten" the existence of children whom they had just left or given to relatives, friends or even strangers. We were asked to adopt as our own several children. Sometimes the wish to have us take children was predominantly motivated by consciously loving wishes. Their parents or grandparents rightly judged that we would be able to take better care of the little ones than they could. Usually the practice is rationalized on economic grounds, but our experience revealed that it occurs with great regularity even among the most acculturated parents, including those who are by no means impoverished, whether or not they indulge in excessive alcoholic intake.

It was mentioned earlier that Apache men were free to leave the band with which they were associated if they disagreed with the decisions reached by the leader. At times, men who left took their nuclear families with them, but it appears that in general their wives preferred to remain with their female kin. But mothers, too, deserted their families at times, for example when they became enamored of other men, although such behavior was strongly disapproved.

When the Apache mother is sober and not under the influence of some urgent selfish impulse, her care of the baby is remarkably tender. Every whimper or gesture of discomfort brings the nipple or, more recently, the bottle. Until the birth of the next child, the nursling or toddler is the monarch of the family, within the limits afforded by the self-centeredness of the parents. However, although the child is usually treated with such consideration, the physical effects of infant neglect are apparent in many cases. As a specific example, Clements and Mohr (1961), Public Health physicians on the reservation, found the incidence of subdural hematoma among babies to be very high. It is likely that such cases of hematoma resulted from injuries inflicted by jealous older siblings.

Erikson (1950, 1966) wrote of the role of consistent, loving maternal care in establishing the capacity of the young child to develop a sense of basic trust and hope and a secure sense of personal identity. Among the Apaches, the inconsistent care accorded to the child contributes to its development of an attitude that it must depend only on itself and that it must be suspicious of the motives of others. While these attitudes were adaptive aboriginally, they are counterproductive today.

SIBLING RIVALRY

The next child is born after less than two years, if the Apache is thirty years of age or less. At that time, the former family monarch is abruptly removed from the parents' bed and, if it has not been taken before from the cradle, it is now. The mother's attention is promptly focused on the new child. The crying, bewildered, displaced erstwhile family favorite suddenly becomes a nuisance and is usually treated as such. Its attempts to get attention are most often met by impatience or overt hostility. If its efforts are not ignored, it will hear irritated "Go away! Don't bother me/it/her," and be roughly shoved aside. We have on occasion observed a mother kick her frustrated child in the face.

If the little one seeks solace from a sibling or its father, it may be petted briefly or get the same sort of attention afforded by the mother; it may or may not be solaced briefly or receive something to eat. Usually it is ignored and finds its thumb, a lock of its hair or a crust of bread to suck. For the next few years it will seem to be eating almost constantly. Throughout its life it will avidly seek bodily contact, especially when in altered ego states of intoxication.

The abrupt and sometimes brutal displacement of the toddler results in severe rapprochement crises (Mahler et al. 1975), and heightens rather than reduces the ambivalence between mother and child which had begun earlier. The contribution of unsatisfactory rapprochement to Arctic hysteria and Kiowa Apache ghost sickness have been delineated elsewhere (Foulks et al. 1977, 1978; Freeman et al. 1976). The displacement occurs during the stage of muscular and psychosexual maturation, in which the child must learn self-control and limit its emotions and overt behavior to those proper within his society. It must learn to please and influence those about it. Among these Apaches, toilet training per se has been practically nonexistent. Since its parents are uninterested in its bowel behavior, it cannot influence them through the ejection or withholding of excreta.[2] Although the child is not rewarded outwardly for learning bowel control, it quickly learns another kind of control which clearly involves muscles — that of turning inward the hostility felt toward its parents and siblings.

Thus, the toddler cannot gain support from or control over its mother through regulation of excretory activities. It must demonstrate maturation by learning to accept its displacement by the new rival and to handle its rage and disappointment in other, approved, manners. It soon becomes aware that overt expression of hostility toward the newcomer is taboo. It may for some time direct anger toward its mother herself without being punished by more than a rebuke. Aggression toward the newborn is reacted to by ridicule or, less often, physical retribution. The child will be called "crybaby," "naughty," "bad," "dirty," or "no good."

Mention was made earlier of the tendency of Apache adults to conceal the good qualities of their young from other people, powers and witches, a tendency rationalized as being for the protection of the offspring. From the material just presented, it is clear that such concealment is not solely in the service of expressing love. A poignant example follows, which is unrelated to training the child to behave in an acceptable manner toward a younger sibling. An Apache mother had a son twelve years old and daughters of five and three. She had been left by their father because of her promiscuity and drunkenness. She lived with her children in a shack in the vicinity of the house of her mother. She had frequently left them for days at a time without warning, to "fool around." Finally she just disappeared and had not been heard from for some months, when she wrote a letter home from another reservation where she lived with a man. The letter requested financial assistance from her impoverished mother.

A frequent visitor to the grandmother's house, the author had been struck by the devoted care she consistently gave to her grandchildren. She had spoken only Apache to the younger granddaughter until the following episode occurred.

Her house was on a hill and water had to be carried in buckets from a faucet perhaps a hundred yards below. The youngest child tried in every way possible for her to help her adored grandmother. One day in the author's presence she took a large bucket to the faucet, filled it to the brim and struggled up the hill, spilling much of the water. Ignoring her attempt to be helpful, her grandmother scolded her in Apache for spilling the water and then spoke to her for the first time in English, saying, "Me, Mary, me no good." Turning to the author, she smiled, saying that now she'd teach Mary to speak English.

But let us return to the education of children when there is a last-born present. The displaced toddler is taught that it can attack older siblings or destroy their property with impunity if the parents are about. This attitude of implicit approval of such behavior toward older children persists throughout the youngest's childhood. A teenage boy had saved his money and bought a longed-for guitar. On the evening when he brought it home, a younger sister willfully shattered the guitar while he stood woefully by. He made no effort to stop her, nor did their mother. By the next day his attitude toward the event was stoical; he seemed proud of his self-control. During autumn, Apache children are fond of playing football and participants are apt to include boys ranging in age from six to eighteen; the younger children are allowed to score almost unchallenged. Boys love to wrestle; the smaller and/or younger child is usually permitted to win.

Although hostile behavior toward the younger sibling is strongly discouraged, the displaced toddler is passively or actively encouraged to torment pets, such as puppies, and other young animals and fledglings. Adults are aware of the displacement of hostility from the human to the animal baby. Canines are included among the cultural *bêtes noires*. Almost every family has dogs, to serve to protect them against potential thieves or attackers. Many do not feed their pets adequately, partly because they want the adults to be savage. While Apaches usually do not fear their own puppies, they are truly afraid that they will be bitten by dogs of every age belonging to their neighbors. They manifest ambivalence, too, toward Coyote. Institutionalized phobias abound. The childhood nightmares of the Chiricahuas and Mescaleros are culturally supported.

Within a few months, the displaced child learns that its older siblings will permit aggression toward them and their property when it occurs in the presence of others, but it may not be tolerated when observers are not present. And it has learned that it must take "good care" of the baby and "love it."

The displaced child, then, is systematically trained to develop reaction formations to deal with its anger toward those who are younger and smaller, to project and displace its hostilities onto supernatural and other objects it has been trained to fear, to express its aggression directly but with attenuated intensity to older and larger children, and to express its rages in cruel attacks on harmless or helpless animals. Additionally, from the earliest time when it can comprehend language, it hears adults speak with rancor about outsiders. No doubt this pattern is an attenuation of the old-time need to assume enmity on the part of all strangers.

By the time the toddler is three, he has learned that a tantrum is rarely rewarding, and by the time he reaches four, he looks upon such uncontrolled activity with disdain. But the disappointments still exist in early childhood, so what does a three-year-old do? If he cries, and he usually does, he tries to do so silently, for he has learned by now that a mother will tolerate a quiet child — one who does not "bother" her. Sometimes she may even show affection if he is near, and remains unobtrusive. The unhappy three-year-old may undergo certain distinctive bodily maneuvers. His torso becomes rigid and his general posture resembles that of attack. His knees bend slightly, his fists clench at his sides and his facial muscles become tense. His jaws are locked together. The muscles of his abdomen tighten and, for a brief time, he may hold his breath. In large measure his posture resembles that of a two-year-old, but then a change takes place. Instead of casting himself to the ground or floor, the three-year-old controls his muscular system. Slowly, his fists relax, his arms grow limp, and he stands erect. His face becomes poised, his color pales and his eyes grow deep and disinterested. He seems to retire inside himself. In other words, he has accomplished two things in the course of a year's time: mastery of his muscles and control of his emotions. He has become passive, and he appears unconcerned. This is the first evidence we have of Apache passivity, of the stoicism displayed throughout his life. To be sure, the toddler has varying degrees of success in his attempts at mastery, but a basic pattern of reaction has been created. Later, as an adult, he will often (when sober and insecure and frustrated) assume the facial response and bodily control which he found to be most acceptable in early childhood days. He will look as though he were uninterested. In terms of muscular coordination, the Apache child's ultimate mastery of his reactions to frustration involves "whole-body" passivity, or relaxation, following a period of extreme tension. In many ways, this sequence of controls corresponds to sphincter mastery required in the course of toilet training. Although the focus of the mother's interests are different, an Apache child (just as his white counterpart) must learn *when* and *what* he must "retain," and which muscles he must master. Both societies require a sense of timing and restraint (R. Boyer 1962:238-240; see also J. Briggs 1972).

In the passage cited above, the positive, adaptational aspect of the development of resignation and passivity in Apache children was stressed. However, Winnicott (1961) has noted that the abrogation of rebellion in the face of separation constitutes a reaction of hopelessness and often heralds severe psychiatric consequences. Khan (1962) found that the mother's inability to tolerate the child's shift from primary identity to seeking recognition of independence results in pathological, inconsistent, precocious ego development in the child. It is the need to have their independence acknowledged which characterizes Apaches.

The fourth subphase delineated by Mahler and her co-workers in their consideration of separation and individuation (Mahler *et al.* 1975) occurs during the period when, in Erikson's words, the child must attain autonomy. The main task of the fourth subphase is the achievement of a definite, in some aspects lifelong, individuality and the attainment of a certain degree of object constancy. As far as the self is concerned, there is a rapid increase in the structuralization of the ego and there are definite signs of internalization of parental demands and the formation of superego precursors. The establishment of affective emotional constancy depends upon the gradual internalization of a constant, positively cathected inner image of the mother (Hartmann 1952). Emotional object constancy will be based in the first place on the cognitive achievement of the permanent object, although all other aspects of the child's personality development participate also in this evolution.

The fourth subphase, which occurs roughly during the third year of life, is a most important intrapsychic development period, in the course of which a stable sense of self boundaries is attained. Also, primitive consolidation of gender identity seems to take place in this period. "But the constancy of the object implies more than the maintenance of the representation of the absent love object. It also implies the unifying of the 'good' and 'bad' object into one whole representation. This fosters the fusion of the aggressive and libidinal drives and tempers the hatred for the object when aggression is intense" (Mahler *et. al.* 1975:110). With the ambivalent, inconsistent care afforded the Apache child, the achievement of the goals of the fourth subphase can be achieved only rarely.

In adolescent and adult years, the Apache stoicism and passivity will be used in the service of aggression. They are also used as an unconscious provocation of others to ridicule and otherwise display hostility toward the passive "victim."

While the overt relative passivity of Apache parents toward toilet training results in children's being unable to control them through cleanliness behavior, Apache aversion to excremental products is apparent in the witchcraft beliefs and practices, as was graphically illustrated in Chapter III.

The intense sibling rivalry which is engendered by Apache socialization is insecurely repressed, and reaction formation to defend against it is weak. This has been illustrated in the preceding chapter, in which an example was given of the brutality directed toward a sibling surrogate during intoxication. An instance of direct hostility toward an actual sibling will fill out this picture.

A sister and her slightly younger brother had always had a complementary sadomasochistic relationship, which, according to rumor, had involved actual incestuous relations. We know relationships to be much more common among Apache brothers and sisters than is generally portrayed. The woman, in her early twenties and regularly employed, had owned an automobile which she had lent to her brother, who had wrecked it while drunk. After she had made the down payment on a new car, her brother attempted to cajole her into permitting him to drive it. With trepidation, based on her knowledge that he was exceedingly violent and cruel when his requests were denied, she refused to lend him her new automobile. He flew into a rage, beat her with a large, heavy stick, and, after she was lying semiconscious and bleeding, stomped her body and head with his cowboy boots and raked her with his spurs. Family members and other onlookers (including children) did not interfere, partly because to have done do would have transgressed the proscription against "making trouble" and partly because they feared personal harm. Some days later the sister awoke in the hospital in which she was immured for a fractured skull and concussion. When she was asked to file a complaint against her brother, she was flabbergasted and said, "But he was drunk."

How folklore is used in an attempt to defend against the anxieties aroused by sibling rivalry will be illustrated particularly in Chapter VI.

SEXUAL TRAINING

Erikson (1950:224-226; 1959:74-82) states that the next stage of psychosexual maturation, following the attainment of autonomy, is concerned with the locomotor-genital system, and that it involves the development of initiative. The four- or five-year-old has sufficient mastery of language and muscular motility to permit concentration on a new field: daydreaming (see also Sarnoff 1976). The child now becomes intensely interested in comparisons of sizes and in sexual differences. Erikson (1950:225) calls this the stage of the castration complex, and writes that "the fear of losing the (energetically eroticized) genitals as a punishment for the fantasies attached to their excitements now occurs in full force."

Careful perusal of Opler's account of child-rearing fails to give a clear picture of early sexual training. In fact, this is because his informants were predominantly men and because no women, except an occasional one who is very old and lewd, will discuss such matters with men, particularly outsiders. Their great aboriginal modesty was repeatedly noted by various early chroniclers, who contrasted their nonparticipation in sexual exploits with soldiers and trappers with the relative promiscuity ascribed to women of other Indian tribes.

Aboriginally, a husband might have slit or cut off the end of his adulterous wife's nose. No doubt this practice supported the group ideal of female marital chastity. Yet modern aged men laugh about the prac-

APACHE WOMAN, NOSE MUTILATED BECAUSE OF INFIDELITY
(Courtesy Arizona Pioneers' Historical Society, Tucson, Arizona)

tice, saying that a woman so marked was then considered to be "easy game."

In the psychotherapeutic interviews conducted with both males and females by the author, little direct information emerged concerning early sexual training. Although Ruth Boyer was eventually treated by Apache women as though she were one of them, she was unable to learn very much about even modern sexual training of prelatency children except through direct observation. She did learn from very old women that even tiny girls were formerly trained to avoid exposure of their genitals and to always sit demurely with their legs close together and straight out before them. It was her impression that, even aboriginally, children were taught that anything to do with sexual activity was deemed to be dirty and that touching of the genitals, especially by girls, was strongly disapproved. Virginity before marriage was highly prized.

Today girls are expected to sit in the modest position only during their puberty ceremonies. However, the strong disapproval of genital touching with hands remains. Yet again we are confronted with inconsistency. The mother may spend hours in bathing and oiling the child, and she pays special attention to the cleanliness of the genitals. We would expect that her repeated cleansing manipulations of the genitals would prove to be highly stimulating to her little ones, but we did not find that the children are particularly excited at such times. It should be remembered, however, that the entire bathing procedure, when done by mothers who have sufficient time, is obviously a most enjoyable, sensuous experience for both mother and child. When the little one is old enough to splash around and to seek to imitate its mother's various moves, when it touches its genitals the mother removes its hands and often says, "dirty." The children enjoy being bathed by their fathers, but to a lesser degree, perhaps because these baths are less prolonged and sensual. They clearly relish less those baths administered by older siblings, baths which are sometimes roughly and unwillingly performed.

The sensuousness of the interactions between mother and young child is manifested also in nursing experiences. Two examples follow. In a very crowded, very noisy front room, a young mother was nursing her tiny son. She gradually became totally occupied with the feeding experience, did not respond to direct questions, and entered a rapturous state which lasted for over half an hour. On a different occasion, another woman was nursing her daughter of fifteen months of age. After the little girl had had enough to eat, she stood up, holding the nipple with her teeth. She walked back and forth on her mother's lap, stretching the breast first in one direction and then in the other. Her mother, obviously enjoying herself very much, periodically squealed, "Ooh, it hurts." The game lasted for some twenty minutes.

While manual masturbation is strongly disapproved, parents ignored what was obviously masturbation — a little girl's rhythmic rocking and thigh contraction which apparently even led to orgasm.

Although modesty is highly prized for girls, when boys engage in sexual explorations with their sisters or other girls their actions are treated with tolerance and amusement, although they are told they are being bad. Later, they will be expected to seek to conquer girls sexually and, during their teens and later, they will sometimes be challenged to prove their manhood by sexual servicing of lewd old women.

Apache children indulge in much of their early sexual exploration in the outhouse, to which they always go with other children, often of both sexes. Their excited giggles are ignored by adults.

Playroom activities among young boys and casual observations often revealed serious preoccupation with castration fears. Girls as young as two years express penis envy. A small girl asked her mother to buy her a penis so she "could have a gun like those boys." She wanted to win a contest of urination distance. Tiny boys express breast envy. All sexual activities, and even new underclothes, are uniformly called "dirty."

Preoccupation with castration anxiety is encouraged by some sexual teachings. The one which follows may have arisen as a result of such anxiety. In the past, children were taught that vaginas had teeth, and such teaching has not entirely disappeared. This belief has been and remains common to all Athabascan-speaking peoples. One of Opler's (1969:65) informants said:

> The boys used to get lots of instruction to keep away from women and live right. When I was a kid I was told that women have teeth in there and would bite off my penis if I didn't keep away from them. Sometimes an old woman used to get the boys together and talk to them. An old man might say to the old woman, "You're spoiling those boys." She'd say, "No, it's a lesson." This old woman told us, "You mustn't go with old women like us. We've had our day. If you do anything with old women, you get a big penis and testicles; you have to straddle to cover it up as you go along the road. If you do it to old women, worms will kill you."

The double message involved here is clear, namely, that if you risk the danger of castration by vaginal teeth, you may develop huge genitals which will be irresistible to all women.

Male informants of various ages indicated that they had responded to similar "warnings" as though they had been seductive challenges. An occasional adult joked about dentate phalluses.

We know that some Apache adults have no compunctions about having daytime sexual relations, even in the presence of small children. The crowded housing of earlier reservation life, which exists also today despite the presence of many modern homes which have been built by the tribe, has made it impossible for children to be unaware of their parents' nighttime erotic behavior. Children are supposed either not to see or hear such activities, or to "forget" them. However, even children who are reared in the homes of more modest parents are exposed to primal-scene observations or their substitutes when they are subjected to viewing drunken sexual encounters which occur in public, as has been illustrated previously. Noteworthy is the frequency of combined erotic and aggressive activities in these instances. The tribal bar is amid several housing projects. Women who attend the bar are considered to be there to seek sexual experiences, which occur at times in the immediate environs. At least during the early years of our research, policemen were often charged with having raped drunken women whom they were transporting to jail. Few doubted that the sexual relations had taken place, but to our knowledge only one policeman was reprimanded. He had previously been charged many times with the same offense, and with rape.

Children interpret primal-scene observations in terms of their stages of psychosexual maturation. When they are preoccupied with the problems involved in traversing their oral and anal periods of development, their understanding of sexual observations involves sadistic fantasies: they fear that one or the other adult is going to be damaged by oral or anal means. The actual life experiences of Apache children make it more difficult for them than for most children in many other cultures to eventually separate oral and anal and genital functions. The fusion of oral, anal and genital concepts is overt in everyday conversation and especially in the folklore, which fusion suggests that the work of repression has been incomplete. And hostility between males and females abounds.

Childhood concerns with sexual anxieties are exemplified by a kind of play which occurs each year. Every August injections are given in the upper arm to children who will attend school for the first time. A week or two later, in every home in which there are young children, all dolls except brand-new ones are found to have pencil-made holes in their buttocks, from the children's playing "hospital." We can understand this enactment to mean that the children are seeking to master in play the anxieties stemming from their viewing sexual activities, symbolized by the thrusting of the pencil, in terms of potential anal damage.

Today young children have actual sexual relations. Sometimes teenage boys have intercourse with girls of latency age, and adolescent girls are known to have prepubertal and neopubertal boys service them.

DISCIPLINE TRAINING

As has been hinted before, prelatency behavioral training has always been somewhat indulgent, compared to Western standards. Physical punishment has always been disapproved, although this cultural standard has been breached from time immemorial. Opler (1941:32-33) noted that when other methods of discipline failed, parents resorted to corporal chastisement. "Parents never whip their children unless they won't get up and run a race or something like that." "I have seen her knock her little boy around like a ball. Everytime he got up, she would knock him down again." "Coolness between one father and son goes back to the time, in the words of the latter, 'when he used me just like a slave. He whipped me, made me work, and kept me around the house.' " When a boy refused a gift from his grandmother, he was taught respect for her by a "good box on the ear." Girls were flogged publicly by their fathers for sexual intercourse.

Today physical punishment rarely occurs, unless the parent is intoxicated. Intoxicated, a parent might beat the child with a large stick or even a two-by-four. In a recent issue of *The Apache Scout,* a monthly publication which is distributed to members of the tribe, it was noted that "when alcohol is in the picture, Indians abuse their children eight times more than do other races in the society."

The two principal means of disciplinary training are through ridicule or shaming and through teaching the child that cultural bogies will punish it severely. Either of these techniques is used directly or through the telling of folkloric lessons, particularly episodes from the Coyote Cycle. Examples of the first means have been presented earlier.

Adults are particularly apprehensive of the laughter of whites, and convey this message strongly to their children. The automatic assumption that whites will ridicule Apache thought and behavior involves to some degree the projection of aggression. The Apache word for whites, *indáh,* is that which is used for all enemies.

An Apache ideology is that children are not to compete "too much " with each other. No one is to be conspicuously "better" than anyone else to avoid making trouble, and those who strive to do well in the "whiteman's world" are punished in various ways. Thus an Apache youth who did well in school, both scholastically and athletically, after receiving a commendation on his graduation from high school, was waylaid and beaten by a gang of his peers, and his dog was tortured to death before him. In recent years, a highly moral young woman graduated from college. Her education had been partly supported by tribal grants. She had been promised a job after completion of a course which would qualify her for a tribal position. After her graduation, the position was given to an uneducated woman. Her house was repeatedly vandalized and she was generally ostracized. Eventually she found it necessary to leave the reservation and live elsewhere.

In the school situation, the Apache child is usually exceedingly well-behaved, a timid, passive observer who fears if it speaks up it will be ridiculed by teachers and classmates alike. As has been illustrated, its fear of mistreatment by peers is well-founded. Its anxiety that it will be mistreated by its teachers has been all too often justified as well. In the early years of our study, teachers in the grammar school on the reservation and in the two junior-high and high schools nearby that are attended by a majority of Apache teenagers did not understand native philosophies, feared Indians, and abused the children, particularly through crass public ridicule. This situation has been improved during the past twenty years, in which the older teachers have retired and less-prejudiced replacements have not only sought to learn native traditions but, in some cases, have even tried to learn to speak Apache. Within the past few years, the larger of the two off-reservation school districts has employed a past president of the Business Committee, a highly acculturated woman who remains steeped in lore and customs, as a liaison betweeen teachers and Apache students.

Apache discipline through ridicule tends to produce individuals who choose the negative identity described by Erikson. Accurately perceiveing the hostility behind the ridicule meted out to them by their parents, they seek vengeance by proving that they *are* no good and "don't know nuthin'." At least until recently, their educational experiences have reinforced that negative identity.

Rorschach and other psychological studies of Chiricahua and Mescalero school children have revealed that until a few years ago even those who initially displayed initiative and adaptability emerged from their educational experiences by being increasingly introverted, noncompetitive and impulsive (Boyer *et al.* 1967, 1968; Day *et al.* 1975). This suggests that school structure has tended to re-elicit earlier emotional problems, very far from ameliorating them.

Aspects of the discipline of Apache children serve to displace hostilities initially directed toward the parents onto culturally provided specters. Underlying all forms of danger conceptualized by these Apaches are to be found oral-oriented, primary-process-dominated thinking. Threats of abandonment to a bogey is a most common form of discipline administered to the toddler, usually by the mother. The disciplining adult will tell the disobedient child, *Jajadeh* will get you," or *"Awshee."* As detailed in Chapter III, *jajadeh* is a word for the Masked Dancers; it also is the native word for the whippoorwill. That harmless, pretty little bird is thought to become during the night a woman who carries a basket into which she will place a crying child and carry it away, perhaps to a mountain, if it doesn't stop "bothering" the parent (see Chapter VI). She is reminiscent of the Navaho *bête noire* Spider Lady. The Apache child fears *jajadeh* will eat it; the Navajo child is told overtly that it will be devoured. *Awshee* means "the ghost is coming." Its presence heralds death, as does the owl it is reputed to inhabit. Children are sometimes taught that witches are people who have been inhabited by ghosts and that the ghost may enter the body of a victim through its mouth or nose, during inhalation.

Opler (1941:32) wrote:

> Instead of punishing a child for enuresis, other means are used to treat the difficulty. "If a child wets the bed, we put a bird's nest there and let him wet it. Then the nest is thrown to the east, and the child won't wet the bed anymore."

No doubt the child clearly understood that the bird's nest symbolized *jajadeh's* basket.

Opler did not state at what age enuresis became troublesome to adults. Today it is ignored until the child is eight or nine; then it is ridiculed.

A team of MountainGod dancers consists of four *jajadeh* and a clown, *thlibayeh,* meaning Gray One or Coyote (Boyer and Boyer 1978). Few Apaches are now aware that the clown has a special name, but all know of his association with the *jajadeh,* since the clown has no other role among the Apaches.

To cite Opler (1941:29) again:

> This masked-dancer clown...is one of the terrors of childhood. "The clown is going to put you in a basket and carry you off somewhere." Say this to a child and he is going to mind right away.

The symbolic equivalence of the clown and the whippoorwill is reinforced not only by their having the same name, but by their making similar sounds. Both say *hoo-hoo-hoo-hoo* in sepulchral tones.

EDUCATION FOR ASSUMPTION OF ADULTHOOD ROLES

The adulthood roles of men and women were clearly defined aboriginally. The woman was to be the homemaker, keep the family together, look after her sons until they were of latency age, and rear her daughters to assume their expected adulthood duties. She was to prepare the foods and cook them, make the dwellings and clothes, weave baskets, and do whatever beadwork was done. She was to supply plant foods, whether gathered in the wild or (less frequently) sowed and collected, when the band returned in season. The men — hunters, warriors and raiders — were to make and care for the implements used in those pursuits. Later, they were expert horsemen. They caught and trained wild horses, or stole domestic ones on raids. An important task was to rear sons of latency age and older to assume their prescribed adulthood roles.

Formerly, the treatments of boys and girls were very similar until they were four or five years of age, and for the most part they were dressed identically. Children of both sexes performed like minor camp functions and their parents were very indulgent as to whether assigned tasks were executed. At the same time, the foundations for the sexual division of labor were laid early. Thus little girls were told (Opler 1941:27):

"Your work will be to make baskets and build fires, my daughter. Keep busy like your mother. Watch your mother as she is going through her daily work. When you get older, you will do the same things. It doesn't hurt you to pick up little sticks of wood and carry them in. Stay there by the fire. Watch what your mother is doing."

Concerning aboriginal training for adulthood roles, we need only note that the education of the boys became increasingly rigorous and even involved the learning of a special language to be used on raids and the warpath (Opler and Hoijer 1940). Further detailing of latency-period and subsequent socialization is unnecessary here because the major conflicts which are expressed and defended against by the folklore can be traced to the puericulture of the prelatency period. A few remarks concerning today's education for the assumption of adulthood roles follow.

The clarity of division of the adulthood roles of men and women has diminished appreciably, although the training afforded girls remains more consistent than that afforded boys. Women ideally continue to serve the same functions as previously, although contacts with Western standards have led to some role diffusion for them. Mothers and grandmothers have abrogated much latency-period and subsequent training to school teachers, Christian church leaders and others. A greater change has taken place in the training of boys. The father's role as the educator of his sons has all but disappeared. The fathers who currently engage in the education of their sons for the most part limit their activities to teaching them aspects of the old ways. Thus, they take pride in teaching their sons to do Indian dances and to sing old songs, and encourage them to become artists who will depict idealized aspects of aboriginal ways. Some fathers teach their sons to ride and care for horses, and to hunt. Their involvement in the education of their daughters is largely limited to teaching them to dance. A very few fathers are skillful in the use and care of farm machinery and convey their knowledge to their sons. Some are sincere in their efforts to get their children to do well in public school and thereby attain the skills which might prepare them to compete in the economic world of whites, but most fathers (as well as mothers) only pay lip service to this goal.

NIGHT DANCE OF THE MOUNTAIN SPIRITS AND CLOWN
(Two teams shown)
July 1962, (Courtesy Barbara Funkhouser El Paso, Texas)

THE ATTITUDES OF WIVES TOWARD THEIR HUSBANDS

The maternal attitude toward the father, whether he is physically present or absent, is an important determinant of the child's view of him and his role. The Apache mother's attitude toward her husband has always contributed significantly to the boy's paternal introjects and his unconscious sexual identity.

Aboriginally, the new husband and his wife lived in separate housing near the wife's mother and sisters. Mother-in-law avoidance was practiced, and the husband had specific obligations to perform for his wife's family. Although to a varying extent he was viewed as an outsider, nevertheless, he was highly valued. When men were to return from raiding or warring, or sometimes from hunting, excited preparations were made, and, on their arrival, women met them some distance from camp, singing and dancing. When the father was away, the mother praised him to their children and when he returned he was encouraged to talk and sing of his exploits. The mother's attitude toward her husband was predominantly respectful. Then, the growing boy's paternal introjects were admirable and his unconscious sexual identity was relatively secure, even if his father were away for long periods during the boys's early childhood, had deserted his family or had been killed. In most bands, there were also apt to be honored grandfathers who did not accompany the younger men on their forays; they contributed significantly to the boys' education and development of secure masculine identities.

Today women are largely contemptuous of men, whose roles are clearly less dramatic and more diffuse than in earlier times. Partly because of the women's attitudes, the boys' paternal introjects are less than admirable and their unconscious sexual identities are frequently insecure (Boyer 1964a). At the same time, during recent years some young Apache men are developing into apparently secure men who are successful in both Apache and Western terms. But these men are as yet clearly atypical. It is our impression that those who are becoming or have become successful in both worlds come from families in which the mother's attitude toward the father was predominantly respectful.

Let us turn now to some further comments regarding the personality organization of these Apaches and discuss the interactions between that personality structure and shamanistic religiocurative practices.

PERSONALITY ORGANIZATION

We have noted previously that modern Athabascans everywhere appear to have a common basic personality organization (Hippler, Boyer and Boyer 1976) and we have found that the prelatency child-rearing practices of Alaskan Athabascans share many features with those of the Chiricahuas and Mescaleros, especially as they concern the transmission of attitudes (Hippler *et al.*, N.D., N.D.a). We have postulated that the harsh ecological circumstances of the earliest subarctic Athabascans required the development of a personality which would be adaptive to the milieu, and we supposed, following Lubart (1970, 1976), that a set of puericultural practices evolved over time which produced that personality. We have been struck by the conservatism of socialization processes, particularly as they pertain to prelatency training — that training which, as Erikson (1966) stated, produces the core of character structure.

As was mentioned earlier, the personality configuration of the aboriginal Apaches seems to have been typified by a high degree of aggressivity and stoicism, independence of action, suspiciousness, suggestibility and the capacity to withstand loss through death or desertion without appreciable psychological disturbances. Today's Chiricahuas and Mescaleros who are considered to be typical by their peers have the same personality configuration, except that their former independence has been replaced by dependency and impulsivity. The descriptive psychiatric diagnostic label which would be used to designate their current personality organization most aptly is "hysterical personality with impulsive and paranoid traits," and the label "borderline personality disorder" could be accurately applied to many Apaches (Gunderson and Kolb 1978; Kernberg 1975).

These Apaches are easily subject to altered ego states and highly suggestible, and they suffer from organ neuroses and psychosomatic conditions which can often be alleviated temporarily by faith healing. Their various psychosomatic complaints frequently constitute conscious or unconscious attempts to achieve secondary (epinosic) gains, and are rewarded by the expectations of the group. The usual Chiricahua or Mescalero, beneath a superficial appearance of being independent, is highly dependent, and he directly or indirectly seeks mothering services throughout his life. This trait is stronger among typical males than females. The universality of phobias has been mentioned before. Children of all ages hallucinate or daydream with such intensity that others believe them to have hallucinated. Such characteristics are ego-syntonic and culture-syntonic, although it appears that the "vision quest"of the Plains Indians is not a regular feature of Apache socialization.

The adaptive nature of some of the characteristic personality traits mentioned above has been noted, but a few additional remarks are in order. The aggressivity which is produced by the child-rearing practices and the ambivalence of parents toward their offspring were dealt with previously in manners which have been adequately illustrated. Aggressivity was guiltlessly discharged against actual enemies and projected onto and discharged against imaginary enemies: witches, ghosts and cultural bogeys. However, much was also internalized in manners which evoked group praise and personal pride. The little child who mastered its rage stemming from its displacement by a sibling and became stoical was obviously proud of its accomplishment and ridiculed other toddlers who had not yet achieved such control. Young boys were very proud of their capacity to undergo physical injury and privation without complaint, and their actions were lauded by others. Teenage boys were encouraged to voluntarily suffer certain mutilations without manifesting suffering and took pride in doing so.

A brief discussion of faith healing will indicate how the suggestibility, dependent submissiveness and the capacity to develop altered ego states were adaptive, making these Indians ideal subjects for treatment by the only means available to them aboriginally, the shamanistic practice which was embodied in their religiomedical system.

All methods of faith healing share the basic premise that recovery depends upon supernatural forces that affect all illnesses equally. The construction of a differential diagnosis is thus ultimately superfluous. Healing based on magic and faith utilizes exhortation and mobilizes religious and personal emotional enthusiasms. The healer attempts to create altered moods and to induce changes in the levels of consciousness, to regressive ego states. Since his goal is to remove immediately a symptom or symptom complex and the duration of relief is not a crucial matter, he considers it legitimate both to introduce ideas that challenge the secondary-process logic of the patient and to exercise influence based upon his emotional hold over his client. "Thus the operation of suggestion in this sense is always dependent on the human relationship behind the ideas, a relationship which induces the patient to abrogate his right to judgment " (Kubie 1950:147). Ultimately, the faith healer places himself and his supernatural powers in complete charge over the patient, who is expected to submit passively to his manipulations. Faith demands no evidence. Belief is the direct perception of a divinely revealed truth. Dependence on evidence is irreligious.

The differential diagnosis between hysteria and schizophrenia is often very difficult to make (Marmor 1953; McKinnon and Michel 1971). Indeed, when these Athabascans have psychotic episodes, they have definite resemblances to acute schizophrenia. It was not possible for me to accumulate dependable statistics regarding the actual incidence of chronic, deteriorating schizophrenia among these Apaches. During nineteen years I observed only three instances. Aboriginally, actual psychotics were at times revered and cared for tenderly. Others, flagrantly paranoid or nasty, were executed as witches or evicted from the band, and were often unwelcome elsewhere, unless they had the ego strength to alter their behavior. Those who did not sometimes became "wild men," who were thought to be cannibals.

The superego of this people is typically inconsistent. There are gross lacunae and there is obvious archaic sadism. Their impulsivity and lack of acceptance of moral responsibility are usually egosyntonic. However, it is difficult to evaluate the degree of internalization of superego traits. The element of what is expected by the group must be taken into consideration more than psychiatrists and psychoanalysts are wont to do in Western clinical practice, where superego development is more frequently mature at an early age. These Apaches are not expected to assume individual responsibility for their behavior until they reach grandparenthood; like the Kiowa Apaches (D.M.A Freeman 1968), when they reach the age of between forty and forty-five they have the capacity to do so (Boyer and Boyer 1976). Additionally, in the past when a young man was singled out to assume the role of leader he became responsible (with some notable exceptions, such as the case of the Chiricahua leader Geronimo [R.M. Boyer and Gayton, N.D.]). Such assumption of responsibility was evident in early manhood in the cases of the Chiricahua leaders Cochise, Mangas Colorado and Victorio and the Mescalero leader Santana. The great chiefs of the past were all male. Today there are three distinguished leaders, all of whom assumed responsibility before they reached grandparenthood. Two of them are women.

Among today's males, there is a high degree of unconscious confusion of sexual identity, which leads them to counterphobic Don Juanism. There appears to be little sexual-identification confusion among the females. Although there is evidence that strong latent homosexuality exists among the men, there has never been much overt homosexuality. The *berdache* role which was common among the Plains Indians was unusual among the Apaches, and , during our time with them, the word *hosteen-zun* (man-woman) was applied to only one or two men. Since the prelatency socialization of the past had significant similarities to that of today, we must assume that then, too, there was unconscious sexual confusion among some men. We assume. too, that it may well have constituted an adaptive trait, leading reactively to a great impetus for individual valor and capacity for suffering stoically, to prove manhood.

Obviously, these Indians, such renowned warriors, raiders and hunters, have had a high degree of capacity for reality testing. It may be that such reality testing was largely operationally concrete. At the same time, they felt comfortable in the presence of much primary-process thinking, as is clear in their aboriginally unchallenged belief in the various kinds of magic involved in their religiomedical practices and in the ascribed dangerous qualities of harmless little beings, such as the whippoorwill and puppies.

A Rorschach study of old Apaches produced some interesting results. It will be recalled that the Mescaleros and Chiricahuas underwent deculturative and acculturative processes which were quite different, the Mescaleros having been relegated to the reservation and the Chiricahuas having been held prisoners of war for 27 years, until 1913. Protocols were obtained from all of the accessible Mescaleros who had lived on the reservation for six or more years prior to 1913 and from the available Chiricahuas who had spent at least their first six years off the reservation before that date. The Mescaleros thought much more concretely and were quite comfortable with primary-process thinking. The Chiricahuas were capable of more abstract thought and were less comfortable with primary-process thinking (Boyer, Boyer et al. 1964).

Such concreteness of thought would make one suspect the presence of schizophrenia, but a diagnosis of schizophrenia depends on many elements (Meissner 1975, 1976); as has been indicated, schizophrenia was rare during the period of our research.

It may be that, formerly, adolescents who were on the verge of a psychotic breakdown achieved cures or improvement from assumption of the shamanistic role (Eliade 1951; Lommel 1967). However, no available data confirm this hypothesis. A study of modern shamans does not show such a pattern. If anything, the shamans are more mature and creative than their peers (Boyer, Klopfer et al 1964), and there is no record that Apache shamans had been cured of psychological disturbances through assumption of the shamanistic role.

There is no implication in the foregoing that *individuals* in all periods have not presented a more mature personality organization, viewed in terms of Devereux's (1956) terms of normal and abnormal, but those people have been recognized as atypical by their peers. It is of considerable interest that today's atypical Apaches respond to Rorschach stimuli in manners which depict the modal personality of those who are typical (Boyer, Boyer et al. 1964; Day et al. 1975).

COMMENT

The ambivalent, inconsistent attitudes and behavior of Chiricahua and Mescalero mothers toward their infants hampers id-ego differentiation. Psychoanalysts hold that during early ego development the baby fails to view its mother as a single person. Rather, it perceives the mother who relieves it of discomfort as good and the one who fails to do so as bad. The actual mother is split in the infant's thinking into good and bad mothers.

The socialization of these Apaches encourages them to retain faulty id-ego differentiation and to retain an unconscious split image of nurturing objects (Kernberg 1975; Volkan 1975). Apache folklore supplies such representations, on the one hand, in holy medicine men and in the female chaperones who take part in the puberty ceremony for girls, and on the other, in real or imagined enemies (Erikson 1939), witches (Weidman 1968), ghosts (Spiro 1952, 1953) and cultural bogies, such as the snake, the cougar, the bear and the canines.

According to current psychoanalytic thinking, the individual who becomes psychotic from functional means has been subjected to socialization experiences which have hampered his early ego development; when he regresses psychologically because of life's stresses, the level of regression reaches that of the earliest period of ego development when he felt more security (Boyer and Giovacchini 1967). It is thought that the person who becomes schizophrenic has been traumatized severely psychologically at an earlier age than the person who suffers from a functional affective psychosis. The psychotic breakdowns of these Apaches are almost uniformly variants of the group of schizophrenias (Bleuler 1911). We believe the fundamental factor of greatest importance in the psychosexual and psychosocial unfolding of the Chiricahuas and the Mescaleros to be the inconsistent treatment at the hands of their ambivalent mothers, who were themselves products of like socialization practices.

Such early traumatization of the Apache's potential psychic maturational capacities is compounded by abrupt and sometimes brutal displacement by younger rivals and the drastic results of the repeatedly observed combined sexual and hostile behavior of the adults of the environment. In the case of the males, a fourth serious psychic injury is provided by the absence of an esteemed masculine role with which to identify. The female, more fortunate, has a model for adult role assumption which has remained more intact. Although she, too, often remains psychologically immature, her psychopathology appears to be less severe because of identification with an admired role pattern. Caudill (1949) found that Ojibwa women were less seriously affected psychologically than men by the effects of acculturation, and the Spindlers (1958) confirmed his observation with their study of the Menominis.

Each of the major socialization traumata to which the growing Apache is subjected results in further oral fixations and all of the psychosexual stages becoming fused with orality. In the early conceptualization of psychological maturation, the growing infant was thought to proceed fairly regularly through oral, anal, phallic and genital phases of development. Today, it is well established that there is ordinarily much overlapping of these maturational phases (Mahler et al. 1975). However, in the average expectable environment delimned by Hartmann (1939), the individual can be expected to progress to such a degree that the characteristics which have been depicted as pertaining to the oral stage gradually become less influential and nonpathogenic.

The beliefs associated with the witch's arrow may be seen as culture-syntonic and egosyntonic because of the fusion of orality, anality and phallicity. Preoccupation with penetration and its potentially damaging effects is a dominant aspect of the phallic phase. In the thinking of the child during its anal stage of development, excreta are assumed to be living parts of itself and, because of adult attitudes toward them, they come to be thought of as poisonous or otherwise dangerous. While the thinking of the child is still influenced heavily by the primary process, it still views magic as logical. Piaget (1926) and Sarnoff (1976) have found egosyntonic magical thinking to be commonly discernible in children of the latency period and later. Early on, the child views the adult as omnipotent and omniscient. During the oral phase, the functions of the mouth and the hand are closely associated (Hoffer 1949).

The witch, a representation of the bad-mother project, is omnipotent and can magically send an invisible or tiny but nonetheless powerful arrow, a classical phallic symbol, any distance to penetrate the intended victim. The arrow is made poisonous by actual bodily waste products or obvious symbols of excreta, parts of cadavers or things which have come into contact with them. The shaman, on the other hand, accomplishes his magical cure by sucking or grabbing out the deleterious penetrating object in the form of an arrow or a cartridge which was tainted with symbolized or actual excremental products. In primary-process thinking, opposites are equal. It is noteworthy that another waste product, ash, which surely serves as a symbol of excreta, must be used to ensure the success of any curative ceremony.

For people who have hysterical characterological configurations, as do the typical Chiricahua and Mescalero, genitality remains fused with orality (Marmor 1953). Genital actions serve oral ends. Individuals with this personality composition regress easily to ego states in which the use of primary-process thinking is egosyntonic and the observing capacity of the ego is weakened or disappears — phenomena which make the differential diagnosis between hysteria and schizophrenia most troublesome at times. It would be redundant to review the use by the shaman in his curing ceremony of these hysterical qualities of his clients.

What is of special relevance for this contribution is the commonality of intrapsychic conflicts among these Apaches, conflicts which must be defended against in what ever manners can be developed, to ensure social solidarity and the reduction of guilt and anxiety in individuals, which have persisted from early child-rearing experiences. Their folklore contains a commonality of themes and symbols which, as will be illustrated in the ensuing chapters, assist in these adaptive functions.

V

Symbology in Apache Folklore

It is commonly stated that men and women became culture-bearing animals because they are capable of symbolic thought. Much has been written about the need to distinguish between the pragmatic or operational content of a symbol and its communicational content (M. Leach 1958). Frazer (1894) and Durkheim (1915) used an evolutionary approach to systems of thought assessed for their symbolic references. Later, Radcliffe-Brown (1922), adhering to Durkheim's (1927) basic sociological frame of analysis, interpreted functions of ritual, folklore and other collectively held symbolic representations in terms of social structure; the contributions of individuals were deemed unimportant. Malinowski (1929, 1935) and later functionalists were critical, finding man's collective symbols not only as representative of outer social reality but also as commonly held symbols that in many instances are deeply expressive of inner affective states that cannot be directly related to social structure. This alternative functionalist approach is related to the position taken by psychoanalytic psychology. Each is concerned with man's ontogenetic development within a social group. Both approaches seek to include biological maturational variables involved in individual socialization as well as the social determinants of symbolic expression.

DeVos (1961) discussed some sociological and psychological functions of symbolic communication. He found symbols to be used (1) for precise conceptual economy in communications when concepts are of a complex nature, (2) to convey precisely concepts that are felt to be too complex for comprehension but when comprehension is necessary, (3) to convey complex emotional states, and (4) inadvertently as projections of inner states. DeVos stressed that with the development and evolution of human ego control, the capacity to symbolize comes itself to be under the direction of objectively organized ego functions.

As noted in previous chapters, psychoanalysts have concluded that each theme or element in a folklore representation can be viewed as a symbol, and that symbols, as used in dreams, hallucinations, symptoms, prose narrative, rituals and religions, are products of repressed impulses and inhibiting influences.

Two of the mechanisms used by the unconscious ego are condensation and displacement. In the formation of the dream and the construction of prose narrative, they are supplemented by symbolization, which further obscures the latent thoughts (Altman 1969: 17 *et seq.;* Waldhorn and Fine 1974). Symbolism is a universal primal language representing an association between ideas sharing common properties that are sometimes obscure. Symbols represent primary ideas from which they acquire their meaning. The association is made by the infantile unconscious mind. The child's interests are regularly specific and physical, and the concrete takes precedence over the abstract. Temporal regression, an inevitable characteristic of altered ego states, includes perceptual and conceptual regression, which leads to the formation and use of symbols.

Throughout recorded history, symbolism used in literature, art, religion and oral literature has constituted an acceptable means of communication based on unconscious understanding, but until recently the application of symbolism to dream interpretation has often engendered suspicion.

Each dreamer employs a preferred set of symbols chosen from the multitude available to him, and social reinforcement of some of his private symbols may contribute to their continued personal use. Familiar objects from the past or the present of the individual will be chosen as a rule.

The experienced analyst can sometimes make an immediate tentative translation of the manifest content of a dream, fantasy, symptom, hallucination or folklore item which is related to him, on the basis of typical images which are present. However, individual symbols may have multiple meanings for the individual, and the most relevant temporal connotation of the symbol cannot be determined without recourse to knowledge of the dominant current conflicts, past history and associations of the narrator. Occasionally the symbol may stand solely for itself. Symbols cannot be fully understood in isolation from the rest of the dream or narrated folklore item.

Referents for symbols are surprisingly limited in number. They correspond to the basic and universal preoccupations of children: birth, death, the body and its functions, the sexual organs and people, particularly family members and their interactions with one another.

The student of the dream or item of prose narrative must be well acquainted with the symbols he will meet. To spare the reader of this and the remaining chapters of the book the tedium of an exhaustive listing, only some of those most commonly met are mentioned here. However, it must be made explicitly clear that the interpretations listed here refer to the *infantile* meanings of the symbols, and that identical symbols may simultaneously have equally accurate alternate meanings from other levels of psychological development.

There are a large number of symbols for birth and death, reflecting man's interest in and preoccupation with how he enters and leaves the world. Water and especially immersion in it have been found to refer basically to pregnancy and birth, but the presence of water in a dream or folktale may refer also to a conscious or preconscious wish to travel or it may serve to refer to an actual event in the life of the individual or of the social group. But any flowing substance may also have important oral connotations and be connected as well with urinary or menstrual fantasies and experiences. An Apache informant's associations to pouring lava included references first to an incident in which the eruption of a volcano was alleged to have influenced a battle, and then soon to the hot ejaculation from a tumescent penis, and finally to her frustration as a child that she could not urinate as far as a brother. Insects, tiny animals and sometimes spiders refer *au fond* to semen, impregnation and sibling rivals, but in special circumstances they may be related to the mundane discomfort of being infested with bedbugs or lice. The spider more commonly refers to a complex of feelings pertaining to women, as will be discussed in Chapter VI. Sleep, silence, descending into the earth, dwindling in size, taking a trip, especially westward, and disappearing into clouds or fog all appear as symbolic variants of death. However, such symbols are, as are all others, multidetermined, and may, for example, portray a wish for the re-establishment of symbiotic fusion with the mother.

Human anatomy is symbolized by architectural features, with buildings representing the body, and windows and doors its orifices. Symbolization borrows heavily from nature to represent anatomical parts and zones. Caves portray body cavities and ledges and overhangs usually represent breasts, as do sisters or fruit. All articles which enclose space or can be entered may be understood to have as one of their meanings the female genitalia. The horseshoe renders their shape and jewels their value, although gems often represent the precious male organs as well, particularly the testicles; the meaning of their presence can only be determined by the context within which the jewels appear. Stoves, closets and cupboards refer more often to the uterus than the vagina. Undergrowth and underclothes are genitalia in general, and bushes, leaves and grass frequently refer to pubic hair. Stairways, ladders, tunnels and corridors often allude to female genitalia, although ascension and descension, particularly if struggle and panting are involved, frequently refer to sexual intercourse. Menstruation is represented by the color red, but red also denotes passion, whether due to sexual excitement or anger. Othello's use of green to represent jealousy was probably based on folklore data. Flowers, like eyes, can stand for the genitals of either sex, as can the ship, which both cleaves water and is a vessel. The phallus is symbolized by anything resembling it in form, function or general properties, such as a bridge which joins two bodies of land. A constant symbolic association exists between the phallus and a vast array of animals, from the mouse and tunneling gopher to the largest of mammals. The serpent is tediously familiar, although, again, for individuals, the snake with its teeth can represent the dentate vagina. By extension, we can see why lengths of rope and vines are gross phallic equivalents.

But by now, the reader will have discerned the flavor of what goes into symbol formation; the folklore data which follow will provide more specifics. He will also know that French's (1952: 92) statement, "the uncritical use of such (universal) symbol interpretation can lead to very untrustworthy conclusions," expresses the opinion of today's psychoanalysts. He will be aware, too, that the person who is sophisticated in symbol interpretation will draw tentative hypotheses on the basis of the manifest content of dreams or folk narratives, which he will then seek to validate through the associations of the dreamer or informant and socialization and social-structure observations.

From the preceding data pertaining to Apache socialization, it has been established that Apache childhood experiences produce individuals who are both orally dependent and sadistic.

All children perceive their teeth to be their first weapon which can effectively express aggression. Before the id and the ego are clearly differentiated, the youngster perceives its hostility to have limitless magical powers, but at the same time it projects its range onto its mother, whom it perceives to be omnipotent and omniscient, and it fears punishment for aggressive wishes according to the *lex talionis,* the tooth-for-a-tooth Biblical philosophy (Klein 1957). Psychoanalysts previously understood the fear of the loss of teeth or their falling out in dreams to regularly symbolize castration fears, but with the increasing incidence of child observations and analyses and the dynamic treatment of psychotics, it has become recognized that such loss of teeth more basically represents a fear of loss of power in general and retribution for hostile oral wishes.

In the folklore data to follow, a partial analysis of an Apache story about the acquisition of Mountain Spirit power and a fragment of an

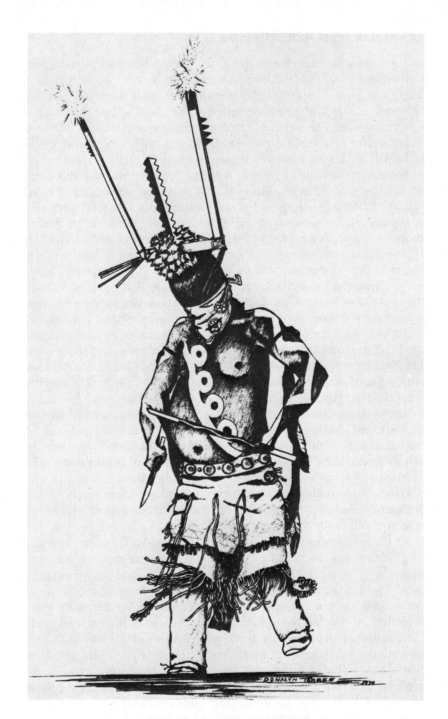

MOUNTAIN SPIRIT DANCER
(Drawing by Donalyn Torres)

origin myth will serve to illustrate some ways in which their themes and elements permitted the expression, without undue anxiety or guilt, of typical Chiricahua and Mescalero intrapsychic conflicts pertaining to dependency and oral sadism. Special attention will be paid to the use of stone as a symbol.

Like the typical dream (Freud 1900), some symbols have been considered to be refractory to comprehension. As recently as 1957, Fliess (pp. 19-30) found stone, as a manifest element of dreams and fantasies, to constitute a symbol in the dreams of Western psychoanalysands which in general defied understanding. Yet Stekel in 1935 had learned that it could represent incest. In 1956, Kestenberg found that stone could symbolize the phallus, feces and the baby, and her findings were supported by Sperling (1961), who added that stone could represent the genitals of the little girl. In 1967, Wilson concluded that "stone at the deepest level in dreams symbolizes the tooth or teeth of the second oral libidinal phase," the stage of psychosexual development which Abraham (1924: 398) designated to be "the most primitive form of sadism."

We turn now to the presentation and analysis of a folktale pertaining to the acquisition of the supernatural power of the Mountain Spirits or Gods. As we know from Chapter III, in the language of both the Chiricahuas and the Mescaleros of today, these holy personages are called alternately *ga^nheh* or *jajadeh*. The consensus of aged reservation members is that aboriginally the Mescaleros called them solely *jajadeh*, and the Chiricahuas only *ga^nheh*.

A STORY ABOUT THE ACQUISITION OF
MOUNTAIN SPIRIT POWER

A very old Chiricahua man told me the following story concerning the acquisition of the position of *ga^nheh* or *jajadeh:*

My father was a great *ga^nheh* leader. Long ago he was out raiding in a small group. They had been out a long time and were doing very badly. They didn't dare use their guns. One afternoon my father went away from camp and sat facing the east, on a big rock. He was looking at *zithtai.*

Zithtai is the Chiricahua name for Tres Hermanas, a three-peaked mountain, a sparsely brush-covered outcropping of stone in southwestern New Mexico. *Zithtai* was considered to be one of the major sites in which the "true," as contrasted with the "made," Mountain Spirits lived.

He heard a man's voice from over his head saying, "Why do you sit there, poor and in sorrow?" My father said he was indeed poor and sad; there were enemies all about and his people were starving. He said he was out there trying to get (supernatural) help for his people. Then he begged the spirit for a glimpse of his hand or his face, so that he would know to who (sic) he was talking. The spirit said, "No. You cannot see me. Just answer my questions." My father repeated what he had said and then said he had only one thing of value, his horse, which was his legs. He asked again to see the spirit. He said, "I pray to you. Bless us. We're starving." The power said, "It will cost you something." My father answered, "I have nothing but my horse." The spirit said, "Go kill that horse. Call your group and feed them from that horse. Return here tomorrow at the same time and place. If you do what I tell you, I will help you." He killed that horse with an arrow, because a gunshot would have attracted the soldiers.

The next day the spirit met him again and this time the spirit said he could expect a big, fat buck to come to their camp that night.

He told my father to meet him again at the same time and place. My father took another man out with him at dusk and they hid behind some bushes.

The narrator paused to comment that the Mountain Spirits always appear at dusk when they perform their dance.

Soon a big buck walked right up to them and my father shot it dead with an arrow.

He again interrupted his recitation, interjecting, "I didn't listen to my father when I was a boy. When I had already come into my manhood, he wanted to teach me to be a ga^{n}heh leader, but I was too interested in baseball. I learned all the songs and all the prayers and how to paint the ga^{n}heh on each of the four days and all of the dances, but I never got the power because I never had a spirit visit me." He went on to state that a younger brother had had a visitation and was the current owner of his father's ceremony. Then he continued his story as though there had been no interrruption.

He told the man with him he had killed that big, fat, iron gray horse for his people, the women, the men. He said, "I give this for the power. I have to give something alive to keep you alive."[1] The people thought he was out of his mind to kill his horse and didn't believe power had anything to do with it. But when he got that deer in the evening, they were all amazed and *then* they believed he had power.

The next day he returned to that same rock and sat facing toward *zithtai*, that holy place. The spirit came. He said, "You're here. Good. You have done well. Now if you want to help your people, you go to *zithtai*. Don't get scared. Someone will take you to that place." He went to *zithtai*, where a clown, *thlibayeh*, approached him. He demanded why my father was there. My father told him all his troubles and said he'd been told to come by the spirit. *Thlibayeh* told him to go into that cave with the narrow opening. He told him that inside there would be some very frightening things, and gave him exact instructions how to proceed. He told him everything he'd see and what to do under each circumstance. He crawled into the cave opening and there he saw big rocks before the door. They were just going back and forth.

As the informant said these words, he moved his hands together and apart repeatedly and simultaneously gnashed his teeth.

If a man went in there, he would be crushed. My father said *sht* and the rocks stopped open. He went through the first door. Then he met a huge snake. It was so big, its mouth covered the whole tunnel. It had long teeth. He could have swallowed my father whole. He said *sht* and the snake's mouth stayed open so he could go right through the second door. There a huge lion growled and snapped his big teeth. *Sht.* Next was a huge bear. *Sht.* When he got through the fourth door, he saw a beautiful country inside. There he was met by another *thlibayeh*, who said mortal men were now welcome there and asked what did he want. He told his troubles again and said he'd been instructed by the *thlibayeh* on the outside.[2] The second clown told him to proceed to the Old Man and the Old Woman who sat far away inside. They just sat there, day in and day out, year in and year out. My father walked toward them. Every step of the way, insects, spiders, snakes, birds and animals of all kinds called to him. Each one said, "I'm God. Take me. I can give you what you want. Take my powers." But my father already knew they were evil and their powers were bad. Like the snake, the lion and the bear, they were *ch?idneh, enti*ⁿ, witches. They had been entered by the ghosts of dead humans. So he paid no attention to them but just walked on to the old couple. Old Man challenged him, as had each of the *thlibayeh*, and he repeated his story and his desire. He didn't talk much because the first *thlibayeh* had told him what to say. The old man told him it was good and if he wanted *diyⁱⁿ* (sacred supernatural power) he could have it. Then my father heard jingles, drums, singing and dancing and the hoo-hoo-hoo-hoo sound those *jajadeh* make when they're dancing. The old man said that was good power from *yusn* and asked my father if he wanted it. He said he did want it. So he went in there where the *gaⁿheh* were dancing, using sabers, not the sticks the men who dress like *gaⁿheh* use, and there he was taught all the songs, dances, how to paint, prayers and everything and there he finally got his power. And it took. He lived 99 years and was always good. He didn't do what the men do now, he did all his good without pay. He had got the power for the good of his people and he used it that way.

A second informant, the wife of a brother of the narrator cited above, presented another version of the story of how her father-in-law had received *gaⁿheh* power. Its sole variation was that the snake, bear and lion who threatened to eat the man as he entered the narrow cave were replaced by three additional sets of huge, grinding rocks which opened and shut until he said *sht*. As she related this portion of the tale, she also gnashed her teeth.

A brother of the narrator presented a shortened version in which there was no snake but instead a panther, a bear and a flesh-eating cervine creature and perhaps an elk. He added an explanatory interpretation, saying the three animals were some of the monsters slain by *tubah-jischineh,* Child Of The Water, about whom information will be given below.

Other versions of the acquisition of *gaⁿheh* power will be presented in Chapter VII.

The myth of origin of the Apaches reveals in its manifest content much preoccupation with dependency and oral destructive activity, combined with wishful resolution of problems pertaining to sibling rivalry and the Oedipal situation. The condensed version which is related here was obtained from a highly acculturated middle-aged informant of combined Chiricahua and Mescalero ancestry. It coincides except for small details with that obtained regularly from present-day informants.

Long ago there was a race of people who, except for a virgin adolescent girl, were slain and eaten by *yeeyeh,* Giant, and four flesh-eating monsters, *bayeh.* Giant wanted the maiden, White Painted Lady, *istsūneglezh,* Virgin Mary, for his bride, and instructed the monsters to spare her. However, White Painted Lady heard the voice of *yusn,* God, and followed His instructions. She undressed, lay on a mountain top and was impregnated by Him when rain entered her vagina.[3] She bore *tubahjíshchineh,* Child of the Water, Jesus, after four days.[4] *Yeeyeh* suspected that *istsúneglezh* had borne a son, but she fooled him into believing otherwise so *yeeyeh* wouldn't kill him and eat him, and the baby grew quickly into young manhood. Child of the Water, aided by other supernaturally endowed Apache-speaking animals, tricked and defeated the monsters. He either relegated them to the wilderness or permitted them to live nearby only after they had agreed not to molest his mother or himself *or their progeny* and to serve as food for the Apaches. Then he slew *yeeyeh.* In their battle, Giant hurled logs or long rocks at Child of the Water, calling them his arrows, but the youth either deflected them or destroyed them with his voice, saying *sht.* Giant wore coats of stone, but *tubahjíshchineh* penetrated them with his smaller arrows or with stones he called arrows, the fourth of which pierced *yeeyeh's* heart.

ANALYSIS OF THE FOLKLORE

We turn now to a partial analysis of the story of the acquisition of *ga^nheh* power. We discuss first the apparently paradoxical equation of the male *ga^nheh* with *jajadeh,* the whippoorwill who turns into a cannibalistic woman at night. The gender-identity confusion of the Apache male was noted earlier (Chapter IV). It is impossible to determine whether similar sexual identity confusion existed aboriginally, but the apparent similarity of socialization practices as pertains to prelatency children makes such a suspicion tenable. The confusion of sexual identity which exists among the Apaches is reflected in their viewing of *jajadeh* as both male and female. As has been illustrated, *jajadeh* is synonymous with both the male figure *ga^nheh* and the female figure of the whippoorwill. It can be no coincidence that the classical cry of the *ga^nheh,* hoo-hoo-hoo-hoo, is said to be in imitation of the actual cry of the whippoorwill.

Viewed one way, the legend version which was presented above recapitulates symbolically the child's quest for its infantile view of adulthood. By being a totally good, obedient child, it can acquire eventually the omniscience and omnipotence it ascribed to its early fantasized fusion with the mother by returning to the womb. Then, after a symbolic death, it can be reborn omnipotent.

In the folktale, the narrator's father is presented first as a hungry, helpless person, symbolically a small child. In the manifest story there is no reference to his rage at having been abandoned. Instead we have the presence of enemies, culturally approved objects onto whom to project and against which to discharge hostility directed originally toward frustrating family members. The oral dependency of the protagonist is obvious.

The initial symbology of stone is that in it, *zithtai,* is to be found the magical gratification of the oral stage. The stone mountain represents the breast. The leader in the manifest content, in an altered ego state and facing the east, from which direction supernatural blessings are thought to flow, first hears the voice of a spirit whom the narrator identifies as *yusn,* God. In renditions of this folktale to be presented in Chapter VII, the first supernatural being to answer the suffering supplicant's plea for help is a *thlibayeh.* We can assume that the clown in this case represents *yusn* and that both symbolize either good-father projects who promise to provide access to the wish-fulfilling mother, or the good-mother project.

Soon it is clear that stone represents the teeth of the oral sadistic phase, affirming Wilson's proposal. Gratification and denotation of danger can be achieved through the vocalization *sht,* reminiscent of the effects of the baby's distressed callings which, to it, magically result in the mother's solacing appearance. Once the projection of oral hostility onto the stones at the entry of the cave as the representation of the teeth has appeared in the folktale, we then find the teeth of the snake, puma and bear without disguise.

The associations of two Apache adults, one male and the other female, to dreams they had related in their interviews with the author indicated that they retained a childhood belief that their mothers had been permanently pregnant, and they used insects, spiders and other small animals to symbolize their unborn sibling rivals. A latency-period boy who had three younger siblings, one of whom was an infant, revealed the same fantasies in play therapy. In the story, the obedient father, representing the questing dependent child, eschews the less than totally gratifying blandishments of similarly symbolized intrauterine rivals. The hostility of older Apache siblings toward the younger child and the undependability of their ministrations have been discussed previously, as has been the Chiricahua and Mescalero fusion of orality with subsequent maturational phases.

Implicit in the legend is the child's entrance into the digestive tracts of a series of bad-mother symbols. Apaches customarily use the word "she" to refer to a mountain, and *zithtai* in the story has a narrow opening which has characteristics of both the mouth and the dentate vagina. Although the narrator failed to mention that the narrow cave opening was covered by brush in his initial rendition, he later supplied that datum. Western psychoanalysands often use the mountain as a female symbol, and the anatomical name *mons veneris* reflects the symbolization of the pubic mound as a mountain and the trees or brush on it as pubic hair. In the story, the power-seeking child symbol gets past the stone-teeth of the cave entrance and enters the gullet of the mountain-mother. Then it gets through the teeth of the snake and enters into its esophagus. The snake is a classic phallic symbol, and its having teeth reflects the Apache notion of the penis with the dentate urethra that appears in the associations of patient-informants to their dreams and to Rorschach stimuli and that is found in an occasional Apache joke.

It is of interest that in some early Near Eastern cultures, when their principal gods were conceptualized as female (Weigert-Vowinckel 1938), the snake was sometimes used as an official symbol of the female. The snake obviously represents the phallic mother in other bodies of folklore. Thus, Chicomecóatl, patroness of the maize crop among the Aztecs, is sometimes depicted with seven interlaced serpents issuing from her neck instead of a head (Ichon 1969).

Then the father gets past the teeth of the cougar and into its digestive tract. The puma is uniformly referred to by Apaches as *she*. When at night they hear its scream, a sound which closely resembles that of a crying woman, they are fearful that they are going to be devoured. To the Apaches, the bear is an androgynous symbol. Here we should recall Lewin's (1950) remarks about the wish to be eaten, thereby to regain fantasized fusion with the mother, and an Apache story about children who sought supernatural assistance. After they were admitted into a holy mountain, these children were cut into pieces on each of four successive nights, and eventually emerged whole (Opler 1942). Opler obtained this story from the same informant who related the folktale of this chapter; all of that Apache's holy mountain caves had gnashing stones at their entrances. It seems reasonable to conjecture that the children were symbolically chewed up, devoured, and reborn cured, owning the omnipotence that young children ascribe to their mothers. To return to the present folktale, the portion which involves the helpless child's getting into the maternal digestive tract, reflecting childhood fantasies of oral impregnation, and emerging at its other end as a powerful figure, closely resembles ideas found in children of Western cultures during play therapy and in associations of adults to their dreams. Among the Chiricahuas and Mescaleros, similar fantasies emerged when individuals of various ages responded to Rorschach-card stimuli and in patient/informants' associations to their dreams. Viewed thus, the folktale can be interpreted as death-and-rebirth fantasy.

In the legend, the path to glory requires re-entry into the womb. The narrow vaginal canal eventually opens up into the intrauterine cavity. But there the protagonist is tempted by symbolic rivals, the insects, spiders and other small fauna. They offer him their powers but are spurned as witches. The small Apache child who has been neglected after the birth of a sibling turns to its older brothers and sisters for affection. But, while they sympathize with its plight, with which they identify on the basis of their own past experiences, they are hostile toward it, as discussed in Chapter IV. That the intrauterine younger siblings can also represent older brothers and sisters is consonant with the presence in unconscious thinking of opposites without conflict (Freud 1915). The temptations offered by the symbolic older siblings of the legend would have been, if accepted, less gratifying than the attentions of the good-parent representatives, the Old Man and the Old Woman.

Referring to the symbology of stone once again, we find confirmation of Sperling's proposal that stone can represent the genitalia of the female. The narrow cave, the vagina symbol, opens into the womb representation; both exist within the stone *zithtai.*

The interpretation of the legend as a symbolic enactment of the wish to obtain fusion with the mother and thereby regain the early fantasized symbiosis is implicit in the symbolized wish to be digested by her. To be sure, individuation is later accomplished when the child is reborn. But its reborn state symbolizes retention of fusion, too, since, as the newborn *ga*^{n}*heh,* it has become omniscient and omnipotent, sharing that fantasized state with the parent-symbols of its infantile imagination.

The legend can also be interpreted as a fantasy of incest and the reversal of the fear of castration. *Thlibayeh,* equated by the informant with *yusn,* God, He-Who-Created-Us, Our Father in Heaven, does not forbid the weak adult-son to enter the symbolic vagina of the maternal representation. Instead, the father uses his supernatural power to make the procedure possible and enable his son to undergo the dangerous procedure and emerge whole and in possession of supernatural power. Such power is often conceptualized by Apaches as being phallic in origin.

The interpretation of the legend as a representation of incest involves use of the *pars pro toto* equation of primary process thinking. The body-phallus equation is common in the dreams and fantasies of analysands. The boy representative, the father of the legend, enters the symbolic vagina; that is, his body as a substitute phallus penetrates the mother representation. That Apaches, too, equate body and phallus is clear in the following joke. Two Apache men were enviously ridiculing a third man, who was generally known as a Don Juan. One said, "He has a big prick." The other replied, "He *is* a big prick."

We turn now to a partial analysis of the Apache origin myth. In the origin myth of the Apaches, there existed a race of people who presumably were the children of He-Who-Created-Us, *yusn.* Except for White Painted Lady, all of them, including White Painted Lady's parents, were devoured by Giant and the monsters. In dreams, crowds frequently represent a single person; in this case and context it seems reasonable to assume that the crowd represents the mother of the maiden. In the identification of Giant, *yeeyeh,* there seems to exist another example of the splitting of the object. Many Apaches translate the myth in Christian terms. At varying levels of consciousness, they perceive God and the devil to be versions of a single parental figure and equate Giant with the devil, thus viewing *yusn* and *yeeyeh* as the moral and immoral aspects of one individual.

In clinical work, we learn frequently that children are encouraged to behave in such ways as to gratify the unconscious wishes of the parents (Johnson and Szurek 1954). Many communications report that parents of both sexes covertly or overtly seduce their children into latent or patent incestuous activity (Rangell 1954). Devereux (1955) reported a counter-Oedipal episode in the *Iliad,* emphasizing maternal sexual seductiveness. He had previously (1953) analyzed the cause of Laius' death at the hands of Oedipus and concluded that Oedipus' cohabitation with Jocasta represented primarily an active homosexual triumph over the dead father. He suggested that, generally speaking, the attainment of full genitality presupposes also an at least imaginary homosexual victory over the father.

In the Apache myth of creation, the interpretation can be made that the father of White Painted Lady, represented by *yusn,* wanted his daughter as a sexual partner. In the overt content of the myth, *yeeyeh,* a representative of He-Who-Created-Us, clearly did so. *Yusn* permitted or directed Giant to kill the mother of White Painted Lady. In Apache socialization, while parents officially disapprove of profligacy of adults and incestuous relations of children, they often indirectly encourage such behavior. While such actions are bitterly denounced and associated with witchcraft beliefs, we heard various stories about sons who had had sexual relations with or married their stepmothers and of girls who had behaved similarly with their stepfathers, on the widowhood of the stepparent or divorce of the couple. Usually such tales were about people in the past, but one stepfather was denounced during the early 1960's for having had sexual relations with one or more of his teenage stepdaughters. Incestuous behavior may occur, too, on a slightly different level. For example, a particularly beautiful adolescent girl was known to have "seduced married men." She had begun such behavior soon after her widowed mother had married a most attractive man, who was some years younger than she but still old enough to be the girl's father. Aboriginally, maidens became marriageable when they underwent their puberty ceremonies, and often married men who were much older than they. Sexual relations between adolescents of both sexes and adults old enough to be their parents are still common.

In the relations among *tubahjíschineh,* White Painted Lady or *istsúneglezh,* and *yeeyeh,* we see a distorted representation of the son's killing his father and cohabiting with his mother: after Giant's death, Child Of The Water and White Painted Lady become the ancestors of all subsequent Apaches. Perhaps we have here, additionally, a validation of Devereux's interpretation that the fantasized fulfillment of the son's sexual relations with his mother involves a homosexual triumph over his father.

The battle of Giant and Child Of The Water, in most versions of the myth, is with arrows. Those of the father-substitute are huge — in fact, logs — whereas those of the chronologically young boy are comparatively very small. People all over the world equate arrow and phallus; the Apaches clearly do in their everyday conversation. It seems tenable to interpret this portion of the myth as constituting a battle in which the father and the son seek to penetrate each other with their phallus-representations, and in which the boy wins.

Thus far we have omitted the identification of the monsters, in our attempt to understand the genital aspects of this story. We have no direct information to assist us. However, since Child Of The Water slays them, in some cases with arrows, and since they perform in the myth functions similar to those of Giant, it seems reasonable to ascribe to them the identity of split-representatives of *yeeyeh,* the immoral father.

We turn now to oral aspects of the Apache myth of creation.

As noted earlier, the symbols found in dreams and myths can be representations of self-images of the dreamer or narrator. In the manifest myth, *yeeyeh* and the Apache-speaking blunderbores devoured the first race of people and sought to eat Child Of The Water; they were, thus, cannibals. We have found only one reference to alleged actual Mescalero Apache cannibalism. Horgan (1954: 263), citing a seventeenth-century Spanish source, wrote:

> From the forests in the mountains about the pueblo of Taxique the Apaches would burst forth and capture Christian Indians and carry them off to their distant encampments. "There they build a great fire, near which they bind the person whom they have captured; they then dance around him, cutting off parts of his body, which they cook and eat, until they entirely consume him, cutting him to pieces alive."

Abraham (1924: 253-8) suggested that the orally fixated individual sometimes has the wish to incorporate the object which has attracted his wish-fantasies, by eating or being eaten by that object or its substitute, as noted before (Lewin 1950: 102-65).

The Apaches use a single word to mean envy, jealousy and greed, and appear to equate the three states. Klein (1957: 6-7) differentiates among them as follows:

> Envy is the angry feeling that another person possesses and enjoys something desirable . . . and goes back to the earliest exclusive relation with the mother. Jealousy is based on envy, but involves a relation to at least two people: it is mainly concerned with love that the subject feels is his due and . . . is in danger of being taken away

from him by his rival . . . At the unconscious level, greed aims primarily at completely scooping out, sucking dry, and devouring the breast: that is to say, its aim is destructive introjection . . . Greed is mainly bound up with introjection and envy with projection.

One facet of the creation myth is that the mother-representatives of the girl were devoured. Although I do not have material from Apache patients or informants which proves that in this myth the wish of the White Painted Lady to be reunited with her mother by being eaten by her has been reversed into the mother's having been eaten by her parents (or parent: *yeeyeh* as father, surely, and perhaps the monsters as mother), I have ample data to indicate that all primary-process mechanisms which are found to be operative in my analytic patients are likewise present in the Apaches. A clear example of the use of reversal to be found in the creation myth appears in a version of the slaying of Antelope monster (Opler 1942: 11). After he kills Antelope, "Child-of-the-Water takes pieces of the meat of the antelope and blows on them, naming and thus creating the various animals as he does so."

Two other facets of the creation merit underlining, in our attempt to understand its relationship to Apache orality.

With the aid of supernaturally endowed, friendly animals, animals which in most instances were likewise the foodstuff of the monsters, Child Of The Water is able to persuade some of the flesh-eating animals to become standard meat for the Apaches. They who had been cannibals agree to become the victims of cannibals. Whom do the friendly animals symbolize in the family constellation of the child? After the Apache child's displacement from the relatively exclusive relationship with its mother by the new nursling, it turns to food and others, including its older siblings, for solace.

In the myth of origin, Gopher as a symbol is overdetermined. In one version, Gopher is one of the flesh-eating monsters. In others, Gopher is depicted as helpful: he assists *tubahjíshchineh* by tunneling under hostile *bêtes noires* or *yeeyeh,* and either bores into them or pierces their armor, thus weaking them so that they are easy prey for Child Of The Water. Gopher, thus, is used to represent both bad and good projects. In some versions of this portion of the myth, Child Of The Water hunts with Killer Of Enemies, another child of White Painted Lady and whose father is unspecified. In his rendition of this part of the story, an adolescent boy said, referring to the episode in which Gopher helps *tubah-jíshchineh,* "Child Of The Water told Gopher he wanted to kill that antelope and *his brother* told him what to do." Here, Gopher clearly represents the loving sibling. It seems justifiable to ascribe to the friendly animals the meaning of siblings who turn in unison with *tubahjíshchineh* upon parent surrogates, onto whom has been projected oral aggression, ultimately bad-mother symbols. If we assume that Gopher, in addition to being a sibling, represents a split-off part of *tubahjíshchineh,* we have a scarcely veiled homsexual triumph over the father. That Gopher is clearly perceived by Apache women as a phallic symbol is exemplified by their repeatedly and quite seriously telling Ruth Boyer not to sit on the bare ground because Gopher would make a tunnel and enter her from below. On occasion, that message would be imparted soon after the relating of a story of Gopher's helping Child Of The Water by tunneling into *yeeyeh* or any of several other monsters. We can suppose that this is an indication that some Apache women unconsciously perceive themselves to be bad-mother representatives, monsters.

In the origin myth one facet is reminiscent of the magical power of the voice which was found to be operative in the legend of the acquisition of $ga^n heh$ power. There, saying *sht* prevented the teeth, upon which had been projected the oral-sadism of the child, from eating the protagonist. In the origin myth, *tubahjíshchineh's* voice could destroy *yeeyeh's* logs/stones/arrows. Attention was called previously to the child's belief in the magic of its voice, which is presumed to have its origin in the mother's response to its calls.

SUMMARY REMARKS

In this chapter, partial analysis of a folktale pertaining to the acquisition of supernatural power and the status of the $ga^n heh,$ and analysis of fragments of the origin myth of the Chiricahua and Mescalero Apaches, suggest anew the general principles that (1) folklore can be understood in terms of the language of the dream, (2) the language of the dream and folklore expresses the rules pertaining to infantile and unconscious thinking which were first delineated clearly by Freud and his followers, (3) folklore serves as a group-supported phenomenon which supplements and enhances the defensive conflicts of individual dreams, and (4) the dominant conflicts which are instilled in members of a group through their socialization experiences are expressed and partially resolved by their prose narrative.

The chapter deals more specifically with questions pertaining to the understanding of symbols. That they are greatly overdetermined and have a plethora of meanings is demonstrated by the multiplicity of significances in the folktale and in the myth of the symbol stone. The many meanings of stone as a symbol in the cited Apache prose narrative are found to coincide with and perhaps even to extend the numerous meanings which have been discovered by psychoanalysts in their efforts to understand the dreams, fantasies and play of Western patients.

A special inference to be drawn from the material of this chapter is that, while symbols appear to have basic universal meanings which depend on the experiences, conflicts and thinking of childhood, an attempt to interpret symbols solely in terms of the manifest content of dream or folklore item may lead to questionable and incomplete conclusions. The temporal relevance of the symbol cannot be understood without thorough knowledge of the developmental past of the individual and the group, and of the current dominantly cathected conflicts of both.

VI

Apache Lore of the Bat

APACHE LORE OF THE BAT[1]

A variety of Chiricahua and Mescalero stories involve bats. In this chapter, analyses of all the known folktales in which that character appears not only demonstrate that Apache folklore serves the defensive and adaptive purposes of traditional oral literature, but also suggest that memories persistent from Apache cradle days are attached to some of the symbols of bat stories.

Opler (1942:28-31, 99-100) recorded the first Chiricahua material pertaining to bats when he recounted the Coyote Cycle. There, bats appear in stories one and eight. So far as has been determined, no Mescalero data were reported until thirty years later (R.M. Boyer 1972). Hoijer's (1938a) texts contain no references to bats.

The folktale that stimulated the initial interest of our cross-disciplinary team and led us to look further was related to Ruth Boyer in 1958 by Old Lady With A Sash, a Mescalero woman in her nineties who was adept at conveying the flavor of whatever anecdote she told. She spoke no English but her gestures made her meanings clear. At appropriate points her arms flapped like wings; the features of her face expressed the mood of each character. Her recital was a performance.

Old Lady With A Sash introduced us to Bat and his fellow bats as the only performers in her tale. Although her story will be presented in detail in its proper sequence for analysis, it can be summarized briefly as follows:

> A bat sitting alone on a tree was being mocked by a group of bats
> on the ground below. The bat in the tree said he was superior, more
> powerful than those on the ground. When a flood came, the bats
> below him escaped. Proud and haughty though he had been, he had
> great difficulty in escaping the waves. Only after considerable ef-
> fort did he manage to "walk on the water" with his wings.

After we had collected tales for a year or so, we recognized this to be
an unusual story, in terms of both plot and characters. Almost no other
Apache could relate any story involving a bat, despite the fact that this
mammal frequents Apache territory and did so aboriginally. Our curiosity piqued, we turned to the literature.

Opler presented two Chiricahua tales and their various versions in
which Bat is associated with Coyote, a character as common in Apache
stories as he is elsewhere among many North American Indian tribes.
There has been considerable scholarship devoted to Coyote, whose complex personality reveals contradictory traits (Angulo 1973; Dundes 1967;
Makarius 1969; Radin 1909; Ricketts 1966; Róheim 1952a; Tsuchiyama
1947; Wycoco 1951; Zbinden 1960). He is a "trickster-transformer-
culture hero" (Boas 1898, 1914) — at one time the creator of the earth,
the slayer of monsters, the teacher of cultural skills and customs; at
another time the blundering fool, a victim of his own inadequacies and
ruses; at still another, a gross, evil and deceitful prankster. He may
benefit mankind by changing the world; he may succumb to his own
stupidity; he may brave the consequences of breaking the most sacred
social sanctions and rules. He is a composite symbol of many aspects of
mankind, illustrating man's weaknesses and strengths, his conscious and
unconscious contradictory nature.

As was discussed in Chapter V, among the Chiricahuas and
Mescaleros *tubahjíshchineh*, Child Of The Water, is the Promethean
culture hero (Boas 1914) who benefits mankind. Coyote is a separate being, a trickster. However, Coyote's actions sometimes complement those
of *tubahjíshchineh*. All Apaches know the character Coyote very well.
As a trickster, a fool and yet a feared individual, Coyote, with his adven-
tures, reflects the ambivalent relationships these Apaches have with one
another. Coyote is feared as a deceitful creature in story, but in real-life
situations as well a coyote is feared — all canines are cultural bogies.
Further, his numerous escapades and postures depict aspects of Apache
life — some laudable, some forbidden. He appears in vast numbers of
contexts, being included in the myths and legends of origin and engaging
in behaviors which in everyday life would be socially ridiculed and
morally censured. He serves the same role in southern Athabascan oral

literature as he does among certain Plains, Great Basin, Plateau and California Indians. Raven or Mink is Coyote's counterpart among the Northern Athabascans and other peoples of the Northwest Coast, as Hare is among the ancient Algonkian, and Bluejay in parts of the state of Washington (Chowning 1962; Ricketts 1966).

In order to obtain a better understanding of the educational and psychological functions of folk myths, analyses will be presented of Opler's tales of the Coyote Cycle that involve the bat, of some recently obtained variants of these tales, and of the story recorded by Ruth Boyer. These analyses suggest some hypotheses regarding the role of the bat in Chiricahua and Mescalero folklore, and regarding the way in which Bat serves individual and group needs just as does Coyote.

In all of the stories that follow, there is a vast overdetermination of symbolic meanings, each of which serves to defend against conscious awareness on the parts of audiences of the forbidden wishes gratified by other symbolic meanings.

Opler (1942:28-31) gives three versions of the first Coyote Cycle tale, "Coyote's Enemy Sends Him Away on Rising Rock and Steals His Wife." In these we have two main overt lessons: first, if a man eschews responsibility for his wife and family while in pursuit of childish pleasures, he risks both death and the loss of his family to another man; second, to steal another man's wife, even with her cooperation, is taboo and punishable by death. Versions one and two emphasize the first sin, while variant three deals with the second transgression. These manifest malfeasances screen others, which are revealed by analyzing the tale as though it were a dream—particularly male homosexuality, disobedience of the Apache proscription against small children's observing parental sexual relations, and mother-son incest.

As will be seen, the first disguising element of the story is that Coyote is depicted in split parts, a technique which mirrors the technique in dreams by which each component represents a projection of an aspect of the dreamer. Seen thusly, each of the coyotes represents a veiled reference to forbidden id components and, simultaneously, defensive ego functions. The role of splitting in oral literature not only serves this function, but it also permits easy expression of emotional ambivalence.

The tales focus on the duties and mental operations of the Apache male, which makes us wonder why so much of folklore refers to the aspirations and problems of men rather than of women. While we cannot amplify here our ideas pertaining to the reasons for this occurrence, we do hypothesize, in agreement with Mead (1949), the Murphys (1974) and the Spindlers (1958), that it reflects a greater insecurity in the males of (at least) nonliterate societies in the process of culture change.

Coyote's Enemy Sends Him Away on Rising Rock
and Steals His Wife
(Opler 1942:28-30)

After gambling for a day or night, the coyotes moved out and
traveled to a place where the rising rock was. The coyotes were
camping right around close to that rock. And in that camp there
was one coyote who had a pretty wife and a little boy.

We see that the tale is introduced by a reference to playing, gambling:
thereby the audience is misled to assume that it is just an amusing anecdote rather than a serious homily. Nonetheless, the entire story can be
viewed as a representation of the problems in the Apache male's growing
up, although the various stages of maturation are presented out of sequence at times — which disguises them. As is so frequently observed in
dream recitations, the initial statement heralds a main theme — in this
case that there is an Oedipal problem to be resolved. This we infer from
the presence of a triad involving a man, his wife and their son.

We shall see later that the rock which could magically rise and descend
represents the transformation of the little urinating penis into the phallus
and back again into its original state. The small child who first observes
such changes in its father's penis is awestruck and ascribes the alterations
in size, position and rigidity to magic. The Apaches ascribe supernatural
power especially to phallic and oral sources. However, we recall that
symbols have multiple determinants and shall not be surprised to find the
rock representing other phenomena as well.

Every now and then these coyotes would go up on the rock. One
would say to another, "You get on that rock over there." And then
some of those coyotes would say, "Rock, rise up with that man."
Then the rock would start to go up, far into the sky. Then they
would tell that rock, "Come down with that man again." So the
rock would bring that fellow down again.

These Apaches view the afterlife as being in the sky; thus we have a
potential veiled statement at this point in the recitation to the effect that
we are dealing with death and rebirth.

Rising Rock would obey the commands of the coyotes. If we view
these animals as substitutes for children, we see the use of denial; it is not
the father and his phallus which are all-powerful, but his children. This
denial reflects the fantasies of omnipotence of the young.

One time this coyote who had the pretty wife happened to be
among the crowd. Another coyote who had it in for him was stan-

> ding in the crowd also. And he told the coyote who had the pretty
> wife to get on that rock. Coyote got on the rock. And the fellow
> who had it in for him said, "Rock, go up with him." And it began
> to go up with him. Then, at the command "Come down again,
> Rock," it came down with the coyote.

Continuing to view the coyotes as symbols of children, we are reminded
of the intensity of Apache sibling rivalry. Before the little child is
cathectedly aware of the sexual union of his parents, he views the father
as a sibling, competing only for pre-Oedipal attentions. This phase of
development was starkly evident in our observations of Chiricahua and
Mescalero socialization, which indicated that many a small child sees his
father primarily as a rival for oral, nurturant satisfactions, and that
fathers often compete with their children for maternal care from their
wives. On another level we may consider the competitive coyotes to
represent feuding between rivalrous Apache families, a condition ram-
pant in early reservation days and previously and which occurs in less
overt ways today. Rivalry was especially obvious between the
Chiricahuas and the Mescaleros after their union in 1913; it should be
recalled that Opler's informants were Chiricahuas who had moved onto
the reservation.

> And that coyote with the pretty wife said, "This is a very fine thing.
> I'd like to go up again." So he was sent up and down until the
> fourth time. Then his enemy told the rock to get up out of sight and
> to stay that way. The rock did so. And all the camp was going on a
> journey, moving. And coyote was up there out of sight and
> couldn't get down.

The number four is used by Apaches, as it is by most North American
Indian tribes, to stress crucial or magical importance.

Not only is the coyote out of sight, but he also can't see the sexual relationships which take place between his enemy and his wife. The small
Apache child must at least pretend it does not view such parental activities, before it may develop the capacity to deny their existence or
repress its knowledge. Neiderland (1964) noted the role of closing the
eyes in the ontogenetic determination of some symbols.

We note also that the coyote on the rock is abandoned. This element of
the story reminds us strongly of the fairly frequent Apache custom of
"throwing the child away," that is, abandoning it with a flimsy ra-
tionalization to whoever will take it. At the same time, the willingness
of the man at this point in the tale to go up and down on the magical
erection may reflect the Apache's eternal quest for a father who will give
maternal care.

In the same story, the going up on Rising Rock is treated as though it were a game for the coyote-husband-child. It is as if he were repeating the youngster's wish to be lifted up in his parents' arms to re-experience reassurance that is thrilling because it is potentially dangerous—it might be dropped. We have seen Apache infants being held aloft, high above their mothers' heads, in moments when the mothers seemed to be relating most positively to their babies, and we have noted the combined delight and fear in the babies' expressions.

Balint (1959) has traced the ultimate danger to the child's fear that it will lose access to the mother's breast, the original source of life sustenance. Arlow (1976), noting the all-pervasive oral fixation of these Apaches, views the thrilling "game" of going up and down on Rising Rock to have its basic roots in anxieties attendant on the fear of loss of contact with the emotional support of the mother. He reminds us that the small child's original model for the little penis which becomes engorged into the phallus and detumesces following the discharge of its contents is the breast, which also fills and empties. That this concept applies to Apache material will become apparent in the ensuing analysis.

At the same time, we have a gross hint of the presence of a negative Oedipal resolution, that is, the giving up of competition with the father for the mother as a sexual object. This is expressed in two ways. In the first, the husband-father finds it a very fine thing to be the libidinous homoerotic object of his symbolic father; in the second, he relinquishes his wife and son to his competitor-enemy. We remember here the problems inherent in the strong latent homosexuality which characterizes typical Apache men.

> As soon as that coyote got out of sight on the rock, the other coyote got his wife. He married that woman and abused the little boy. Every time he brought meat he took the muscle meat, the toughest part that isn't worth eating, and he threw it to the boy. He would say, "Eat that, you! Your father went up on that rock, he went up in the sky." He was mean to him. He told him that every day.

Here, too, we have a veiled statement of the Oedipal conflict. It is not the boy who harms the father and takes the mother sexually, but the converse. But why is this facet of the manifest story necessary, if not to call attention to competition between father and son for sexual access to the mother? And we must recall that many Chiricahuas and Mescaleros both consciously and unconsciously view sexuality in oral terms.

If we view the ascension on the substituted erection as representing the ecstasy of intercourse, we have a continuation of the child's wish that the father be punished for his sexual behavior with the mother. We note also that when the father is in the sky, dead, one of his symbolic sons gains sexual rights to the mother.

> Now we come back to the boy's father. He was up there on that
> rock. And he saw some bats playing around there above him.
> Coyote called to them, "Hey, you folks up there playing with your
> children, come down here! I want to see you."

The portrayal of the bats playing with their children seems to represent
an idealized version of the child-parent relationship. It is a wish that
there were no hostility among Apache mothers, fathers and offspring.
We note that the bat family or families were above Coyote, more heavenward,
more nearly in paradise. Then the situation changes, and the focus is on
the bat siblings, as one bat looks down toward earth, just as he might
look down on a younger brother or sister.

> And one of the children said, "Wait! Someone's saying something
> down below."

Apache children often alternately empathize with and enjoy the
discomfort of the toddler who has been in effect abandoned at the birth
of the infant. These older siblings sometimes seek to give the toddler
solace and at times try to get their parents to pay more attention to it.

> The coyote yelled the same thing again. Then they heard him and
> went down there. And he began to beg help from those bats. He
> said to one of them, "Old man, won't you please carry me down?"

The displaced toddler, despairing of getting attention from its mother,
often turns to its father for tenderness and emotional support, which it
gets inconsistently.

> The bat told him, "We might fall." But he kept begging him,
> "Carry me down." So the bat went away and got a basket. And it
> was fastened across his head and hanging on his back. The first
> thing the coyote did was to look over this basket and the strings to
> see how strong it was. The bat had a thin string, just a hair, as a
> rope for that basket.

The similarity between the bat basket and the cradleboard is obvious. In the tale, the bat's role changes to that of parent.

Here, attention will be called only to the coyote's doubt of his potential rescuer's good will. This clearly reflects the Apache child's semi-
mistrust of his parents, a distrust which seems to increase with age and
manifests itself later in ascription to shamans, good-mother represen-

tatives, of the intention to do harm to or even kill their supplicants.

> The coyote said, "What kind of string is that? That's going to break with me; then I will fall." The bat answered, "This will never break." The coyote said, "All right, let's see you put four big rocks in it and jump around with it here." So the bat put four rocks in and did what the coyote asked him to do. It didn't break. Then the coyote said, "That will be all right." The bat, before the coyote got into the basket, told him, "I'm going to tell you just one thing you must do: shut your eyes after you get in the basket and keep them shut all the way down. If you open your eyes, we're going to fall and break our legs." The coyote said, "All right." So they started going down to the ground. When the bat started he said, "Rock, stick, stick, stick." He just kept saying that all the way down until he was just a little way from the ground. Then the coyote began to yell, "I just have to look." The bat said, "Don't you do it, for then we are going to fall." The coyote insisted, "I just have to open my eyes." The bat begged him not to. But the coyote looked and they fell, and the bat hurt his shin. But they were down, and the coyote went on his journey.

Thus he abandoned his injured parent-rescuer, just as Apache parents throw an unwanted or seemingly burdensome child away — another reversal but representative of the vengeance toward their parents that Apaches feel. The choice of negative identity, which leads to personal destruction and societal anomie, has been cited before as a manifestation of that vengeance.

In the second tale of the Coyote Cycle that Opler (1942:30-31) presents, "Coyote Seeks His Family and Kills His Rival," a coyote is killed for a manifest wife-stealing, a veiled Oedipal transgression.

Another version of the Rising Rock story, which includes elements of the second legend of the Coyote Cycle, deviates in the following particulars (Opler 1942:28):

> Coyote is living with the family of another man. In order to possess this man's wife, he sends her husband up on a rock during a hunt. He then tells the woman that her husband is lost and they might as well live together. Meanwhile, Old Woman Bat brings the husband down in a basket secured by one stand of a spider's web. Coyote has just obtained a promise from the woman that she will come to him later that night, when the husband is heard approaching. Coyote jumps from the woman to his old place behind the fire. As the husband comes in he greets him, saying, "See, I'm taking care of your wife just as I used to do."

It is overt in the story that the woman only pretends that her husband is dead and willingly enters into cuckoldry. Apache men aboriginally practiced polygyny, preferably sororal polygyny. Even more commonly they had wives in various camps on their hunting and raiding routes, and the several women often resented the double standard. Although even military accounts stress the "fidelity" of Apache women, that some of them reacted by cuckolding their husbands is implied in the earlier practice of slitting the nose of an adulterous wife, an interesting example of symbolic *lex talionis* retribution. An old Apache man once said: "When she went with the other man, she took away her husband's manhood. Then he cut off her nose." A moment later he laughingly equated nose and phallus.

The *double entendre* of "taking good care of your wife" is familiar to Apaches.

It can be no coincidence that a strand of the web of a spider appears in some of the stories. As do so many other peoples of the world (Abraham 1922: Graber 1925), the Apaches use the spider as a symbol of ambivalence toward the mother. Frequently the spider represents the castrating or cannibalistic vagina, and its web is seen as a trap. In this instance, the web strand seems to denote the umbilical cord, the sustaining symbol of rebirth.

A third version of the Rising Rock tale, also combining elements of stories one and two of Opler's Coyote Cycle, shows the following difference (Opler 1942:28):

> Coyote is on his way to visit a family when he meets its head and sends him up on the rock. He marries the man's wife and abuses his son, addressing him as "son of the man who went up on the rock," and forcing him to carry meat in from the hunt.

We recall that Chiricahua and Mescalero children are taught to fear *jajadeh,* the whippoorwill, when they are misbehaving. They are told that *jajadeh* will come at night, perhaps in the guise of a woman, with a basket into which the child will be pushed while asleep and in which it will be carried away to be eaten on a mountaintop. The bat, also a night animal, and the whippoorwill are overtly equated by some Apache informants.

But Bat, too, is a contradictory figure in Navaho lore. He has both beneficent and fraudulent aspects. Like Coyote and the clown, Bat is a personage associated by this tribe with Darkness and Night, ultimately symbolizing death, and he is believed to live in the nether world. He is a helper, often a guardian in sand paintings and rituals, a mentor who bridges the distance between man and god and who plays a role in instruction. In the Navaho myth of creation, Bat Woman rescued Monster

Slayer, a figure similar to *tubahjīshchineh,* from the ledge where he had destroyed the Cliff Monsters. This was done by means of a burden basket with a tumpline the width a grocer's string, which no doubt represented the source of food and basically the umbilical cord. Bat is believed by the Navahos to have a "wing hook" or a "vagina wing" by means of which she clings to rocks when she makes an "embarrassing sound." The negative side of Bat includes his disobedience to a culture hero's instructions. Further, in a Navaho story, Bat whispered the answers to examination questions which those under his protection would otherwise have failed. We are, of course, reminded of the protecting instructions of *yusn* or *thlibayeh* to the quester for gan^nheh power (Chapter V), and recall that *thlibayeh* means both Coyote and clown. Thus, among the Navahos, Bat personifies deception. In one story, bats kill Coyote, grinding up his skin with soil and scattering the mixture in all directions (Reichard 1950), recalling to us the southern Athabascan concealment of feces in the wild and the afterbirth to avert their being used for witchcraft purposes. The Navahos clearly view both Bat and Spider Woman with ambivalence.

We recall Arlow's (1976) view of Rising Rock as a symbol of the breast. We have further inferential support for his judgment. In Chapter V, it was noted that among Western analysands ledges typically represent breasts; Bat Woman rescues Monster Slayer from the ledge where he had destroyed the Cliff Monsters, which we can easily comprehend as symbolic sibling rivals. Lewin (1950) and Klein (1957) wrote of the infant's projection of his oral sadism onto the breast, which is sometimes viewed as desirous of eating the nursling. In a Navaho story, Spider Woman is depicted eating the child on the mountaintop. But Spider Woman is commonly used as an everyday disciplinary agent. The Apache mother merely tells her child that, unless it behaves, it will be carried away by *jajadeh,* perhaps to be eaten. Navaho mothers are even more graphic. In Canyon de Chelly there is a single stone spire, called Spider Rock, which rises abruptly for many hundreds of feet from the canyon floor. It is red, except for a top layer approximately eighty feet thick, which is white. Navaho mothers take their unruly children to Spider Rock and tell them that, if they do not behave, Spider Woman will take them in her basket up the spire and eat them on top; the white layer is the bones of children she has devoured.

The use of the mountain as a symbol of the breast is well known throughout the world. An aged Apache, speaking of *zithtai,* Tres Hermanas, Three Sisters, said they looked to him like breasts.

In 1959, Flitting Bird, a Mescalero woman in her sixties and the daughter of Old Lady With A Sash, told Ruth Boyer another variant of the Rising Rock story. It is recorded here simply for purposes of completeness. Its analysis would be redundant.

Another coyote had a pretty wife and a young girl, his daughter. They moved around a lot; lots of people then had horses and camped and moved a lot. One day the coyote said , "You all go. I will look for something to eat and then I will follow you with some meat." He did. Actually, they only moved a little way. He looked for his wife but could not find her.

Some people said, "She was going with a man. We thought it was you."

So that man followed their tracks. He could see that they had stopped there when he saw a poker on the ground. He asked that poker, "Talk to me please. When did my wife leave? Where did she go?" And the poker just pointed the way.

So the man followed the poker's directions. He saw a little puppy. It pointed out the way for him to go.

He waited until he saw some coals in the fire. He asked the coals, "When did my wife and another man stay here?" One of the coals rolled out of the fire in order to show him the way. So he walked that way.

He saw a little rock. He stood on the rock. They were on the other side, his wife and that man. He sat on that rock. The man with his wife said, "Grow up with that man." He said it four times and the rock began to grow taller and taller with the man on top of it.

The wife and her friend were going off. They camped for two days and two nights. That is just like four days. The man wanted to get off that rock but the rock was way up in the air with him. He could see a lot of bats flying, flying, flying with their children. They were trying to get on the rock.

The man said to the bat, "Take me down, please help me." One of the bats had a little basket on his back. "I will take you down. You get in my basket and I will take you down, but if you open your eyes, you will fall out."

So they started down. He said four times, "Sticking on the rock."

As soon as the man was off the rock, the rock dropped to its normal size. However, the man started to get tired as they began to go down. He opened his eyes and fell from the bat's basket. He was not hurt and began to follow his folks. The bat flew away.

Finally, he found those two. He did something to that man. He killed him, I guess.

In Opler's first version of the Rising Rock story, Bat warns Coyote
that if he opens his eyes during the descent, "we're going to fall and
break our legs." But when Coyote disobeys the injunction, he escapes
unscathed, and the shin of the bat is injured. In Flitting Bird's version,
Coyote also escapes injury; no mention is made of Bat's legs. In Opler's
eighth Coyote Cycle story, "The Eagle-Killer Rescued by Bat," to
follow, Coyote is again unhurt, but Bat's legs are broken. The leg is used
frequently by these Apaches to symbolize the phallus.

The son's looking during the descent is thus designated as potentially
castrating both to Bat and to himself. Just as it is taken for granted that
Apache children will ignore their parents' sexual relations and "forget"
them, in the Rising Rock story the pretty woman's husband is enjoined
against opening his eyes while father bat descends to mother earth, calling, "Rock, stick, stick, stick," an obscure phrase, the meaning of which
will be clarified later. In the castration threat to both the father and the
son we have a reflection of the boy's wish to demasculinize his father and
his *lex talionis* fear of castration. In the tale, only the father's leg is injured. This, even in the story, follows Coyote's proclaiming himself to be
helpless and pleading for help, an aspect which will be discussed below.
It also serves as the gratification of an infantile wish.

Other meanings of the closed eyes will appear in the discussion of the
"Owl-Killer's Rescue by Bat," to follow.

It is perhaps redundant to mention that the presentation of different
aspects of a single theme in connected but ostensibly separate story in-
stallments serve disguising, defensive purposes, which permit their expression without stirring disquieting anxiety in listeners. The same purpose is served for the individual by the fragmentation of one night's
dream into separate dreams with varying manifest content as it is recalled, and which can be brought together only through analysis of their latent content.

The very material which analysands use to deny the presence of forbidden wishes or activities often unwittingly constitutes an admission of
guilt for the transgression in question. We find this phenomenon in
Opler's second version of the Rising Rock story. There "Coyote jumps
from the woman to his old place behind the fire" when the husband approaches. Fire is frequently used to symbolize passion, especially sexual
passion. The Coyote's claim is that he is just behind the fire, that is, he is
not sexually involved with the man's wife, in denial of the facts given in
the tale. Coyote's assertion in the story can be seen as a claim that he is
only a child observing the sexual union expected when a man comes
home to his wife after a separation.

In Opler's third version of the Rising Rock story, Coyote is killed as punishment for having illicit intercourse by having to swallow hot rocks. Opler (1942:28) introduced the Coyote Cycle with a story explaining how death came to the Chiricahuas.

> Raven said that he didn't want death in this world. "I'll throw a stick in the river. If it sinks, there is going to be death, but if not, everything will be all right," he said.

> Then Coyote came along and said, "I'll throw a rock in the river. If it sinks, people will die. If it doesn't sink, there will be no death."

> Raven threw the sticks and they floated off. Then Coyote threw the rock and it sank. After that, people began to die.

As is common elsewhere, these Apaches use both the stick and the stone to symbolize the phallus and water to represent the womb.

In the explanation of the origin of death, then, penetration of the female genitalia is punishable by destruction. This theme is found occasionally in the dreams of Apache patient-informants.

In Jicarilla (Opler 1938:44-47) and Lipan Apache (Opler 1940:28) folklore, Raven is held responsible for death. In both their and the Chiricahua versions, a male figure with magical powers is blamed for death, which implicitly constitutes punishment for illicit intercourse — ultimately representing, we assume, mother-son incest. The male figure represents an externalized superego introject.

Opler's (1942:99-100) eighth Coyote Cycle story is the next one of his series which includes the bat in its manifest contents.

The Eagle-Killer Rescued by Bat

> The people had nothing to eat. When they hunted for deer they set a fire around the mountain to kill the deer. A boy went after the deer. A bald-headed eagle took him. Another day the eagle took a girl. The people thought the best way was to kill a horse, clean the gut, and put the blood in the entrails. So they did this and put the entrails over the shoulder of a boy. And they gave him a sword. They built a fire around the mountain so the eagle would come.

Thus far, highly overdetermined elements are present. We note first the recurrence of fire, this time surrounding the symbolic erection. The setting is similar to that of the hungry people, children substitutes, who hunt in the legend of the acquisition of ga^nheh or $jajadeh$ power (Chapter V.)

The bald-headed eagle, of course, is not really devoid of feathers on its head. It only has the appearance of having the caput uncovered, like the retracted foreskin. Those eagles are no more common than those with brown heads in the homelands of these Apaches.

We know that the irrationality in folklore is the failure of its formal structure to obey the laws of Aristotelian logic and its following, instead of the Von Domarus principle (Arieti 1948). When we interpret the use of the bald-headed eagle in this context, we conclude that it is specified in the story because it can more effectively represent a phallus.

Again we have allusion to our observed ambivalence of Apache parents to their children and vice versa, with the ascription to the eagle, a father representation, of cannibalistic desires. We assume these desires are partly projected onto parents by their children, who seek to release aggression toward their parents by oral means and simultaneously to achieve fantasized physical reunion, a re-establishment of the symbiotic phase. From the socialization data, we know that Apache parents envy their children and have oral aggressive wishes toward them.

Among the Apaches, the horse is often equated with phallic power. In the ga^nheh power-acquisition tale, the man sacrifices his horse, "his legs," that is, renounces his adult masculinity and becomes a helpless child, before he can succeed in the quest (Chapter V). We are reminded also of the Biblical sacrifice of the lamb rather than the son to appease a vengeful god.

The function of the entrails is not entirely clear. Presumably the eagle is to be fooled into accepting as food horse rather than human blood. The entrail bag itself is reminiscent both of the basket carried by *jajadeh* in the story told to naughty children and of the basket associated with the bat in its rescuing function. Viewed thus, both the bad cannibalistic mother-surrogate and the child hero carry containers of food which is forbidden to Apaches. Elsewhere we have written of food taboos of these Apaches, who will not eat anything which unconsciously reminds them of cannibalism (Boyer and Boyer 1972:55-56); these taboos would be unnecessary were there no unconscious wish to eat human beings.

Further reference to the intestines of horses will be made in the discussion of "The Owl-Killer Rescued by Bat," which will follow.

The eagle took the boy and flew away to his home on top of a high mountain. The eagle saw more smoke and prepared to leave the nest. The little ones said, "This man said 'sh' to us." The eagle said, "Never mind, eat him. He's been shot; that is why he makes that noise." The eagle went away.

It was noted before that the bald-headed eagle might have been chosen because he can more easily represent a phallus. We should not forget that earlier Rising Rock itself constitutes that symbol, as does the fire-surrounded mountain in the Eagle-Killer story. We are reminded of the small child's sometimes visualizing its father's erection as being surrounded by light (Boyer 1971; Greenacre 1947).

We wonder why the concept of man's having been shot is introduced, when it seems so out of context in the manifest material. Obviously being shot refers to penetration. Thinking from this standpoint, we are reminded of the use of Rising Rock as a phallic symbol. In this frame of reference it may not be too farfetched to suppose that the "sh" represents an anal noise and that the boy's being raised by his father substitute also represents anal penetration by the phallus. In the *jajadeh* power-acquisition account, the sound "sht" is used to ward off evil.

> Then the boy got up and killed the little ones with his sword. He left one little one. "When does your father come back?," said the boy to the little eagle.

> "My father will come back when the cloud is on top and it thunders."

> "When he comes back, where does he sit first?"

> The little eagle pointed to a rocky point. The boy sat down there.

> The eagle came back carrying another boy. As soon as the eagle lit, the boy killed the eagle. Then he said to the young one, "When does your mother come back?"

To borrow a phrase from *Alice in Wonderland,* events grow curiouser and curiouser. It seems strange that the little eagle is so cooperative, in view of his by now being fully aware of the intention of the boy to kill both his parents and his siblings. We can deduce that the eaglet must have hostility toward all the other members of his family.

But why does the boy wait until the father eagle has sat down on the rocky point before he slays him with his sword? We have another reference to penetration while on a rock, perhaps a substitute for Rising Rock, the phallic symbol, which is duplicated by the sword.

As noted in Chapter IV, the earliest genital sexual behavior which we observed, aside from masturbation, occurred in the outhouses, in conjunction with toilet activities. Both sexual and excretory activities tend to be lumped together as "dirty," as are the anatomical areas concerned and even clean underpants. Such explorations no doubt serve to reinforce earlier childhood fantasies which link sexual and anal functions, which are so often conceptualized, by children who may not yet know of the existence of the vagina, as consisting of anal penetration and anal birth.

Returning to the analysis of the Eagle-Killer story, it seems reasonable to assume that Coyote's penetration of eagle with a sword symbolizes anal intercourse, reminiscent of Rising Rock's penetration of Pretty Wife's husband.

"When little clouds are all over and there is a little fog."

"When your mother comes back, where does she sit?"

The little eagle told him. Pretty clouds began to be all over. Rain without thunder is female; rain with thunder is male rain. As soon as mother eagle spread her wings to light, the boy killed her.

In the Chiricahua and Mescalero myth of origin, *istsuneglezh* is impregnated by *yusn*'s rain when she spreads her legs or vulva on a mountaintop (Chapter V). In the Eagle-Killer legend, the mother eagle spreads her wings and is penetrated by the sword, a symbolic re-enactment of the Oedipus theme, after the father is killed.

As yet, we have no direct clue as to why the clouds and fog are introduced into the story. We do have some idea as to why the explanation of female and male rain is introduced. Thunder is accompanied by lightning. Lightning power in Apache folklore is equated with snake power because of the similarity of the shape of forked lightning to the appearance of the snake in motion. Both are quite consciously associated with phallic power by Apaches.

Although we do not have direct confirmatory associations from Apaches, evidence from other cultures leads us to suppose that thunder also serves to symbolize phallic and anal functions. Jones (1914) lucidly articulates the symbolic transformations of the expulsion of intestinal gas. He maintains that males create by a blowing movement, that is, by breath or sound, or by wind. Jones rarely made categorical statements, but he wrote (p. 278): "that the idea of thunder is exceedingly apt, in dreams and other products of unconscious fantasy, to symbolize flatus, particularly paternal flatus, is well known to psychoanalysts." Derek Freeman (1968) affirmed his conclusion from work done with members of other cultures, and Dundes (1976), who studied the symbolism of the bull roarer in many cultures, noted that the noise made by that object is frequently said to represent thunder and concluded that the bull roarer ultimately symbolizes the flatulent phallus.

But the boy did not know how to get down. He looked down and saw a little thing walking. He called to it to take him down. The little thing then said, "Who are you? Where are you?"

Knowing the sympathetic magic connected with the utterance of certain names, we can conjecture that his calling "the name of the place," a name so secret it is omitted from the story, defines the place as an especially endowed mountain, where people used to go to acquire power. The acquisition of such power was traditionally accomplished only by the supplicant's undergoing an ordeal during which he proclaimed himself to be helpless (Chapter V). We have here an implication that Coyote's undergoing the ordeal on Rising Rock gives him supernatural power, and we suppose that it is the acquisition of such power which allows him to emerge without being castrated, despite his disobedience of the proscription against looking, and to harm his father's legs without retaliation.

When even very aged Apaches mention their ambivalent fears of *jajadeh,* the whippoorwill, they speak in awed and somewhat embarrassed tones, saying, "I'm still afraid of that little bird, that dusty, helpless, gray little thing."

That one he called to was a bat. So the bat came up. She had a basket behind her; she used one horse tail hair as a strap. The boy said, "Maybe if I sit in the basket, the horse tail hair will break."

And he might fall and be symbolically castrated, that is, having his legs broken.

The bat said it would not break; that she used it to carry fruit and she piled it to the top. But the boy was afraid and told the bat to test the basket with big rocks and to dance with it. Bat did so and it did not break. The bat told the boy to get into the basket but not to open his eyes while they were descending. Bat danced down the mountain and sang, "My vulva sticks to it."

First to be noted is a further indication of sibling rivalry. No effort was made to rescue the second boy who had been brought to the mountaintop. Both he and the little eagle were abandoned.

We note that eagles are carnivorous and do not carry fruit to their young. The presence of fruit in the eagle's basket both identifies her as a human surrogate and constitutes a denial that she carries children to be eaten.

That she symbolizes the whippoorwill seems evident. We might remember that when the Apache mother is disciplining her naughty youngster, she implies that not she but the *jajadeh* is angry and will deal with the bad child. The eagle's claim that she carries only fruit proclaims her to be a good mother surrogate. As in the Rising Rock tale, it is the father, the male eagle, who punishes for transgression. But thus far only one sin has been identified: the boy's penetration of his mother after his father has been killed.

The equation of horse-tail hair with spider-web strand is again clear, as is the symbolization of the cradle by the basket. Coyote's demanding that the strength of the strand of hair or web be tested by placing rocks in the basket reminds us of his having forecast the existence of, or brought about, death by throwing stones in the water.

In a Jicarilla story, "Why Bat Has No Feathers," Old Woman Bat rescues *jonayaiyin* from Eagle, who had carried him to the aerie as food for the eaglets. (Wherry 1968). Her basket is held by a "spider-thread handle." *Jonayaiyin* is the Jicarilla equivalent of *tubahjishchineh*. *Jonayaiyin* rewards Old Bat Woman by filling her basket with eagle feathers, warning her that if she carries them about, they will be stolen by birds. She is so happy to exhibit them that she forgets his caveat. After the fourth time he gives her the feathers, and she loses them to the birds. "From that time bats have had no feathers" (Wherry 1968:131).

In this Jicarilla story, the rescuing bat is equated with the eagle, which in the Chiricahua tale we have seen to be the equivalent of *jajadeh*. We note also the presence of the spider-web component of the basket in the story.

Let us return to the Eagle-Killer story.

The allusion to dancing we can suppose to be connected both with the dancing of the Mountain Gods, the mortal representations of supernatural spirits, in their use of power for good purposes, and also with sexual potency. The "true" ga^nheh in the cave of *zithtai* thrust true swords about. During the first day of the puberty ceremony for girls, a girl's female "chaperone" and her male singer—parent surrogates— instruct her as to the proper behavior for a wife and mother. At dusk, the team of "made" *jajadeh* approach her in single file; the leader first makes a cross over her head with his wooden swords and then thrusts one of them directly at her in an obviously phallic manner.

In the Eagle-Killer story, we have again the interdiction against the boy's looking. That the sanction is against viewing sexual activities is supported by Mother Bat's next statement, that her vulva stick to the mountain, now clearly identified as a phallic symbol. It reminds us also of the Navajo belief that the bat has a "vagina wing" with which to cling to rocks. Father Bat's "rock, stick, stick, stick" in the Rising Rock story has also been explained.

We now suspect the clouds and fog as representing darkness which will hide the parental sexual activities. But an additional meaning is possible. Speaking of flatus, an Apache man said, "It's so thick, you could cut it with a knife." Perhaps the clouds and fog also symbolize gas escaping from the bowels when the anus has been penetrated. This would be consistent with the interpretation of the sound "sh" as escaping flatus. In a personal communication, Dr. Werner Muensterberger informed us that he had found stone to symbolize the feces-covered phallus after anal intercourse.

Later we shall see that bat wings were once worn by Apaches to help them stick to horses, another common phallic symbol.

But informants regularly state that the skin of a bat should be hung on the cradleboard to protect the baby from being frightened and from "hearing anything bad." Can we not now assume that in this case the "anything bad" that the child must not hear and will frighten it is the excited and exciting noise of parental sexual relations?

> Twenty feet above the ground the boy opened his eyes and the basket fell with the bat. The bat broke her legs. That is why the bat's legs are so short. This funny song saved the *man's* life. As the bat lay there, the boy left her. (Authors' italics.)

In this story, too, the rescued boy abandons his parent. And again we have the boy revivified. We recall that in the Rising Rock story, the man on the mountaintop was referred to as dead. He is symbolically reborn. This allows us to interpret his being in his mother's basket as his being in-inside her womb; using the body-phallus equation, we see that we have here a repetition of the mother-son incest theme, which can also be seen as a return to fantasized symbiosis.

Bat's getting short legs as the result of the descent with the boy in the basket, now seen as mother-son incest, results in his becoming a *man* in the manifest story material. Her symbolic castration reflects a notion which is commonly held by small children, namely, that the penislessness of the woman results from her having been castrated during intercourse. This idea is certainly a part of the reasoning of Apache children. In dream analysis, going up or down mountains or staircases has often been found to symbolize intercourse, as is clearly the case here.

> The boy did not know where he was. This was when the world was first made. There were few people. He went to a deserted camp. There were wickiups there, with the branches on them still green. This showed that the people had left not long before. The poker started to talk to him and said, "The people went away not long ago, but they did not say where they were going."

In dreams, statements such as "This was when the world was first made" constitute the dreamer's use of remote time to represent his earliest remembered childhood. "There were few people" is sometimes used to indicate that the latent content deals with a period when only his nuclear family mattered to him. The sentence would have been more complete had it read "This was when and how the world was first made."

In dream analysis, to enter a wickiup with green leaves could easily symbolize the entrance into a vagina surrounded by pubic hair. We have then in the legend an almost explicit statement that the wickiup does represent the vagina when the poker, the instrument which is used to stir up the fire, an obvious phallic symbol, talks to the boy. Its message can be read as the boy's having come just too late to have observed sexual relations, and a denial that he did indeed observe them when the vulva were sticking to the mountain. The poker in the wickiup can be understood as evidence that dentate vaginas can be used by women to regain penises removed from them. Sexual relations castrate not only women but men as well. The concepts, quite conscious to Apaches, reflect the degree of intersexual hostility which can be observed so easily during field work with them.

> He left there to follow the people. He found a robber fly. It was sitting on a rock and he came across it by accident. The man started to talk to it. "I'm hungry and suffering. The eagle took me away. I have eaten nothing. Have you seen my people around here?"

Many Apaches know that robber flies and their larvae prey on other insects and their young. We do not know whether they consciously conceptualize robber flies to be cannibals as well, but such a notion is common elsewhere. Thus, at the end of the story, we find another allusion to the cannibal on the mountain, reduced in size. The man-boy's proclamation that he is just an innocent victim who had not gratified any forbidden wishes allows him to be reunited with his actual family.

Thus far we have not stressed the symbolic roles of defiance and repentance, with self-abasement and pleas for help. These phenomena have always been important in the Apache legal system. The sinner who refused to admit his guilt and promise to reform was punished severely. As an example, the person who proclaimed himself or herself to be a witch might be forgiven and considered to be an acceptable member of society after vouchsafing repentance. The one who was defiant and continued to threaten to practice witchcraft toward enemies would be either cast out from the group or killed.

We recall that, in the myth of origin, *tubahjıshchineh* relegated the defeated monsters to the wilderness if they were unwilling to serve as food for the Apaches.

In each Apache bat story, before the transgressor-protagonist is rescued and restored to his family, he proclaims his helplessness and abases himself via his pleading for succor. We believe this action represents his repentance for the various malfeasances he symbolically commits.

In 1958, Old Lady With A Sash related another version of the Eagle-Killer story to Ruth Boyer. It was presented as an example of a tale which was told to children to educate them properly, "to teach them to behave," but its lesson was left obscure. Old Lady said simply: "This is the story of how bad owls were killed. That is why the Mescaleros have been able to multiply. The Eye-Killers were all killed and the people have been saved."

The Owl-Killer Is Rescued by Bat

Long ago there was an owl sitting in a tree. At that time they were called "Eye-Killers." No one dared to get near them, because if you look into their eyes you will surely die. No man dared to come near them because they kill by staring. However, up close their eyes are not powerful. One man decided he would get close.

The other Mescaleros came around and they killed a horse. They wrapped the intestines of the horse around the man. Many of the people at that time were being killed by wild animals and they wanted to do something about it. They wrapped the man's arms and legs with the intestines. They covered him all up. Then they put him out in the open.

The owl flew down. He picked the man up and took him to the cliffs to the young owls. The little owls tried to tear off the intestines from the man. He pretended he was dead and lay there. The owl flew off again. The young tried to feed on the man with the intestines wrapped around him, but each time they tried they could hear a hissing sound come from him. They would turn away. They wondered about the sound. He got up. The little owls looked at him but their eyes weren't strong and they couldn't kill him. Their eyes didn't do anything.

Now the owl had some intestines hanging on the line, and this man told the owls he was hungry and wanted to eat the intestines hanging on the line. The little owls got them down and built a fire to cook them. He began to drain the fat off the intestines onto a rock. This fat was very hot. The man threw the fat at the little owls and blinded them. He took a sling and killed all of them. The man was all alone on this high cliff. He didn't know how to get down. He stood there and after a while some bats flew around. A father and a mother bat came by. He called to them, "Father bat, mother bat, will you come help me?"

The father bat told him to wait there and he would get a basket. Finally the father bat came back with a basket. He told the man to get in. He told the man he must close his eyes and not open them or he would fall and so would the bats and they would all be killed. If he kept his eyes closed all the way down, they would all get down safely.

The man closed his eyes. The bat started to go down slowly with the basket on his back. The man closed his eyes until they were very near the ground and then he opened them. They began to fall but it was not too far to the ground and they did not get hurt.

In Apache myths pertaining to the remote past, all fauna are considered to be the devourers of Apaches and all speak their language. We can view them as bad-mother projects. Through the actions of *tubah-jíshchineh,* the son of *istsúneglezh* and *yusn,* which include the slaying of monsters, some animals and birds accept the role of being friends of the Apaches, serving as sources of their food or providers of other services. They become good-mother projects. The eagle renounces its hostile role and agrees to provide its feathers for ceremonial purposes. The owl continues to be their enemy.

As delineated in Chapter III, the owl holds a special place in Apache folklore. It is greatly feared as a herald of death or as a death-dealing agent. It approaches an intended victim and says, "I am going to drink your blood." It may be sent by a witch, be the embodiment of a witch, or be itself a witch. When an Apache dies, his departed spirit inflicts "ghost sickness" on a living person or people. The owl may be the messenger of the ghost or it may inhabit the owl.

Before we heard the Owl-Killer story, we were unaware that the owl is thought to be able to kill with its evil eyes, although we had long known of the Apache fear of hearing or seeing the bird.

We had wondered whether we would ever find in Apache folklore a closer resemblance to the original Oedipus myth than merely the killing of the father and sexual union with the mother. It will be remembered that in Freud's interpretation of that myth, the transgressor of the taboo against mother-son incest is blinded as retribution. We may have in the Owl-Killer story a disguised representation of that element of the Oedipus myth.

That the small child who resents its father's sexual activities and bodily closeness with its mother wishes him to lose his penis and fears castration in return is well known. The penetrating aspect of sight is equated with phallic penetration in primary-process thinking, and patients' associations to their dreams have made it amply clear that blindness often symbolizes castration.

Still further supplementing the killing ability of the owl, we recall that Apaches have customs which remind us of belief in the Evil Eye (Chapter IV). They will protect a favored child from the supposed envy of others and of imagined malevolent supernatural powers by hiding its beauty from their vision. They also fear that the glance of the witch may kill.

Elements from the Chiricahua and Mescalero stories of the Rising Rock, The Eagle-Killer and the Owl-Killer and the Jicarilla tale of "Why the Bat Has No Feathers" are reshuffled in a Navaho folktale. It is summarized here without analysis, which would be long and redundant.

Feathers for Bat Woman
(Newcomb 1970:61-66)

Older Brother, dressed in leather armor and holding a concealed bow and arrow under one arm, wrapped himself in a blanket to resemble a small animal. A Great Bird carried him high above a great rock and dropped him into its nest. He was protected from injury by carrying a medicine bundle in each hand. He took medicine from a bag and spread it in the rock; its resemblance to blood fooled the parent bird into believing he was dead and suitable food for the birdlets in the aerie.

He turned one fledgling into an eagle and another into an owl; both flew away. Their fallen feathers were to be of use to the People in their ceremonies. Seeing their empty nest, the Great Birds flew south to find a higher mountain on which to build another nest.

Unable to descend from the cliff, Older Brother begged Grandmother Bat to carry him down; she agreed to do so in return for the feathers in the nest. There were so many feathers that they could fill her basket; she planned to use them in her own nest. As he got into the basket, it expanded to fit him. He closed his eyes in accord with Bat Woman's command, but when he heard a queer noise which aroused his curiosity, he opened them and he and Grandmother Bat fell rapidly. He obeyed her command to close them again and they descended slowly and landed with a slight bump. Bat Woman clambered up the crag to collect the soft feathers for her nest but the wind blew them away. She had no use for the large wing and tail feathers which remained and half flew and half scrambled down the steep rock and gave them to the youth who would turn them into birds which were useful to the People. He would take some of them to his mother to show her he had really visited the home of the Great Birds. Bat Woman hid from him the fact that she had lost the soft feathers, by keeping her basket closed.

Older Brother turned south to begin his long journey home but looked back to see Bat Woman wending her way home on a dim path that led through a dry lake bed which was overgrown with yellow flowers. He warned her not to go through the bushes which had grown on the old lake bed, but she pretended not hear him and continued on her way.

Now let us repeat and amplify some Chiricahua and Mescalero socialization data. Until recently, and once again in rejuvenated "Indian identity," all Apache children spent much of their early daytime lives in the cradleboard, where they were wrapped securely and only their faces and sometimes their arms were visible. Even the face was partially hidden and also protected by the surrounding basketry hood of the cradle, unless the viewing person were quite close; nor could the infant or toddler see the faces of those around it unless they were near. The security of the cradle was clearly felt by the enfolded baby and was acknowledged by mothers, who stated openly that it helped protect the baby when siblings became rough. When it was unhappy for whatever reason, a child who was more than a few months old would cry until it was replaced within the cradle.

We recall that whereas intoxicated people of many societies tend to assume the fetal position when they sleep, drunken Apaches generally lie in the cradleboard position, with their legs kept straight and, frequently, their arms held parallel to their sides. Until lately, most Apache adults have preferred to wrap themselves in blankets for sleep, rather than to lie between extended coverings as in white man's beds, and most Apaches prefer to enfold themselves in blankets rather than wear coats, either when they are even a little bit cool or when they are anxious. Certainly, shawls and blankets are in profuse evidence on ceremonial occasions.

Many Chiricahua and Mescalero children used to have access to the haven of the cradle until the birth of the new rival.

When children of over three years of age are about, most sober Apache parents conduct their sexual activities discreetly at night. However, as we know from actual observation, they feel little or no visible compunction about engaging in such activities in the presence of younger children, who are generally put out of the way by being placed in the cradle, and who are believed to be incapable of knowing what is going on.

For the young child, security is experienced particularly when there is physical closeness in an atmosphere of acceptance. Before the birth of its rival, the Apache child can usually achieve some closeness at will. Thereafter, however, when it seeks such proximity, it often receives manifestations of hostility or indifference. The angry looks it receives remind us of the killing eyes of the owl.

However, the child's experiences while in the cradle are not all solacing. To begin with, to be there is to be separate from physical contact with the mother or some surrogate for her. The little one is placed in the cradle only during the daytime. At night it is ordinarily cuddled against its mother. And during the day it is subjected frequently to angry interchanges between its parents or sometimes to their exciting and frightening sexual relations, which it could only interpret in terms of its pre-Oedipal stages of psychosexual maturation, as orally or anally hurtful. Further, the cradle often restricts all movement of the child's legs and lower torso.

In each of the tales presented before the Owl-Killer story, obvious direct or indirect allusion is made to forbidden adult sexual activities. In those cases in which the protagonist goes up on Rising Rock, he symbolically re-enacts the exciting and frightening sexual actions that the actual Apache infant and toddler watches and misunderstands and wishes were not occurring. The hero's experiences on the magical erection can be viewed as a fulfillment of the common wish of the small child to share the parental sexual embrace and excitement. In every instance, having gone up on Rising Rock or its equivalent, such as the cliff in the last-mentioned tale version, the boy becomes frightened and helpless and pleads for succor, which is regularly supplied by Mother or Father Bat, who brings him to safety in a basket — a vagina or womb symbol. In the manifest content of most of the stories is a reference to a horse-hair or a spider-web filament associated with the basket. Apache mothers in the past wore their hair long and hanging; an infant could touch the pendant strands and feel reassured.

In the Eagle-Killer story and its variant, the Owl-Killer tale, the protagonist is also protected by holding or being held in intestines. The old Apaches had no repulsion for intestines. Today many Indians continue to prize them as food. There are obvious similarities among hairs, spider-web threads and the nonmuscular parts of intestines. It now seems reasonable to hypothesize that they all represent the protective wrappings of the child's early cradle-held life and its sometimes touching the maternal locks. Within the cradle, the child is protectively wrapped securely and the buckskin sides of the cradleboard are held together by strands of sinew or narrow thongs of leather. The baby's head is encircled by a basketry framework hung with amulets that dangle on threads of sinew, beaded strands or other thin cords. *Jajadeh's* basket and that of the bat can now be seen as representations of the cradle and the child's mixed emotional states while it is lying within.

Jacob (1976) judged that the bat stories, with their involvement of the spider-web symbol of the umbilical cord, serve also to assist in alleviating persistent unconscious anxieties attendant upon actual childhood viewing of birth. Among these Apaches, childhood anxieties pertaining to childbirth are no doubt heightened by both their being prevented from seeing childbirth and their parents' either ignoring questions about it or giving evasive answers. They have ample opportunity, however, to see animals bear young and to know of the connection between birth and that cord. As was mentioned in Chapter IV, before childbirth took place in the hospital there was a custom of preserving the umbilical cord, which was wrapped in a small leather package decorated with beadwork and then either hung on a tree branch in some concealed area or hung as a dangle from the headboard of the cradle. Either course was accompanied by ritual prayers. Customarily, the cradle was used for only one child and was itself on a tree in some hidden place, although occasionally it was used a second time for a child of the same sex. No doubt an emotional as well as a cognitional equation of cradleboard and umbilical cord was established.

During the period of its life when it was cradled, the child's emotional life was perceived by it largely in oral terms. The wish to eat and/or be eaten by the loved one has been mentioned previously. Balter (1969) wrote of the wish in the myth cycles of Oedipus, Perseus and Jason to acquire power through oral incorporation of the mother. That the same wish is expressed in the potlatch ceremony of Alaskan Athabaskans has been noted before (Hippler *et al.* 1975).

Early on, the thinking of the child is dominated by the primary process, as is that in dreams, some daydreams and hallucinations or delusions. In such thinking, the wish to express frustration by biting or eating is externalized, and the child, dreamer or psychotic fears oral destruction via the *lex talionis*.

The fear of the person who is remote physically and the loss of dread when he or she is close is reflected in Apache attitudes toward *jajadeh*. At a distance, the little whippoorwill is an object of terror, particularly to the young, but the aged, viewing a *jajadeh* nearby, are struck by its prettiness and softness and speak of it tenderly, while admitting with a kind of shamed giggle their earlier terror and continued apprehension when its name is mentioned.

Their attitudes toward bats are equally ambivalent. They say, "That little bat is soft and friendly, and when you want it to smile all you have to do is tell it and it will smile." And they say, "We all used to catch bats by throwing a moccasin into the air or a stick. The bat would go into the shoe or cling to the stick and come down and you could play with it." But they also say, "It is mean and poisonous and it bites and it can kill you." When questioned about bats, informants usually initially shuddered. At the same time, when they were asked to name ominous birds and animals, the bat was never mentioned. Flitting Bird said, "After you catch it, you skin it and you can use the skin in various ways. You can take several and string them in a bracelet. You wear that kind of bracelet when you want to tame a wild horse. That horse will never run away with you if you are wearing those skins. You will stick on that horse just like the bat clings to the ceiling. This is Indian medicine." The association of the bat with the control of livestock is prevalent among Apache groups, including the Lipan (Opler 1940:31).

In the Owl-Killer story, it will be noted, there is no obvious allusion to sex. Old Lady With A Sash, while startlingly bawdy in her everyday life, was very reluctant to talk about sexual matters, and when she related stories she customarily omitted various elements. This is despite the fact that she often sang lewd Apache songs while being driven in the car. It may be that she elided an introductory portion of the story, on pertaining to sex. Be that as it may, she claimed to be the sole possessor of bat power among the Apaches, and her assertion was generally accredited. She had a power dream and learned bat ceremonies from her maternal grandparents. She had but two living relatives, Flitting Bird and his son. She would not transmit bat ceremonies to either of them because neither had had a power dream. For various other reasons as well, Old Lady With A Sash, a highly respected woman, considered both unsuitable to become shamans or to share her ceremonies.

Old Lady With A Sash had once been part of a large kinship group many of whom had been killed on the warpath. It is possible that she had used her shamanistic powers in an effort to protect them and, having failed, feared that either her powers had been nullified by witchcraft practiced by others or that she herself had unwittingly killed her kin by some error of ritual. In any event, a reason she gave for omitting parts of stories was that they were so "strong" that if she related them in their entirety, the listener might be damaged. Ruth Boyer felt there was an undercurrent of fear responsible for the omissions—fear of power reprisal and/or of further diminution of results. In any event, Old Lady refused to tell her bat tale, summarized early in this presentation, in its entirety, to Ruth Boyer, saying with a friendly smile, "If I told you the rest of the story, you would hang to the ceiling like a bat."

The story as Old Lady With A Sash told it follows. She stated that this is a tale to be told to children, that it would teach them "not to mock."

The Bat and the Flood

There were a group of bats on the ground. There was one bat sitting alone in the tree. He was above the bats below. The bats on the ground began to make fun of the bat in the tree. They began to laugh at him.

Then the bat in the tree said, "Who do you think you are to be laughing at me? I am mightier than you are, and I am way up here while you are down there. If it rains, it won't matter to me. I don't have to worry. If there is a flood, I will be safe."

But the bats just made more fun of the bat in the tree.

Finally a big flood came. The bats on the ground were able to get away. But the bat in the tree fell off. The flood began to sweep him away. He flapped his wings hard. He flew with his wings flapping and getting very wet in the waves of the water. The water swept him this way and that. Then he was walking on top of the water. Slowly he began to soar upward, and this is what he sang:

> "Bat wings, I am walking with,
> And now I am old
> And my children will get old, too.
> I am walking on the water.
> I am walking on the water."

He sang this song about his wings.

Old Lady With A Sash told this story when she was relating other tales and a bat happened to fly by. After relating it, she ignored questions on other matters and pursued her own line of thought. She first gave common ideas about bats, such as those which have been mentioned before. Finally she said she knew bat medicine but that she would not convey it to her daughter or grandson, although she recognized that it would disappear with her death, as indeed it did.

She mentioned only one cure or remedy: "There are certain kinds of bugs that bite you. They hurt you. You heat the bat and place it on top of the bite. The bat has been prepared previously by having its insides removed, so that only the skin parts are placed over the bite. You keep the bat body—*and especially the wings*—in a buckskin bag." She referred, of course, to the bag filled with amulets and carried by all shamans and also by some other people.

As noted previously, we heard Old Lady With a Sash's story early in our field work among the Apaches, at a time when we were relatively naive about their beliefs. It was only much later, and unfortunately after the death of the raconteuse, that what had seemed a simple tale took on a new significance. Then we knew it to embody religious concepts, interpersonal relationships, and dispositions toward success and leadership in meaningful combination.

Additionally, during over twenty years of work with these Apaches, no other individual used the character Bat in narrations, with the exception of Flitting Bird in her one story. And no other tale that involved a flood was related to us.

All other Apaches who were questioned about bats initially ascribed evil qualities to them, in contrast to their being conceptualized as beneficent creatures by Old Lady With A Sash. However, the Apache ambivalence toward the bat has been mentioned before.

Flitting Bird said that the bat had been greatly feared aboriginally and that the Mescaleros had stayed in the Guadalupe Mountains to avoid the flying mammals that hovered about the mouth of the Carlsbad Caverns in the dusk. Their name for those caves can be translated as "The bats come out of the cave so thick that it looks like smoke coming out of a hole."

We are reminded of the smoke and fog in the Eagle-Killer story and our perhaps too-tentative guess that one of their meanings in that instance pertains to flatus. We wonder whether the smoke in that story refers also to the bats' emergence from Carlsbad Caverns, with its characteristic stench. We recall also that, among Westerners, disappearance into clouds sometimes symbolizes death.

In 1969, the tale was read to a class of sixth graders on the reservation to determine what message, if any, they perceived. Five of the sixteen children noted that it meant "you should not make fun of people or talk about them." This is the lesson Old Lady With A Sash had suggested, and it appears to indicate that some children were familiar with that concept. Three students said bats would bite them, kill them or give them rabies. The other eight responses were noncommittal. In no instance was there any idea of assured success, such as "I think I can." This is reminiscent of the absence among Apache youth of the sense of omnipotentiality which is customarily found among white adolescents (Day *et al.* 1975; Pumpian-Mindlin 1965).

Then the story was read to a number of reservation adults. Some mentioned that it pertained to leadership and to the amount of "fussing" that Apaches direct at their tribal leaders. Typical responses follow. "A leader is always ridiculed. Others are jealous of him." "It makes it real hard for the leaders here. But *this* bat succeeded even through all its difficulties. And he felt contentment because of it."

Aboriginal Chiricahua and Mescalero males underwent arduous training to prepare them for their role as hunters and warriors. Among the Chiricahuas, near the end of his training period, a young boy would be taken to someone who knew the Bat Ceremony, to insure his competence in taming and riding wild horses (Opler 1941:71). We do not know whether the same procedure was routinely carried out among the

Mescaleros. That it may have been is implied by the previously cited words of Flitting Bird.

"The Bat and Flood" can be approached from the point of view of the ever-present reciprocal ambivalence between Apache leaders and their followers. Leadership among them has always been tenuous. Insofar as a man can direct a cluster of individuals, the group members listen to his counsel. Fine oratory matters indeed, but more important are his successes, particularly in terms of outwitting enemies. A leader is required to prove himself continually and might be deposed at any time, apparently especially by someone who is thought to possess more skills, which go hand in hand with supernatural power.

Additionally, a man's right to leadership is always viewed with some skepticism. No man should consider himself to be better than another. A man or bat has no business sitting on a limb above the other bats, and Apaches expect that a person who holds himself to be superior to others will eventually fall. Part of everyday gossip includes potential failures of "know-it-alls."

Nevertheless, every man has a right to leadership just as he has the right to obtain power. Superior intelligence and capabilities have always been recognized. But the degree of his success might be the result of a supernatural power acting through him. Hence, to mock such a leader might be interpreted as criticism of his power and thus be dangerous. Children must therefore be taught not to mock. They must be educated, and the vehicle for this and other education is often the tale told to them at bedtime.

When "The Bat and the Flood" was read to adults, the most dramatic response was given by Bitter Mouth, the only reservation Apache generally considered to be a witch. As soon as the character Bat was mentioned, she giggled and hid her mouth with her hand. Although she denied having heard the story previously, she clearly recognized its progression and anticipated its next steps. After she told some familiar bat lore, she then said the tale reminded her of the *jajadeh* stories. Then she implied there was more to the story and openly ascribed it to Old Lady With A Sash, saying the remainder of the folktale had not been told because of Old Lady's fear that she would lose some of her bat power were she to complete it, thus corroborating Ruth Boyer's feelings. Old Lady had related only the "safe" part of the story. To know its remainder would be dangerous to a person who did not own bat power. Bitter Mouth, a very modest and prudish woman, did not say that to speak of things sexual is outside the realm of Apache decorum, but this may also have been a factor in both her own and Old Lady's reluctance to tell the entire tale. No doubt both women were aware of sexual implications in the "clinging" of the bat.

We have no way of knowing what was omitted. As the story was told by Old Lady, the idea of wings was stressed. "He sang this song about his wings." This appears to be the key to the power. During her narration, Old Lady raised her arms up and down vigorously each time she identified with her Bat supernatural. We may speculate that she thereby sought to rise above her adversities. In the Eagle-Killer story, Old Lady Bat said her vulva stuck to the mountain; we have concluded that her wings were the symbol of her vulva, and perhaps the flapping with orgasm. Thus we might wonder whether at least Old Lady With A Sash equated her supernatural power with her sexuality. We know that when she was in her nineties she flirted outrageously with the author in front of his wife, saying to her, "If I meet him in the arroyo tonight, you'll never get him back." The author was then just past forty years of age.

Bitter Mouth and Old Lady were members of feuding families and there is no doubt that Bitter Mouth feared her.

During the years 1969 through 1973, Bitter Mouth refused to speak further about the bat. Then one day in 1974 we visited her in her house where her much-loved but much-hated husband, toward whom she was exceedingly possessive, was dying. It was obvious that she was fearful that his illness and impending death had resulted from her hatred and/or powers. It was then that she requested that the author serve as the family shaman.

We reintroduced the bat story and she became immediately uncomfortable and clearly feared supernatural retribution if she were to disclose information to which she was not entitled. Rather than complying directly with our request for further information, she related another story, one clearly part of her associations to the bat theme.

How the Apaches Got Fire

In the days before the Apaches got fire, they had to eat their meat raw. And all the animals could converse in Apache.

Coyote was dancing on those embers and had a brush attached to his tail. The other coyotes and animals warned him that if he continued to do so, his tail would catch fire and he would be damaged.

He continued to dance and the brush caught fire and he was frightened. He ran across an arroyo and came to a steep place, where he was trapped.

Some Apache children were atop that steep place, playing with bows and arrows. He called to them to throw something down to him to help him get out.

The piñon helped him. As soon as he got out of the arroyo he went around setting fire to yuccas, those trees you're not supposed to burn, that have the big stalk sticking straight up in the air, which were before the caves. There were all kinds of animals in those caves, and they all got roasted except the bat, which was able to flit from side to side of the chimney and to cling to the rocks and eventually to escape.

Bitter Mouth stopped at this point, saying she could not tell the rest of the bat story or its portentous significance. We understood her to have related a portion of Old Lady's story which had been previously omitted, a part which may well have preceded the bat's sitting in the tree in a position of leadership.

In "How the Apaches Got Fire" Coyote escapes punishment for his forbidden sexual escapades — that is, only the brush, and not his tail is destroyed. Then Bat escapes from the heated, smoking chimney — the vagina, cloaca, anus. Perhaps in the combination of the two stories, "How the Apaches Got Fire" and "The Bat and the Flood," the bat is an alternate representative of Coyote. The latter tale begins with Bat sitting in a tree. In the dreams of Western analysands, a bird sitting in a tree often represents a penis in a vagina, or the clitoris. If we interpret the opening of the story thus, we can see Bat's position there to have resulted from his having acquired supernatural power through his ordeal and being above the incest taboo. In any event, whether we accept that interpretation or not, he has become a leader as a result of obtaining supernatural power.

In "How the Apaches Got Fire," the first message pertains to the Apache prohibition against eating raw meat, which pertains to their taboo concerning cannibalism. In the Jicarilla story mentioned before, "Why Bat Has No Feathers," the eaglets represent Apache children. *Jonayaiyin* is saved from being eaten by them by giving them blood from giant Elk, whose horns are later used as a phallic symbol. Combining these elements, we assume that the reference to raw meat and blood refers to the small child's cannibalistic desires both to express its oral aggression toward the bad-mother part object and to ingest the good-mother part object and thus achieve fantasized symbiosis.

Then appear many references to sex. Coyote is dancing on fire and risks symbolic castration, the burning of his tail; thus his dancing is defined as being involved with forbidden intercourse, which we can infer to allude to incest. Then we have the common themes of the earlier bat stories, but represented in an opposite manner. Coyote is not atop a mountain, unable to get down. Instead he is in a hole and can only be rescued by being lifted up. Apache children rather than bat children empathize with him, and branches of a magical piñon tree descend to carry him up. We do not know if he sits on them as though in a basket, but their equation with the bat of the former stories seems evident.

In the earlier stories, Coyote, who is rescued, then abandons his savior, the bat, who is the parent surrogate. In this one, Coyote is evil in another way: he proceeds to enflame symbolic erections before caves which hold animals; all of them but a bat are killed.

As noted in Chapter IV, Apaches who fear competition from newborn rivals sometimes conceptualize their mothers to be constantly pregnant and in their fantasies and dreams depict the fetuses as various small animals, birds and insects. They hold the belief that phallic penetration of the vagina-womb will kill its occupants. In "How the Apaches Got Fire" only the bat was saved, by use of its wings and its capacity to cling to the walls of the "chimney." In this story, the bat does not cling to the symbolic erection, Rising Rock, with its wings-vulva, but rather to the inside of the vagina. We are reminded of the symbolization of stone as the inner female genitalia. Only the bat can be born, that is, succeed over its rival siblings and assume the position of favoritism or leadership.

This interpretation seems supported by Old Lady's use of bat wings to cure the evil effects of bothersome insects. Insects very commonly symbolize siblings.

Recalling the oral aspects of Apache concepts of genital sexuality, it is of interest that the two plants mentioned, the piñon and the yucca, are sources of especially favored Apache ceremonial foods.

In summary, then, we believe we have uncovered at least a major role of the bat in Chiricahua and Mescalero Apache folklore. This small flying animal emerges as a symbol by means of which some of the most crucial of pre-Oedipal and Oedipal Apache emotional problems can be presented in the oral literature in a manner which allows their expression without the arousal of excessive guilt and anxiety. These problems are related primarily to the ambivalence of the earliest mother-child relationship and to the birth of the next sibling.

Mother/Father Bat is a nurturant, comforting symbol. It is the opposite of *jajadeh*. Apaches refer to *jajadeh* as "that little gray dusty bird." Although we have no such information for the Mescalero and Chiricahua, we know that the Navajo equate the color gray with "evil," "dirty" and "despicable," and that they refer to the bat as being brown (Reichard 1950). Certainly, many Apache and Navajo words and concepts are similar. In any event, among the Apaches the bat is a good-mother project, a rescuer, whereas the whippoorwill is a bad-mother project, a cannibalistic destroyer. The bat can be likened to the shaman who practices good medicine, while *jajadeh* is related to witches and their agents, to owls who say, "I am going to drink your blood."

Both of the winged creatures use baskets. That of *jajadeh* transports the naughty child away from the family, repeating the Apache custom of giving an unwanted youngster to just anyone — in effect, abandoning it. The basket of the bat is used to restore the symbolic repentant, frightened self-abasing child to the bosom of its family. And yet the Apache attitude toward each figure is ambivalent. While the whippoorwill is feared, in later years Apaches refer to it somewhat tenderly. The rescuing bat is seen as both orally aggressive, perhaps poisonous, and also soft, furry, smiling and friendly. In each legend the rescuing bat is injured as a result of the disobedience of the child, and is abandoned. The Apache shaman is always feared also as a potential witch.

Similar contrasts and ambivalent attitudes involve the basket element. *Jajadeh's* basket can be viewed as a symbol of the devouring dentate vagina, and the bat's as a representative of the protective and nurturing womb from which the child can be reborn good, sin-free and worthy of reacceptance into society. At the same time, the basket of the whippoor-will symbolizes the disagreeable aspects of the child's isolation and helplessness while in its cradle, where, especially in the absence of mater-nal supervision, it is subjected to the hostility of its jealous siblings or where, in a kind of captivity, it may be aware of the pervasive interparen-tal hostility which manifest itself even in its parents' '' sexual activities. Opposing these disagreeable associations, the basket of the bat represents the feelings of safety and solace experienced by the youngster while it is encompassed in its comforting wrappings, the supporting thongs and the basketry headboard of the cradle.

In Chapter IV, the ambivalent attitudes of Apache mothers and their startling inconsistency when handling their young were delineated. Also stressed was the intense traumatization of the Apache toddler when the next child is born and it is removed both from the mother's bed and the cradle. We consider these two psychological injuries to be the most im-portant events in the child's psychical maturation; and we believe that the way the child is treated with the birth of the next baby fixates its un-satisfied oral strivings for the rest of its life.

Today's Apaches, and the protagonists of the recounted stories, seem constantly to be searching for nurturant and loving support from people they hope they can trust but of whom they suspect hostile intent. When their emotional and sexual attachments prove insufficiently satisfying, they must turn elsewhere. In their life situations, they turn to seeking various oral satisfactions, such as constant smacking and sucking among youngsters and a tendency toward widespread drunkenness among adults. These solutions give only temporary relief from the deep-seated deprivations encountered throughout childhood. Often the Apache re-mains pessimistic and unsure of himself. Frequently he turns part of his aggression inward, behaving in manners which lead to self-destruction and social anomie.

We suggest, then, that the bat stories depict symbolically the ambivalent Apache views toward parental authority figures. These qualities of insecurity, resentment, abandonment of others, fear of failure, defiance and repentance, oral needs including alcoholism — all of which are lamented by the Apaches themselves — result from circumstances encountered in infancy. In disguised form the lore of the bat permits release of resultant tensions in verbal expression.

One element highlighted by the analysis of the bat stories is that memories persistent from very early socialization experiences are symbolized quite clearly, a phenomenon that is demonstrated graphically by the consistent presence of the spider-web strand, which symbolizes emotional conflicts pertaining to the umbilical cord and the cradleboard.

Throughout this chapter, emphasis has been placed on the overdetermination of symbols in bat stories. D. M. A. Freeman (1976a), extrapolating from material obtained in field work with the Kiowa Apaches, noted that the tale of the rock that grows can be understood as a representation of issues and stages in the course of the Apache male's growing up. He focused on post-latency stages of maturation and adaptation.

Among the Kiowa Apaches there was a traditional adolescent vision quest, a seeking for a guardian spirit, which appears to have been more consistent than among other Southern Athabascans. Freeman views the Rising Rock story as a symbolic recapitulation of this search. Radin (1909) recognized that the trickster tales of the Winnebago were arranged by *them* in a particular sequence which represented a series of developmental stages. As delineated in Chapter II, Arlow (1961) discussed the hierarchical arrangement of fantasies in the inner life of individuals, reflecting the vicissitudes of individual experience as well as the influence of psychic differentiation and ego development. An individual's fantasies are grouped around basic instinctual wishes, and each group of fantasies is composed of different editions of attempts to resolve the intrapsychic conflicts attendant on those wishes. Each version corresponds to a different "psychic movement" in the history of the individual's development. Systems of fantasies tend to become organized and relatively constant after the passing of the Oedipal phase. The shared fantasies or oral literature of a group are similarly hierarchically arranged and also correspond to different defensive and adaptational editions of attempts to resolve common intrapsychic conflicts. They represent different developmental stages in the intrapsychic experience of individuals who grow up in that group.

Freeman suggested that the Rising Rock story with its variants epitomizes the critical intrapsychic reorganization which occurred when the Apache male finally settled down after his chaotic, reckless warrior years and became a responsible stable elder in the grandparental stage, following the prolonged adolescence common to Southern Athabascans.

Freeman called attention to the similarity in function of Grandmother Spider among the Kiowa Apaches and Bat among the Chiricahuas, Jicarillas, Lipans, Mescaleros and Navahos. He spelled out the reasons that the emergence of the superego proper, true guilt and "guilt-type depressions" was delayed until the latter part of the warrior stage and the advent of grandparenthood. He wrote:

> Two important sentences are added to the end of one of the Kiowa Apache versions of this myth: "This is the last of the Coyote stories. It's the last time that Coyote associated with human beings." [The Rising Rock story and that of Grandmother Spider] is a myth of death and rebirth. It represents, at the first level, the child's abandonment during rapprochement and rescue by his grandparent (or other parent substitute); at a second level, his vision quest during adolescence when he is weak and alone begs for rescue by a guardian spirit; and finally his ultimate successful completion of his Oedipal resolution when he sets aside the reckless, chaotic, id-ridden Coyote-man portion of himself... his years of aggressive recklessness, license and promiscuity. He identifies with his now-departed grandparental ancestors and parents, takes responsibility for his wife and children and grandchildren and assumes the role of responsible stable elder.

VII

Folktale Variation in the Service of Defense

FOLKTALE VARIATION IN THE SERVICE OF DEFENSE

Early in the practice of their science and art, psychoanalysts discovered that patients introduce folklore data into their "free" associations and use such information as they do their other verbal and nonverbal communications. This discovery was one of the two main stimuli which focused psychoanalysts' attention on the study of folklore (see Chapter I). Subsequently, much oral literature obtained in this manner has been studied systematically in the context of its use by patients. However, to my knowledge no examples exist in the folkoristic, anthropological or psychological literature of the systematic analysis of folklore data which have appeared in the associations of non-Western patients, although some therapists have presented fragmentary examinations of such information within the context of the prevalent transferential situation within which it appeared (Devereux 1951).

At one time during my work as a psychiatrist among these Apaches, a woman and her grandnephew were being seen individually. The great-aunt introduced a folktale, which had been previously unrecorded for the Chiricahuas and Mescaleros, as a "free" association. She subsequently related it to her grandnephew, who later related his idiosyncratic version as a part of his associations. This chapter consists of a systematic analysis of their variant presentations of the folktale and demonstrates how they used the prose narrative to express their dominant common and individual intrapsychic conflicts in manners which defended them against disturbing anxiety and guilt.

Better To See You attended psychoanalytically oriented psycho-therapeutic interviews lasting an hour each for six months, being seen face to face five times weekly. She was a middle-aged medicine woman whose services had been formerly sought frequently, but her shamanistic status had waned during recent years, following her having to begun to drink heavily. She suffered from chronic osteoarthritis and diabetes and had begun to develop cataracts. However, she refused stan-dard medical care because of her conviction that illnesses resulted solely from the resentment of affronted powers (*itseh*) or the actions of witches or ghosts. Accordingly, she had sought shamanistic treatment for her physical illnesses, without successful results, both from local faith healers and from renowned practitioners from other Indian tribes.

Several factors had combined to cause her to have lowered self-esteem and perhaps to question her identity as a shaman, and contributed to her regressively seeking solace in excessive alcohol intake; their relative im-portance cannot be weighed. Her latest husband was younger than she and, finding her progressively less attractive, he had begun to consort with other women and to threaten to divorce her. Her daughters, for whom she had had puberty ceremonies conducted and of whom she had unrealistic positive expectations, had disappointed her with their behavior. The repetitive failures of faith-healing treatments for her disorders had led her to have deep-seated doubts concerning the efficacy of shamanism, doubts ordinarily repressed but disturbingly conscious following each fruitless ceremony.

Better To See You's stated motives for seeking interviews were that she was curious about why other Apaches came to talk with the author and that she needed the small fee which the researchers were required by the tribe to pay informants. However, one of her relatives was a shaman who came for interviews after he failed to cure a man who subsequently was helped through psychotherapy with me. That shaman thought his reputa-tion had been diminished and stated openly to others that he had come to kill me through witchcraft (Boyer 1961; Klopfer and Boyer 1961). Thus it is highly probable that her desire for interviews had also been motivated by a wish for a shamanistic cure for her physical ailments, her drinking problem and her depression.

During the first few weeks of interviews, she developed a strong transference relationship of a mixed nature. She reacted to me both as an ideal father surrogate and as a son who had received supernatural power but who had yet to be trained in religiomedical ceremonies. It was in the context of this transference situation that she related the folktale which provides the raw data of this chapter. She told the tale in such a manner that during much of the first of the three hours of its recitation, I thought she was relating a dream.

Soon after she came for therapy, her thirteen-year-old grandnephew, Peter, who lived with her, and who was the son of her sister's daughter, also came to see me. He had earlier established a strong transference reaction in which I was an ideal father surrogate, and he was in open competition with one of my sons, a boy of his own age and Peter's classmate, for my favoritism. Soon after Better To See You told me the story, she related it to him and he in turn presented his individual version in his interviews.

INCIDENCE OF GROUP AWARENESS OF THE FOLKTALE

A year after their treatment had been terminated by our departure from the reservation and when I was no longer seeing Indians in therapy, I surveyed the incidence of awareness of the story among the reservation Apaches. Until that time, we had not heard the tale from anyone but Better To See You and Peter. Twenty-seven percent of fifty-one people who were fifty-one years of age or older knew a variant of the tale, and fourteen percent of forty-eight who were twenty-one to fifty years old. With two exceptions, the Chiricahuas, Lipans, Mescaleros, and San Carlos Apaches who knew the story believed its protagonists to have been members of their tribe. Probably only one who was twenty years old or younger had known the tale before the survey was begun. The commonest presentation of the story follows:

The Man Who Turned Into A Snake

Two adult male friends were hunting or raiding in Mexico and had lived on berries and occasional rodents for several weeks. They were tired, hungry and depressed. One evening they made camp by a lake and found some large eggs. One partner warned the other that eating the eggs might be supernaturally dangerous. Nevertheless, his reckless companion roasted and ate one or more of them, without having first performed a little ceremony to avoid affronting the "power" of the eggs.

The following morning he had turned into a black snake some thirty feet long and two or more feet thick. The transgressor had become one of the Underwater People and was thus sacred, but, at the same time, he had the ability to perform evil at will. He told his companion to return to their band, to tell the snake-man's relatives what had happened and to inform them that he would remain in the area of his new abode where, if visited by members of the band, he would perform ceremonies to bring them good luck and perhaps confer supernatural power onto some of them.

The partner obeyed the monster's instructions. A brother of the snake-man believed the returned companion had committed murder. Accordingly, his kin group went to the site of the alleged transformation. There they found huge snake tracks and exonerated the messenger.

Two endings of the story were of equal incidence: (1) the people who visited the lakeside never found the snake-man; they returned home and "forgot" their relative and (2) the kin group found the water monster, who conferred good luck on them and gave some of them supernatural powers.

Opler (1941a) synthesized Aarne's (1913) fifteen determinants of the changes to be found over time in folklore. He designated them as (1) fortuitous changes resultant from a reshuffling of myth elements, (2) deviations reflecting culture change, and (3) divergences apparently induced by predominant interests or personality traits of the narrators. An analysis of the story which had been obtained in the survey by direct questioning under optimal conditions indicated that it could be interpreted meaningfully only within the realm of Opler's first two categories. For data pertinent to his third classificatory element, it appeared that folklore narration must take place in a particularly favorable position of rapport, in which the transference relationships between the informant and the investigator are well known and the narrator's associations to the folktale are obtained and can be assessed (Boyer and Boyer 1967a).

After the survey was done, I reviewed the world literature and found variants of the tale to exist in the folklore of many Indian tribes in the United States, in that of some Indian groups in Central America and perhaps in Tierra del Fuego (Boyer 1975). Analysis of the manifest content of the folktale, based on conclusions drawn from its interpretation from the evidence to follow from Better To See You and Peter, indicated that the folktale was used particularly to help individuals defend themselves against anxieties resultant from unresolved sibling-rivalry problems.

THE FOLKTALE VARIATION PRESENTED BY BETTER TO SEE YOU

Better To See You essentially introduced herself during her first interviews by spontaneously relating a dramatic life history. According to her

personal myth (Kris 1956), her father, a violent, notorious Chiricahua
buffalo hunter, had come across her mother, then an unmarried teenager,
and her mother's sister while they were gathering berries on White
Mountain (the imposing 12,000 foot peak which is the central landmark
of the Mescalero homeland). He had tied them to trees but otherwise
treated them well. After a few days he selected the mother of Better To
See You as his bride. He persuaded her to join him and took her into the
wilderness of northwestern Arizona. They and their ensuing children had
wandered about, avoiding other Indians, since the kidnapper had been
banished from his own tribe as a "wild" man, inferentially a cannibal;
they lived on the spoils of his hunting and plundering. He was slain by
Anglos when Better To See You was three or four years old, after he had
murdered one of their companions while looting their camp. His wife
burned his body to a mass of charred bones, which she scattered lest they
be found and used for witchcraft purposes. She and her three daughters then
arduously trekked southwestward, seeking to return to the reservation.
When they reached the Río Grande it was in flood and they had no way
to cross. However, at that time a maternal uncle of Better To See You
consulted a shaman, who divined the location of the mother and her
children and magically enabled them to cross the river and the waterless
white sands, and eventually to return to Mescalero. There, the four lived
with the mother's brother for a time, and the young girl came to view her
uncle as her father. He lovingly reared her after her mother remarried
and took her other children with her. When Better To See You was a
young adult, a half-brother was killed by a gunshot by an "envious"
man.

Better To See You's mother had told this story to each of her children;
we were told that each related a variant version.

Over the years, we learned information from other sources which
modified Better To See You's highly cathected, personal myth. According to more objective observers, the violent Chiricahua had abused and
kidnapped both of the teenagers. The mother's sister had escaped after
they arrived in Arizona, and remained on another reservation with a man
she met there. Later, the mother had also gotten free and gone with
another man. Who actually sired Better to See You was moot. Subsequently, her mother had become homesick and written to her brother,
who went to get her and her children. The "wild" Chiricahua was probably killed by white men after he murdered their companion when he
was caught stealing their provisions. When they returned to the reservation, the family included a baby boy who subsequently died. We can
assume that the infant was treated by the mother as her favorite. The
maternal uncle had not reared Better To See You after she was left with
him by her mother. Nevertheless, she often visited her uncle, who always
treated her with consideration. He informally adopted her. During her

childhood, Better To See You had always been jealous of and hostile toward little boys. There can be no doubt that she had heard all of the data presented above at various time during her life, but her need for a different past had caused her to either deny or repress information contrary to her personal myth, which had become for her an historical reality. Her belief that her uncle reared her required repression of the fact that she had been shifted from family to family. In Chapter VIII, we shall note that the repression sometimes failed.

We shall not attempt to analyze in detail the intrapsychic meanings of her personal myth, because we have too little associative data.

During the course of her life, Better To See You had sought one father after another; she had hoped that each would perform both fathering and mothering functions. She had been left by two husbands who found her dependency and jealousy intolerable.

It is common among these Indians for a person who "knows" a ceremony to impart it to one of his or her offspring. Better To See You deemed her children to be too immoral and unstable to be shamans, and none had had a power dream. She had begun to teach her ceremonies to Peter, through the means of story-telling, but he, too, had had no power dream. Her desire to transmit her knowledge to me was motivated in part by her regarding me as a son to teach. She was one of the shamans who wanted me to accept the new position of chief Apache shaman, in order to have me serve as a good, strict, omniscient father "for all future generations of Apache children." During the early weeks of her therapy, she asked me to learn all of the songs of the puberty ceremony (Bourke 1890; R. M. Boyer 1962:295-299; Nicholas 1939; Opler 1941:82-134), in order that I would be able to serve as the singer for a grandniece during her ceremony, which was planned for nine years thence.

Soon after she asked me to become an Apache, rather than just a white shaman, and to sing for her grandniece, she related the folktale. Her actual rendition involved much redundancy. An abridged recounting follows:

> Long ago, two Mescalero guys went to Mexico to hunt buffalo. One night at a lakeside, Grasshopper Boy ate a *big* egg and turned into a *big* black snake. His partner had warned him not to eat that egg without first performing necessary rites, because it might be supernaturally dangerous. The other guy returned to White Mountain and told Grasshopper Boy's relatives what had happened, but they thought he had murdered his partner. So he took the brother of Grasshopper Boy down there. The Snake-Man told his brother what had happened.
>
> Some years later the brother of Grasshopper Boy went to see him

again. As he hunted deer, the brother heard a shot. Two Comanches had killed the water monster, so the brother returned home
and they all "forgot" about Grasshopper Boy.

Later some Blackfoot Indians went to Mexico. They found the
snake bones and used them for poison for their arrowheads. They
went north and attacked a camp of Mescaleros near White Mountain.

Three men, some ladies and some children got away. They were
hurt and poisoned by the bone powder of the snake, but they went
to a shaman who made medicine and saved them. Two of his
daughters had been kidnapped; the man who got well found and
recovered the girls while the Blackfoot Indians were feasting and
drinking *tiswin.*

For Better To See You, her telling of the story was at least
preconsciously associated with her wish to educate me, and its content
was not perceived by her to have any relationship to her life or intrapsychic conflicts. Her mood was largely euphoric, reminding me of a
hypomanic reaction; the psychology of such reactions includes denial as
a predominant defense (Lewin 1950).

An interesting event took place during the recitation of the story, one
which revealed her ascription of omniscience to the possession of the
penis. It occurred immediately after she said her uncle had arranged for
the return of the family through the aegis of an all-knowing shaman. Her
interview was followed every day by that of a man. Engrossed in her
recitation, I had not noticed that I had permitted her to remain beyond
her hour. The man, who knew she was there, knocked on the door and
entered the consultation room unbidden. He feigned surprise at her
presence, saying to her, "I'm sorry, I didn't know you were here."
She replied, "I thought you knew everything. Your third leg hangs to the
the ground."

It is interesting to note that in many societies the use of the leg as a
symbol for the phallus occurs at a young age. For example, a girl of
Western European derivation early in her third year referred to her
genital region as her "hurt" and, speaking of her imaginary penis,
pointed to her knee (Mahler *et al.* 1975:146-150). As mentioned earlier,
very young Apache girls verbalize the wish for a penis.

Soon after Better To See You had related the story, she began to talk
about the half-brother who had been shot. Her envy of him and particularly his penis was starkly evident, and it was clear that she had had
transiently conscious wishes for his death before he was killed. She said
another man had shot him because of envy, although the facts were that

he was murdered in the course of being robbed of recently acquired money. During the period when she was talking of her half-brother, she was anxious. In fact, she had had little contact with her half-brother, but she was clearly jealous of his having been his mother's apparent favorite. Her ill will toward her sisters and half-sisters who lived with Better to See You's mother, and her hostility toward her mother were successfully denied through two rationalizations: (1) her uncle was so fond of her that he would not let her go with her mother, and (2) her mother's new husband was poor and could not afford to take care of so many children. Then she transiently remembered that her younger brother had accompanied the family on their trek to the reservation. It was obvious that she had displaced her resentment of that child to her half-brother and then displaced that jealousy with the envy she ascribed to the murderer of the half-brother. In her interviews with me, Better To See You spoke English. It was clear that her use of English often involved direct translation from Apache. The Apaches have but one word for envy and jealousy.

We should remember that the family returned to the reservation when Better To See You was three or four, when we would expect her to have been at the height of her castration anxiety and earliest penis envy.

It will be noted that her variation of the folktale contains two major additions, that involving the snake-man's having been shot by Comanches and the sequel which involved the Blackfoot Indians and the shaman. No other informant mentioned either group of Indians in his or her narration.

Included in the Mescalero Tribe are a few Lipan Apaches who came to the reservation at the turn of the century, after they had been decimated in Texas and northern Mexico by Comanches and Kickapoos (Sjoberg 1953). In pre-reservation days, contacts between the Comanches and the Chiricahuas and Mescaleros were generally hostile, although there was occasional cooperation between the Comanches and those Apaches on bison hunts. Especially during this century, there has been increasingly friendly contact, and today many reservation Apaches have Comanche ancestors (Boyer 1962: Appendix 1). Nevertheless, as recently as fifteen years ago, in an impromptu event at the annual puberty ceremony, a Comanche and a reservation Apache had a brutal fight representing ancient warfare, and the Comanches are still called *indāh,* enemies. It is possible that the Lipan Apaches and the Blackfoot Indians had contact on bison hunts in Texas, but there are no reservation Indians known to have Blackfoot heritage. In any event, it is very unlikely that Better To See You could have included the Comanches and the Blackfoot Indians in her variation as the result of diffusion, since the folktale has not been recorded in the literature of either of these groups. We must assume, therefore, that she included the Comanches and the Blackfoot Indians for personal reasons.

Although my hypothesis is based on inferential information and not from direct associations to the Comanches and the Blackfoot Indians by Better to See You, I believe she included the former group as substitutes for the white men who shot her father and the Apache who slew her half-brother, and the latter because their name includes black, the color of the snake and the alleged charred bones of her father. As will be seen later, Peter called the latter group "those black-footed Indians."

When we examine Better To See You's presentation, we also find a number of variations of the type Opler designated as fortuitous. Thus, as an example, it was a brother of the man who was turned into the water snake who accompanied the hunting partner to the site of the transformation. For reasons which will be amplified below in the discussion of Peter's version, I believe Better To See You and the others who included a brother in the manifest content of the legend thus exhibited repressed sibling rivalry, discharged safely through the protection of the folktale. Suffice it to say at this point that Grasshopper Boy was killed in the manifest legend not by fratricide but by tribal enemies. We shall see below that Peter conceived of the hunting partners as brothers from the beginning. He was in actual life closer to active sibling rivalry than were the adult informants, and his resultant conflicts were more nearly conscious. It is entirely consistent with the socialization data and considerable information from the case study of Better To See You, omitted here for the sake of brevity, to assume that the original hunting partner was indeed in her mind a sibling surrogate of Grasshopper Boy. We recall that both her half-brother and her father were shot and that many young Apache children view their fathers in part as rivals for maternal attention.

Factual historical data are sometimes included in legends and even folktales. We do not know to what historical period the tale was ascribed by the informants. Some said "long ago," but the majority dated the occurrence to the middle or latter portion of the nineteenth century. During that period, not only the Comanches but also the Blackfoot Indians and the Apaches had guns. However, the Comanches had acquired guns much earlier than either of the other two groups, from the French, a bit of information which may have been learned at some time by Better To See You and then "forgotten." She dated the time of the event to "before the days of the reservation." Can we not assume that her giving the guns only to the Comanches and her choice of having the snake-man killed by gunshot stem from insecurely repressed sibling rivalry?

The Blackfoot Indians found the bones of the dead water monster and used them for witchcraft purposes, which were subsequently neutralized or overpowered by the workings of a Mescalero shaman. Why did she not have the Blackfoot Indians appear sooner after the demise of the snake-man and use some other part of his corpse for witchcraft purposes? Let us remember that in her personal myth her own father was burned, so that only his bones remained, her mother scattered those bones so that they would not be found and used for witchcraft. We believe these data give credence to the supposition that Better To See You equated the buffalo-hunting Grasshopper Boy with her notorious buffalo-hunting father. *Her* legend version was the only one in which the companions were hunting bison. Her father was a "wild man"; wild men were always thought to possess supernatural power which they used for evil purposes. Again, during pre-reservation days, most if not all Apaches were thought to possess powers, or at least ceremonies which might themselves carry power.

She never explained why she called the protagonist of the legend "Grasshopper Boy," but her interview associations indicated that she chose that name because her father was one who "jumped" from place to place.

But Better To See You went through life seeking a replacement for her dead father. Why then should she equate a dead shaman with her father, since we would expect her to restore her father and rejoin him in her legend version? She was "adopted" by a much loved uncle after her return to the reservation. She grieved greatly at his death, which occurred in her adulthood, and during a long period of her interviews she spoke of him in such terms that it was clear that her cherished uncle, the first father surrogate, still lived in her mind. She married and lost two husbands whom she had striven to make into father replacements. In the Blackfoot raids three Mescalero men got away. Can we not assume that her choice of the number three refers to those three men? This is partly conjectural, but soon after she related the legend she introduced the subject of her dissatisfaction with her third husband, whom she partly wished to be dead, and her relative satisfaction with her uncle and two previous husbands. Perhaps in her individual legend variation she thus restored the three loved and lost former father surrogates.

The return of the mother and daughters to the reservation after the death of her father was, in her personal myth, due to the workings of a shaman. In the folktale as she presented it, it was a shaman who saved the three men (as well as others). However, we then find a curious statement, namely, that two daughters of the shaman himself had been kidnapped and found through his employment of supernatural powers. In fact, one of the conditions of his practicing shamanism for the poisoned camp members was that the men promise to return his daughters to him. The mother and maternal aunt of Better To See You were kidnapped. In a sense, Better To See You and her sister were too, since their proper place was with the Mescaleros. This would seem to form an unmistakable link between Better To See You's account of the legend and her personal myth. If so, we have then the undoing of the death of Grasshopper Boy, who became a shaman and, in her mind, her father. At the end of the legend, she, as one of the recovered daughters, was reunited with her father.

The Folktale According to Peter

The following is a verbatim account of Peter's rendition of the folktale, omitting only repetitions.

Two guys went to a pond. One of them ate an egg and turned into a big black snake. The other guy went home. Ten years later two brothers went hunting buffalo. One of them went off and got kill-ed. The other was scared he'd done something that had killed his brother. He went to a medicine man to learn how his brother had died. The medicine man told him to carry an eagle's stomach filled with water so he'd never be thirsty and so his brother's ghost wouldn't kill him. He said the boy's father had been killed by a mountain lion. He went home.

Two other guys went out hunting. They came to that pond. The snake talked to them and scared them. One of them dropped that stomach full of water. Then the snake told him, "You are my boy."

Two Comanches killed that snake. Ten years later, those black-footed Indians found the bones and made poison of them. There were only three men and one woman left after they raided the Mescaleros. They went to a medicine man and he told them the whole story. He made medicine and those men got well and got his two sons while those black-footed Indians were feasting.

Having been abandoned by their parents over a year previously, Peter, 13, and his two brothers, aged 2 and 4, lived with their maternal grandaunt. During his first interview Peter had falsified grossly his past and present lives. He said his parents lived happily together in a nearby town where they lovingly cared for him and his brothers. According to his story, he lived alone with his grandaunt during the school year and idyllically spent summers with his parents and brothers. He said his parents had given him a bicycle, factually non-existent, identical to one owned by my son.

During the first seven interviews, three themes emerged: (1) his longing and seeking for a powerful and nurturant father, (2) his rivalry with his brothers for their grandaunt's attention, and (3) his ambivalent rejection of his mother. One manifestation of his competition with his brothers for the grandaunt's favoritism was his attempt to have a "power dream," which would qualify him to become a shaman.

In the eighth interview he expressed the desire to be adopted by white parents who had a son of his age, and to move with them to California, where he knew my family to have our regular home. He also related an hypnogogic experience, dating it to a year earlier when he had thought his father dead. In it, he had seen the ghost of an Indian man and feared the ghost would kidnap him in a bag made of bed sheets. When I questioned a maternal aunt as to whether she had known of his "dreams," she said she had, but he had not mentioned the bag made of bed sheets. In the ninth interview he presented a recent frightening hypnopompic experience in which the ghost of an Indian commanded him to jump rope, an activity which was being learned by his four-year-old brother. Then he related the legend.

As mentioned, Peter longed for a father and competed with his brothers for their grandaunt's attention. The "dream" of the man with the bed sheet was recognized by him to be a veiled wish to be taken away by his father. The intimacy of the desired relationship is indicated by the presence of bed linen. Sheets were not used in Peter's family at that time, but he knew them to be used by mine. The second "dream" is more obscure. Peter wanted a strong father who would support his attempts to be a good boy. He knew me to be relatively strict with my son. One of Peter's brothers adored me and his affection was returned. Perhaps the rope-jumping represented a desire to regress and compete on the level of that younger brother, in addition to a wish to be made to behave well. The first interpretation is the product of Peter's associations, but the second is conjectural.

Peter's distortions of the legend from the version presented to him by Better To See You reflect the same intrapsychic conflicts as had emerged during the first seven interviews. In her version, the theme of finding the lost father appeared only in the latent content, and that of hostility toward the mother was absent. In the manifest content, there was a hint of sibling rivalry. Grasshopper Boy's brother accused the companion of murder but then abandoned and "forgot" Grasshopper Boy. Let us examine Peter's version. There, the cardinal psychological theme of the manifest content is the finding of the lost father. In addition, there is obvious sibling rivalry. A hunter is killed and his brother accuses himself of murder, that is, reveals his guilty wish that his brother be dead. However, the ego defense mechanism of undoing finds expression in Peter's having an externalized superego figure, the shaman, absolve the guilty brother of the murder by stating that the death resulted from the actions of a puma. We shall return to this detail later. A second example of the need to undo the unconscious wish to murder the rival follows.

In the manifest content of Peter's rendition, a second set of brothers goes hunting. However, the presence of the eagle's stomach identifies them as being the first pair. Thus, the murdered brother has been revivified. The wish that the sibling had been eliminated is still fulfilled, however, because the snake-father then claims only one son as his own. We find further, less obvious indication of sibling rivalry. Better To See You had stated that men, women and children survived the massacre. In Peter's story no children live, since he first says there are only three men and one woman left alive. At a later time he reverses the implicit denial of living children by stating that two boys survive. As we remember, Peter has two younger brothers. There is but a hint of distortion, which coincides with his ambivalent rejection of his mother. First he reduces the number of surviving women to one; then he says, "He made medicine and those men got well." The one woman who was left is thus eliminated.

Peter's variant production of the tale related to him by his greataunt presents a thinly veiled confession of and resolution of some of his personal conflicts. It was clear he wished to be the son who lived and refound his father. Let us examine one facet in some detail. The shaman who absolved one brother of the murder of his rival can be equated with the father, because the snake-man who said "you are my son" had become a shaman, a personage who lived partially in the spirit world and had supernatural powers he could use volitionally for good or evil purposes. The shaman avowed that the mountain lion had killed the unwanted brother. Every Apache with whom we spoke about pumas, including Peter, preconsciously equated those cultural bogies with women, presumably dangerous mother surrogates upon whom oral aggression had been projected.

Peter's use of the puma as the murderer, then, can be understood to be a distorted way of saying that a neglectful, greedy woman, surely reminiscent of his own mother, had slain his sibling. It seems more than fortuitous that he chose to have a carnivore kill his rivals. Cougars kill by biting and clawing. The individual who has not yet resolved his oral dependent conflicts is wont to dream of removal of his enemies by oral aggressive means. In the unconscious thinking of all patients with whom the author has dealt, whether white, yellow, black or brown of skin, teeth and nails or claws are equated. In Peter's version the father was a shaman. It is probably relevant that I was regularly accorded the position of shaman.

DISCUSSION

It will be noted that the interpretation offered for the legend version presented by Better To See You is less completely convincing than that for Peter's. I believe this can be explained on the basis of the greataunt's having been older and having had much more time to defend herself against the psychological problems which have been demonstrated to have motivated portions of her legend variation, and to use the products of conflict solution for adaptive purposes. Peter was still in the regressive period of his puberty, and stimuli continued to activate conflicts against which his defenses were less adequate. Thus the evidences of his unsolved conflicts were more apparent, because less successfully distorted.

There can be little doubt that the variations manifest in the renditions of the legend by Better To See You and Peter were consonant with modifications in social structure resultant from acculturation and also reflected deep personal needs of the narrators. In the survey in which we sought to determine whether the legend had changed consistently over several generations in similar manners, we obtained inconclusive evidence. Two principal factors may be at fault.

One, the *research technique,* inasmuch as the legend was obtained originally in a situation of rapport in which the anxiety of the informants motivated the production of validatable "free" associations, whereas the survey was conducted under favorable conditions but nonetheless conditions which did not produce such validatable associations.

Two, *culture lag.* The socialization processes of the Mescalero tribe are consistent not only currently but probably over time, with certain relatively superficial variations. Thus one would expect theoretically to find a generational continuity in the basic personality conflicts of the Apache which would be reflected in folklore and rituals.

Two problem complexes resulting from child-rearing practices of the Apaches are those produced by the psychologically unsatisfying father and insecurely repressed sibling rivalry. These problems were reflected in the legend variations which were produced by the informants who had the opportunity to provide easily validatable free associations. Additionally, there were demonstrated some of the manners in which the legend served as a self- and societal-protective device, which enabled individuals to discharge strivings which had been suppressed or repressed, and thus to live with unconscious or preconscious conflicts without feeling overwhelming anxiety and guilt.

The unconscious fantasy life and wishes demonstrated in the legend which has been presented here are common in the mental life of children who have been displaced early in life by younger siblings. A few examples will suffice.

(1) It can be no coincidence that the egg was associated with water, a constant female symbol in dreams. We recall that various Apaches revealed a wish to kill unborn rival siblings (Chapter IV). The symbolic unborn younger child was killed by being eaten, by the use of teeth, the first effective means by which the young child can inflict actual harm.

(2) The wish to reenter the mother and thereby be in close contact with her in a state of symbiosis is represented by the disappearance of the snake into the water. I do not wish to minimize the obvious fact that the snake is a phallic symbol. Our clinical data make clear that these Indians use their so-called "genital sexuality" in large part to resolve oral problems.

(3) The fear of retaliation, which in our culture is reflected frequently as the main determinant of cancer phobia, is represented in the folktale by the fear of ghosts, witches and the snake.

(4) The fear of being poisoned by the remnant of the destroying sibling is a logical corollary of (3).

EPILOGUE

The psychotherapeutic interviews of Better To See You and Peter resulted in a sharp reduction of their intrapsychic conflicts pertaining to the dominant problems which were expressed in their legend recitations. It is probable that this was due in part to the stories' being brought into the treatment situation and analyzed as though they had been dreams. It is of interest that when Better To See You first introduced the legend, the author was confused for the better part of an interview as to whether she were relating a dream.

Better To See You was able to decathect to some degree her search for a father. She was able to extricate herself from a most unsatisfactory marriage, to which she had previously clung because of her desperate quest for a loving and supporting father. No doubt her actively divorcing her husband helped her repress her hostility toward me for deserting her and contributed to her ability to resolve her split transference relationship with me into an abiding friendship.

Additionally, sibling rivalry with other shamans lost its intensity. She was able to face her decreasing shamanistic status with more equanimity and to give up the active practice of shamanism, coming to restrict her activities to those of practicing herbalism with little implication of the involvement of supernatural power. She continued to utter appropriate incantations when administering everyday native medicines but could acknowledge that they were merely necessary form statements. She continued to be in demand as a chaperone at the girls' puberty ceremony but now considered herself simply an educator who gave instructions to the debutantes as to how to live a good and useful life.

Peter's quest for a father lost its urgency and he was able to become more self-dependent, apparently as a result of his internalization of qualities and attitudes he observed to exist in me and others, more idealized, which he had projected onto me. The intensity of his sibling rivalry was sharply reduced and he renounced his ambivalent attachment toward his mother, whose narcissism had led her to desert her children. Nineteen years later he remains one of the few young men of his generation who has never been jailed and has not become a drunkard. He works steadily and consistently looks after his needy relatives. His transference relationship with me has also resolved itself into a continuing friendship.

VIII

Folklore Knowledge as an Adjunct In Understanding the Psychiatric Patient

INTRODUCTION

Transcultural psychiatric research has sought to determine the influence of social structure and socialization processes on the etiology and symptomatology of personality disorders and to establish general principles which might assist psychotherapists in their efforts to better understand and more successfully treat people from divergent sociocultural backgrounds. Such research has become worldwide in its scope. Recent studies of the psychological illnesses of U.S. immigrants in lower socioeconomic groups have indicated that their form and dynamics can best be understood in terms of the folklore of their native lands. Thus, a common psychological constellation found in Philadelphia among Italians is clearly a derivative of *malocchio* (evil eye) beliefs, and a condition found among Puerto Ricans stems from the *ataque* syndrome (D.M.A. Freeman 1976).

During the past thirty-odd years, increasing attention has been paid to the sociopsychological problems of North American Indians. In the course of this research, it has become obvious that those who seek to do psychotherapy with people of non-European derivation benefit from undergoing training which helps them rid themselves of ethnocentric prejudices which lead inevitably to countertransferential problems (Boyer 1964), and that they must acquaint themselves with the specific bases which determine their patients' or clients' culturally bound modes of communication. Various studies have been devoted to demonstrating the utility of learning about native folklore elements, such as traditional oral literature and ceremonies, in an effort to understand their influence on communication styles used by Indian patients (Devereux 1951; Hallowell 1941; Hippler *et al.* 1975; Johnson and Proskauer 1974; Seward 1958).

A clinical vignette shows that deep awareness of the folklore bases of a patient's communications make understandable an interview which might be incomprehensible to a psychiatrist who does not have such knowledge.

CASE PRESENTATION

Better To See You, whose personal myth and variation of "The Man Who Turned Into A Snake" were presented in Chapter V, had become progressively more crippled and she had had serious eye and ear problems during the ensuing sixteen years. Nevertheless, she had continued to refuse standard medical care. A few months before the clinical vignette to follow, she had fallen and sustained an abrasion of her left foot and had once again ignored the medical advice offered to her by physicians at the reservation hospital and their Apache outreach personnel.

Although her psychotherapy with me had not improved her osteoarthritis and progressive blindness, it had relieved her of much of her depression and her drinking had diminished. However, our relations were influenced by her retention of the hope that I would cure her physical disabilities shamanistically. When that did not occur she became progressively more disappointed and her feelings toward me became ambivalent. Additionally, she had transferred the high aspirations she had had for her daughters onto her granddaughters, and they had become undependable, even before puberty, to the degree that she chose not to have puberty ceremonies for them.

Following her treatment with me, Better To See You had continued to undergo unsuccessful shamanistic ceremonies. In 1965 she began to consider seeking the help of a highly publicized white faith healer, Mr. Smith. In 1970 she became convinced that he could cure her without her actually going to see him. She reasoned that, since witches could cause illness by shooting invisible arrows from great distances, he could treat her by correspondence. Accordingly, she mailed him money to help her. His written blessings proved ineffective and she became depressed again, although she did not relinquish her faith that he or I would cure her at some time.

The abrasion on her foot became infected and gangrene developed.

Although she was warned by local physicians that she should receive immediate attention, she went alone to a distant city without an appointment and against all medical and family advice. She did not see the white faith healer. She returned home and her foot was amputated. After a few months, it was possible to fit her with a prosthesis.

When we heard of her recent amputation, I remembered how her variation of the story "The Man Who Turned Into A Snake" had reflected her dominant intrapsychic conflicts and allowed her to express them without anxiety and guilt, and I decided to determine whether another rendition of the same tale might include new elements which would reflect her current concerns and her efforts to cope with them. Upon arriving on the reservation, Ruth Boyer and I found Better To See You to be a patient in the Indian Hospital, learning to use her prosthesis. Members of the staff said she had occasionally been disoriented as to place and time during the night, and that she had talked in Apache, which none of them understood, to apparently hallucinated individuals. She was in a private room and received no external stimuli, except for noises in the hallway and occasional visits from members of the staff and her family. No confusion was observed in the daytime. She was receiving no medication.

In her everyday life, Better To See You took care of children of various unmarried female relatives and was often with other kin. Under those cirmumstances, she had apparently been in complete contact with reality. When her kin were briefly absent, at times she lapsed into altered ego states during which her fantasies served to defend her against loneliness, feelings of helplessness and various fears. During the years of our contact with her, following her psychotherapy, the complex transference relationship of her treatment months had continued, along with our personal friendship. She had come to view Ruth Boyer as predominantly a good-mother or sister surrogate. We had been with her on dozens of occasions and, during each visit, she had communicated with us as though we were relatives who were totally aware of Apache history and lore.

When we entered the room, Better To See You appeared to be in an abstracted or mild trance state. After we greeted her and were warmly welcomed, I said we had heard that she had gone to see Mr. Smith. She immediately entered into an altered ego state, as would be expected of a person undergoing faith healing, and began to speak in a "story-telling" voice which reminded me of her mental state and manner of speaking when she had related the story of the snake-man, although she did not on this occasion manifest the euphoria that she had displayed on that previous occasion. Nevertheless, I was alerted that what she was to tell us might be influenced heavily by primary-process thinking and could therefore be interpreted largely as if it were a dream. She responded to my question, saying, "He called me over there seven-and-a-half years ago, and when I went he and his wife were together and she was a nice-looking lady but they didn't do anything for me. I didn't know anything until now but now I know everything." That event was totally imaginary. She had never seen Mrs. Smith, except possibly in a photograph. She had often referred to Ruth Boyer as "a nice-looking lady." She spoke immediately of her present difficulties. "That C.H. (a female to whom she was distantly related through her father) came to my house. I was in the kitchen, cooking good food. My (teenage girl relative) had gone to a movie at the center. She hadn't wanted to go. I fell down and I couldn't get up. I was lying alone on the kitchen floor. Then John (C.H.'s son) came and put his face right against mine. It was all white." She touched her left cheek with the palm of her hand. "I don't know why he done that. I didn't know if he was alive or dead." She anxiously asked me, "Is he dead?" and continued, "I don't know why he done that because I never harmed anyone, never killed anyone." At this point she became acutely anxious, obviously because of her concern that his ghost might harm her, and sought to divert herself and us by trying to get us to take her to her house so that she could show us exactly what had happened. She complained that the young female relative who, she believed, was to have come to take her home several hours earlier had not done so.

I then asked her whether she remembered the story of the men who went to Mexico and found the egg. She nodded agreement and said the story had been told to her by Old Lady W. "Old Man W. had two daughters, no, two wives. The ladies had trouble between them and they left him. Each lady fell in love with someone else and they went away." Without transition, she referred to her own personal myth, saying, "My mother came back from over there with my father. Poor thing. She brought back four people with her: a boy, Alfie, a girl, S., me and another girl I can't remember." Without pause she went on: "When I was in school I had a dream of two men, God and Jesus. I was just sick. I was over there in the house by the underpass. There was no roofing. The sun was just bright. It was about this big." As she spoke, she first made a circle about 7½ inches in diameter and then moved her fingers rhythmically, indicating that the image was pulsating. "Then it got all cold and dark and then the sun came back. I felt myself all covered with ashes. It was all bright."

I understood that she was covering herself with ashes in an attempt to ward off ghost sickness, but wondered whether she were simultaneously referring to her life history and its unconscious fusion with the story of "The Man Who Turned Into A Snake." Accordingly, I asked her whether she meant the ashes of her father's bones, burned up by her mother. She promptly agreed. Then, referring again to John, she asked anew, "Did he die?" Then she said, "I was lying in the ashes in the black coals. There was no roofing. The sun came up. Morning was the color of (red) clouds. Soon I saw the sun clearly. The father of Jesus.''

Again without temporal discontinuity she continued, "I dreamed I was on top of East Mountain in *this* bed [the hospital bed]. Two boys were talking. Then both of them fell on the ground and this bed was right there. I was in bed with the two boys. The sun was bright, right on top of East Mountain, talking to me. 'Hi, hi,' he said. He was laughing. He said, 'You are going to be all right. You are going to get well and live for a long time.' I was dreaming. I woke up. The sun was [she made the pulsating motion with her fingers] and laughing. It was a dream I had a long time ago. I was six or seven years old. I'm all right. I told you, 'You are going to live.' I was in school. Through all the clothes, steps, smothered me to death. East Mountain, on top. Someone calling me, Mr. Smith calling me. He said, 'Get up!' Does she remember me? I was in the hospital. I dreamed that way. Smith brought me the book and I was just reading it.''

Again without pause she said, "There are two bees. Sunflowers. Bees, red, and yellow. You know their name?" I asked if she meant bumblebees, since of the bees and wasps on the reservation, only some bumblebees have any red coloring. She shook her head no. "They was fighting." I assumed she was relating a recent power dream and asked if they bought her power. She nodded agreement. "I was really unhappy. I was going down. My uncle came. He took me outside. The bees were fighting real hard for me. They came and brought me sweet stuff like candy, honey. They put the honey in the palm of my left hand where they were fighting. They were eating meat." I asked her to describe the bees again; she made it clear they had now changed to wasps and were biting little pieces of flesh from her left palm. "They foretold I would spend half of my life in bed. I was just praying and praying. Then I got sick again. S.P. was married to my mother. Then it was the same thing again. The butterflies were fighting. They were big yellow butterflies, with black on the edges, beautiful, yellow. One bee was dead. One butterfly, he flew away, safe, and didn't get hurt. The other one was killed. The butterfly came from the east. Yellow is for happiness." She spent some time repeating this material in various ways, making it clear that one bee killed the other while fighting "over" or "for" her and that one butterfly did the same to the other. Although the interview was being recorded in shorthand, she mumbled now and spoke so softly and rapidly that no verbatim account exists for a period. However, we understood her to say she had been raped by two boys who fought over or for her on East Mountain while she was a girl and had had a nightmare recollection of the experience the night before we saw her, while in the hospital. Then she spoke with less pressure and anxiety.

"The school children all got sick. The girls got in fights. There was no hospital. Influenza. Just go off and die. Went to see God. Lots of things happen I dream about. I got a vision that came to me. My uncle came to me on a porch. He sat with me. It's about the beehive.''

I was certain by this time that she had just related a power dream, and that she believed she now possessed a new supernatural power, and asked her how she used the power after she accepted it. Rather disgustedly, she replied, ''I told you before.'' I did not contest her statement, believing it to be possible that she had done so symbolically earlier in the interview and would amplify later. She continued, ''I know lots of things, but I hold myself back. I could become ... I saw a picture of me. I am not dead, but I have no head.'' I asked whether her bee power enabled her to put herself and others back together when they were in parts. She nodded yes. Then she hummed briefly, identifying with her bee power as Old Lady With A Sash identified with her bat power by flapping her arms as though they were wings, and said, ''The beehive is really good and the butterfly is really bigger and more beautiful than the wasp. ... Bees are different from wasps. They bring honey and wasps eat raw meat. ... The bee was trying to kill the butterfly but she got away.''

At this point, Better To See You became acutely anxious and would not continue to talk about bee power and its acquisition, nor did she refer again to ''The Man Who Turned Into A Snake.'' She sought again to have us take her home. We informed her we could not, after having been forbidden to do so by a nurse in her presence. As we said goodbye, she looked frightenend and said ''Not goodbye.'' She rubbed the long black sleeves of Ruth Boyer's blouse, now noticing the color for the first time, since the blouse was partially covered by a tan vest. Startled, she asked, ''Why did you wear *that*? You go home and wash it white.'' As we left, she asked again why John had touched her with his white face.

DISCUSSION

In order for the reader to understand the analysis of the clinical vignette which follows, it may be advisable to reread Better To See You's personal myth and variation of the story of ''The Man Who Turned Into A Snake'' in the last chapter, omitted here in the service of space.

After I said we had heard that she had gone to see Mr. Smith, Better To See You replied that he had called her to see him some seven years before. It was then that she first began to think about consulting him as a faith healer. It may be that she did not expect her message to be taken literally. It is frequent for a prospective client of a shaman to state that he has had a vision in which the shaman called to him to apply for succor, although such visionary claims are often fictional and recognized as such. Some seven years previously she had dreamed that we had called her to visit us and when we went to see her some months later she said the dream had forecast our visit and that she hoped that

I would cure her of her various ills. Her disappointment and only partially hidden anger because no cure occurred appear to have persisted and to have been expressed in her statement, "I didn't know anything until now, but now I know everything." In point of actual fact, the year before she had prepared a dinner for us without letting us know she expected us. We had spent the evening, and Better To See You had known it, with a sister surrogate whom she predominantly hated, as she felt more hostility toward C.H. than affection. Better To See You had pouted like a neglected child despite our apology. Such manifest evidence of her ambivalent feelings toward us was not new even then. She had previously had us to "lunch," taking great pains to cook "good food," and had come to demand that we visit her *first* when on the reservation. When we did not do so, she sometimes whiningly complained, and, on occasion, she briefly refused to visit with us when we did call on her.

After Better To See You said, "Now I know everything," she spoke about a distant female relative toward whom she felt intense ambivalence. C.H. had been her expected guest when she was cooking the "good food," but had not appeared. Had she been present, C.H. could have looked after Better To See You, who could not get up from the floor when she fell. Just as I had neither cured her nor prevented her developing further blindness and arthritis and we had failed to come for the meal she had prepared, so too had C.H. failed her.

John, C.H.'s son, was alive and healthy, yet Better To See You repeatedly expressed fear that he was a ghost. John was also the name of the little brother who had died after their return to the reservation and of whom she had been so jealous. During one period of her psychotherapy, she had become aware of persisting death wishes toward him and of her fear that his ghost, displaced onto that of the half-brother who had been shot, would harm her. That fear had been repressed anew and, to our knowledge, had never come to consciousness again until, as I assume, it re-emerged during this vignette, displaced onto the favorite son of C.H. In this last interview, she misremembered her long-dead brother as Alfie, rather than John. It will be recalled that in the life story she presented in 1959, she had omitted her brother John's having come with the family on the return trek to the reservation. During times when she was feeling hostile toward C.H., Better To See You had previously sometimes "feared" that her son John would be harmed.

She responded to the question concerning whether she remembered the story of "The Man Who Turned Into A Snake" by stating that it had been told to her by Old Lady W. Then came a slip of the tongue in which she equated Old Man W's wives and daugthers. In her treatment period, she had once made the same parapraxis, calling her mother her father's daughter. We were unable to determine whether old Man W's wives factually deserted him, but we remember that the sisters who were kidnapped by the "wild man" left him and went with other men.

Then followed a revision of her personal myth. She remembered that her uncle brought her mother back from Arizona. I assume that this temporary return of the repressed resulted from her identification with her mother as a "poor thing," realistic because of her current plight as a helpless old woman who had had an amputation and was unable to accustom herself to the use of her prosthesis. To observe her awkward efforts to do so was truly heart-rending. It seems likely that her loving identification with her mother allowed her, for the moment at least, to repress once again her hostile feelings toward the bad image of her mother and to focus them on other people, particularly the girl who failed to come to get her, C.H. and us.

Better To See You then promptly turned to a dream she claimed to have had at six or seven, in which two men, God and Jesus, appeared. At that age she had been sent to live with a family who lived near the school "by the underpass," and introduced to Christianity and the lesson that God and Jesus were fathers in the sky who loved and would protect and save their mortal children. With her move and new experiences, she felt unprotected, and we can assume that the roofless-house symbol in the dream had as one of its determinants her feeling exposed and helpless.

As the interview continued, she stated that she had had the dream during the previous night. It seems reasonable to assume that she had had such a dream during her childhood and that it probably recurred periodically in times of stress. No doubt she hoped for rescue when she was raped as a child, whether the rape occurred in fact or was only desired and feared. Sexual assaults on small girls by teenage boys are common today and took place then as well, although apparently less frequently.

We can guess that at least one other element contributed to her dreaming that she was found desirable during the previous night. She had always been a sexually active woman and had been deprived of intercourse for several years. She must have felt particularly unattractive following her amputation. No doubt she suspected that the teenage girl had not come to see her because she was on a sexual assignation. We recall how she had sought to deny her hostility toward that promiscuous girl earlier in the interview, when she had asserted that she was absent against her will at the time of the drunken mishap.

At least in cultures in which the main deity is conceptualized as male, regressed patients often equate the sun with God; a famous example is to be found in the Schreber case (Freud 1911). The equation of God and the sun is common in the world's folklore. However, Better To See You was without doubt also referrring to the puberty ceremony for girls, which traditionally has taken place on the reservation at the foot of East Mountain.

During the puberty ceremony, a man who knows relevant ritual songs is hired to sing them for the maiden whose "coming into womanhood" is being celebrated and sanctified. Although he may not be accorded the status of shaman at other times, during that period of five days and four nights he is often so deemed, because of "the power of his songs." On the morning of the fifth and most sacred day, he paints a picture of the sun on the palm of his left hand with yellow pollen, and some red and black. He opens his hand and holds the palm up toward East Mountain at the moment of the sunrise, and the representation on his hand is though by some to make the sun come up. From a short distance, the exposure of the picture of the sun looks like a yellow butterfly when he opens his hand.

The girl who is "coming out" also has a female attendant, who instructs her in the lore of the ceremony and supervises her ritual behavior. Her behavior must be impeccable for the successful outcome of the ceremony, which is designed to make her become a moral woman and a good wife and mother, and to give her fertility and a long, happy, healthy and productive life.

On the fifth morning, when the sun appears over East Mountain, the girl is symbolically reborn as *istsúneglezh,* White Painted Lady. It will be recalled that *istsúneglezh,* bore *tubahjíshchineh,* Child Of The Water, after being impregnated by rain from *yusn,* God, as she lay atop a sacred mountain with her legs spread apart. The female attendant forbids the girl to bathe during the days and nights of the puberty ceremony and tells her to keep her legs close together for the sake of modesty. Recently, a chaperone told us that the girl should keep her legs so and forego bathing in order that she not become pregnant. She did not state that the message is conveyed overtly to the maiden. At the same time, the debutante drinks only through a cylindrical tube, a bone or a hollow reed, an object which is about six inches long, perhaps a reflection of childhood fantasies related to oral impregnation. On the final morning, the maiden is briefly accorded the shamanistic status; she blesses many people and paints the tops of their heads and their cheeks with yellow pollen and/or white clay. Some of them are thought to be cured or protected against various afflictions as a result of her actions. One woman was said to have sought fertility through receiving the blessing from a symbolically newborn *istsúneglezh.* Part of of the girl's face is colored with white clay; her cheeks are painted with a ring of red superimposed upon which is a spot of yellow pollen.

Let us return to the vignette. The significance of the sun's pulsating can be but conjectured. Extrapolating from information from analysands in our culture, we must wonder whether Better To See You was symbolically depicting preconsciously experienced vaginal sensations as she recounted the dream of being sexually assaulted by the two boys,

Her having mentioned them immediately after she spoke of dreaming of God and Jesus leads us to suspect that the dream had a disguised incestuous element involving her uncle-father and herself. The two boys who were fighting over or for her were replaced promplty by two bees who were fighting over or for her, and while talking of them she said, "Through all the clothes, steps, smothered me to death" and "My uncle came." Knowing of the sexual symbology of steps her speaking of smothering and bedclothes surely depicts discomfort pertaining to anxieties in the bed, and suggests that both the boys and the bees symbolized her father-uncle; we may even suspect that she thus veiledly expressed her wish that I would assault her sexually. One time some years previously when we were partying together, I ventured to introduce the subject of butterfly power. Better To See You said only the yellow butterfly was associated with love magic. Her teenage grandnephews and others sobered immediately and fled from the house, and Better To See You became acutely uncomfortable. It was obvious that all assumed that I had suggested that Better To See You or one of the girls have sexual relations with me; they were embarrassed both because my wife was present and because I had come to be considered to be a relative.

Flitting Bird was of the opinion that when two yellow birds flutter near a person's head, their presence is the result of love magic. Better To See You said the shaman need send but one.

Better To See You had used actual sexual relations primarily in the service of being held and nurtured. In the vignette, she said, "My uncle came to me on a porch. He sat with me. It's about the beehive." Porch is often equated with ledge in dream language and may symbolize the breast. The three sentences appear to fuse sex and nurturance.

Another phenomenon may be applicable as well. In the lives of tiny Apache children, it has always been scarcely possible for them to avoid seeing the erections of adult men. We recall that Greenacre (1947) noted that little children of our culture, first viewing an adult erection, sometimes see pulsating bright lights. We do not have information concerning this among the Apaches, but the possibility is worth considering.

By now Better To See You had ceased alluding directly to the story of the snake-man. However, its associative links to what followed clearly include the themes of sibling rivalry and magical rescue from death, symbolized by dismemberment. She turned, immediately following the dream recitation, to talking about the new acquisition of bee and the reacquisition of butterfly power.

As mentioned earlier, supernatural power is acquired by these Apaches when they are in altered ego states via dream or hallucination, and most frequently the changed level of consciousness occurs during an ordeal, often self-imposed. Better To See You was undergoing an involuntary trial because of her amputation and her immense difficulty in learning how to use the prosthesis. Her "I was really unhappy. I was going down" can be understood to represent an inner experience of ordeal. In her life history and at various times during her therapeutic interviews she gave evidence that she viewed her uncle as one who rescued through magical means, a representative both of God and her father. The vignette material was confusing as to when she had had the power dreams which endowed her with bee and butterfly power. However, since we had known her well and she had never previously mentioned owning bee power, we must assume that its presumed acquisition had occurred in the very recent past, perhaps during the previous night, if, indeed, it did not occur during our being with her. She may have preconsciously conceptualized me to be her singer-shaman and Ruth Boyer to be her chaperone.

We can ascribe the sequential acquisition of the new bee and the old butterfly power to the condensation and the negation of the existence of time, which are typical of unconscious thinking.

Let us turn to the subject of the bees. At first they were red and yellow; later they were yellow and black. We note the similarity to the colors used on the singer's palm when the sun was painted on it, and also to the colors painted on the maiden's face, and we infer that there may be a connection between these phenomena. While the color red has no single meaning to these Apaches, a red paste or clay is important in certain aspects of the puberty ceremony, and it is sometimes thought that the red-tinged early morning clouds herald a good day and good luck. Earlier during the interviews Better To See You had said, "Morning was the color of (red) clouds." Yellow, as she mentioned, customarily represents happiness and good luck and is equated with the pollen which is used to bless the maiden and which she uses to bless people on their first and fifth mornings of the ceremony. Such pollen is to be found in the medicine bags of shamans and others and is always sprinkled on the person who is to be treated for an illness. Black has two meanings. It is an unlucky color and, when it occurs in dreams, it is thought to herald misfortune. At the same time, one of the four "gifts" required by the shaman before he undertakes a healing ceremony is a black object, usually a black-handled knife, and the product of fire, ashes, which are first black and later gray, are always used in the treatment of ghost sickness and ailments which are thought to have resulted from witchcraft. Black neck-scarves are still worn by some elderly Apaches as a precaution against evil, misfortune and ghosts. But red is also the color of blood and, in the context of the vignette, we must wonder whether its early inclusion should be connected with the bleeding which was to be expected when the wasps were eating her flesh, during her amputation and during childbirth. Let us not forget, however, that red, yellow and black are predominant colors painted on the maiden's face and the shaman's left palm.[1]

It is of interest that Better To See You did not speak of the acquisition of wasp power but referred only to bee or beehive power. The bees/wasps were both good and bad agents, reminding us of the opposing aspects of Apache shamans, who, while they are rescuers, are latently witches/murderers. The shaman and the witch of many cultures are thought by various observers to constitute societally acceptable good- and bad-mother projects. The bees brought her honey and good food, and ate her flesh. They can be understood to indicate the psychological developmental stage to which she had partly regressed, fusing castration anxiety with oral dependency and sadism.

But why did Better To See You fuse the acquisition of bee and butterfly power? In the vignette, she said, "I saw a picture of me. I am not dead, but I have no head," and then agreed that bee power gave her the capacity to restore dismembered bodies.

Taking into consideration the regressive pictorial representation of ideas which is characteristic of the dream (Freud 1900, Chap. 7), we can view her statement "I have no head" to denote the amputated foot. This must be a signal clue related to her new acquisition of bee power and her wishful statement in terms of Apache folklore that she has the capacity to regain her lost member. We recall her earlier equation of the leg and the phallus (Chapter V) and know of the symbolic representation of the penis by the head, the container of the thinking brain. Considering the overdetermination of symbols, we conjecture that she sought simultaneously to solve several problems, including her long-sought acquisition of a penis, the possession of which she hoped would remove the guilt and fearful aspects of her sibling rivalry with her younger brother John.

She never revealed how or when she had acquired butterfly power. However, her services as a shaman had been sought from the time she was about forty, from within a year after she had lost her second husband to another woman. She presented no clear details of how she came to lose him, but she once alluded to a belief that had left her for a woman who had hired a shaman to cause him to have love sickness.

Love sickness can be inflicted only by a shaman who possesses butterfly power. We may assume that then, during another intrapsychic ordeal, she hallucinated the acquisition of butterfly power in the service of wishful restitution of an external love object, as she apparently believed during the interview that she had acquired bee power to replace another love object, a body part. To acquire butterfly power would make her totally sexually omnipotent. We can but conjecture that there was a relation between her acquisition of butterfly power and the coincidence of the picture of the sun on the singer's left palm and its looking like a butterfly when he opens his hand to cause the sunrise. It may be important that all references to body laterality in the vignette refer to the left side. We can only guess that her choice of obtaining bee power, previously unkown to Apaches so far as we know, had a relationship with the letter B., as in Bryce and Boyer, by both of which I am commonly known on the reservation. She certainly envied my ascribed supernatural power, power so great that it prevented my being killed by witchcraft by her shaman relative.

Let us deal with but four further aspects of the vignette. First, following her indication that the possession of bee power hopefully gave her the capacity to reconstitute her body as entire, she said, "The beehive is really good but the butterfly is really bigger and more beautiful than the wasp." Bee power has now been changed to beehive power.

When beehives have appeared in the dreams of my Western analysands, they have symbolized pregnancy. Among the Amazonian Kagwahiv, to dream of a pregnant woman is stated to mean that honey will be found and, conversely, to dream of finding honey symbolizes a pregnant woman (Kracke 1977). Additionally, honey in a dream is overtly stated to denote both semen and oral impregnation. To the Kagwahiv, to dream of a wasp indicates the wish to be kissed by a woman, and a dream in which a woman is kissing a man signifies the threat of being stung by a wasp. She Who Uses A Cane used the wasp to designate a flesh eater, no doubt a symbolic representation of a projected cannibalistic wish. When we studied the potlatch ceremony of the Alaskan Athabaskans, we learned that their repressed cannibalistic wishes directed toward mother figures represented, in part, a wish to regain fantasized symbiotic reunion (Hippler *et al.* 1975).

Both the Western analysand and the Kagwahiv use the beehive to symbolize pregnancy partly because of the larvae which teem inside the beehive, which is said to have the shape of a pregnant abdomen. While such symbology has not been discovered explicitly among the Apaches, its presence can be inferred from one belief which rationalizes their traditionally having murdered one of twins soon after their birth: twins were thought to result either from witchcraft or from immoral behavior on the part of the mother, who was thought to have indulged in "too much sex" or to have had intercourse with more than one man. Each of these latter acts would involve the presence of excess semen. Some Apache children conceptualize their mothers to be constantly pregnant. Taking these data into consideration, it seems reasonable that the larvae inside the beehive may be equated both with semen and with intrauterine babies. An occasional Apache has wondered whether semen were homunculi. Despite their obvious ambivalence toward babies, Apache mothers usually consciously want them and refer to them as "sweet."

We can, then, assume with some degree of confidence that Better To See You, with her allusion to the puberty ceremony, one function of which is to make the girl fertile, referred to a wish to have the capacity to, anatomically intact, become pregnant and be reborn. Apaches, like Western analysands, sometimes equate the baby with the penis. Were she to become pregnant, she could resolve her conflict regarding sexual identity by symbolically being both male and female. Additionally, we recall her equation of leg and phallus. For her, it seems likely that to have a baby would be the psychological equivalent of restoring her lost foot (leg).

The statement that the beehive is good but the butterfly is bigger and more beautiful than the wasp is highly condensed. It implies that the capacities to make dismembered bodies whole and to become fertile/pregnant via ordinary intercourse, the result of "love-sickness," are perhaps differentiated from the forbidden wish to become orally impregnated. During her therapy, it had been evident that Better To See You feared taking a penis into her mouth lest she bite it off.

Better To See You then said that the bee was trying to kill the butterfly, but she got away. It was clear, when she hummed, that she identified with her new supernatural power. Again we can but offer suppositions. Perhaps she feared that the acquisition of bee power would remove repression of cannibalistic wishes and displace her butterfly power, the use of which surely depicts a more acceptable, less regressed phase of psychosexual development. But Better To See You indicated at various times during her therapy that she retained the common Apache fear that sexual relations were potentially damaging to both partners.

It is very likely that Better To See You feared continuing to talk about the bee power of two reasons. Other shamans have refused to complete their recitations of their experiences of power acquisition because they fear that telling the whole story would endow the hearer with the power and thereby result in shared ownership and a lessening of the quantum of power held by the narrator. At the same time, they sometimes cease their recitations in order to protect the listener. Thus, Old Lady With A Sash would not complete a tale she was telling about her bat power, because, "If I told you all of it, you would hang to the ceiling like a bat." (Chapter VI).

Finally, at the end of the vignette, when our separation was imminent, Better To See You associated our departure with death. It was *not* to be goodbye. Her thought of death became associated with the newly noticed black sleeves which were supposed to be washed white, as though their change of color would magically undo the separation-death threat. But she had an insoluble dilemma. Earlier in the interview she had designated the face of the ghost to be white (like our faces). Apaches do not generally picture ghosts as being white, but rather black or gray. In the Apache language, the word *indáh* means both enemy and white man. It is my conjecture that the ghost of the son of her distant female relative, which we have shown to be equated with the ghosts of her two dead brothers, became fused with us and the hostility she projected onto us. Thus, whether the sleeves were black or white, her fear of death through separation would have remained unsolved.

The sparse psychoanalytic literature pertaining to the bee illustrates that as a symbol the bee has various meanings and that individual patients use it to express and defend against problems pertaining especially to the fusion of oral and phallic wishes and sadism and to sibling rivalry. Fenichel (1927) wrote of a male patient who felt guilty because of incestuous wishes toward his mother and who had unresolved sibling-rivalry problems. For him, bees represented phallic stingers as well as dangerous children, castrating germs and spermatozoa. Being stung was feared as a punishment for his wishes toward his mother, and his associations included the death of the male after copulation. Fenichel's last words in his article were that the bee is an apt metaphor for dangerous pleasure. Moore (1958) wrote of an eleven-year-old boy who was preoccupied with conflicts about active and passive sexuality. He feared the bee sting would poison him or lead to cancer, that is, impregnate him, and believed that he would lose his "stinger" when he had active intercourse, as the bee loses its stinger after it stings. Evans (1955) wrote of a latency boy's response to being stung by a bee. The boy equated the tooth, the bee's stinger and the phallus and indicated his fear of castration as a punishment for forbidden sexual relations. Bradley (1965) wrote of a patient who projected his oral-sadistic attack onto the nipples, initally symbolized by bees. He called attention to Mellaart's (1963) statement that the priestesses of the many-breasted goddess Artemis of Ephesus were called *melissai,* bees, and noted that the stinging bee expresses sadistic oral-phallic wishes in the poetic image of a woman's bee-stung lip. Bradley (1973) wrote further of the bee as symbolizing the nipple onto which oral hostility had been projected, and also noted that beehives until recently have been traditionally constructed in the shape of breasts in many cultures.

It would be redundant to spell out the multiple manners in which Better to See You's and the Kagwahiv's uses of the bee and the beehive coincide with their symbology as found in Western analysands.

Apache folkore abounds with stories which encompass most of the basic expectations evinced by Better To See You in her quest to regain her health, to be cured of her blindness and arthritis and to regain her lost leg/phallus. The Apaches of yore were ignorant of the existence of endocrinological disorders, and today's aged people are unable to understand either its existence or physiological origins. A few examples will follow.

According to a well-known story, in the remote past a blind boy carried a legless boy to a sacred mountain, where they hoped to be made whole by the Mountain Spirits. After undergoing an ordeal, each was cured of his disability (Hoijer 1938a:33).

Long ago, a woman was deserted because she was blind and deaf. She sought the help of the Mountain Spirits and, after she had undergone an ordeal, she could not only see and hear well but was endowed with supernatural power (Hoijer 1938a:33).

In a modern version of an old story with many variants (Chapter V), two boys set out in quest of supernatural power. They were taken to a holy cave and subjected to a series of ordeals by the Mountain Spirits. During the fourth night they were totally dismembered, probably the result of being eaten by symbolic sibling surrogates. On the fifth morning they emerged from the cave, symbolically reborn, not only completely reconstituted but possessing supernatural power.

When we were on the reservation subsequently, Better To See You refused to talk further about her bee and butterfly power acquisition. We learned from a female relative who lived near and looked after her, and from the devoted grandnephew Peter, that she had not mentioned her acquisition of bee power to them. Each said, "She must want to keep that private for herself." Such secret retention of self-assigned supernatural power is common among these Apaches. They had heard her ask occasionally and without explanation, "Why did that boy's ghost do that to me?" Better To See You denied to me that she had experienced further power dreams or contacts with ghosts. I learned from them that she had returned from the distant city very angry with Mr. Smith and had denounced him and his curative powers. Subsequently, however, she had resumed her attitude of adulation toward him and was again praying to him for renewed health and longevity.

A last word. According to Opler, as mentioned in Chapter III, a set procedure was involved in the acquisition of supernatural power. The *diyi^n* of the familiar object in the environment which offered its powers to the mortal-aspirant, delineated the practical utilization of the power and gave instructions pertaining to its administration. In view of the material which has been presented regarding the acquisition of bee power by She Who Uses A Cane, we must suspect that Opler's informants had given him an idealized picture of what actually happened, which had been grossly revised by culturally supported secondary elaboration. However, the possiblity remains that Opler's description reflected the facts as they existed during the 1930s and that, with deculturation, individual conceptualizations of the procedure involved in the acquisition of supernatural power now vary. The only Apache who was willing to tell me of his actual experience of acquiring bear power was the subject of Opler's (1969) *An Apache Odyssey;* it was obvious that his recounting had been doctored to match descriptions of power acquisition that he had read in the anthropological literature pertaining to the Plains Indians.

SUMMARY

This chapter aims to illustrate the constant interplay between the total environment of a society, particularly its expressive modes of communication, and the idiosyncratic thinking and behavior of the individual participant within that culture. To understand in fullest richness the content of conscious and unconscious motivations and the activities and fantasies of a patient of a different ethnic background from that of the psychotherapist, it is essential that the latter become thoroughly familiar with the sociocultural bases of the person seeking aid.

The clinical vignette presented in isloation exemplifies what the therapist might hear in a single interview. This is augmented by including Better To See You's personal life history and psychological configuration, and finally by taking into account pertinent data from Apache culture as a whole. The patient's seemingly bizarre eccentricities are imbedded in a wealth of "normal" shared Chiricahua and Mescalero folklore, religious beliefs and ceremonies, and it is only in that perspective that the data become fully intergrated and the "rational" and the "irrational" can be segregated and evaluated.

It is strongly suggested that the psychotherapist interested in the mental health of any patient of non-Western derivation look to the culturally influenced defensive and adaptive mechanisms of that society as whole. A good starting point is in the comprehensive knowledge and analysis of that group's folklore.

IX

Reflections

It is time to reflect on the value of the philosophical orientation of this research and its methodology to anthropologists, folklorists, and psychologists. Because of the highly personal nature of the volume, it seems appropriate to include some of the events which contributed to the development of my viewpoints and elucidate certain influences which have bolstered my convictions.

As long as I can remember, I have been vitally interested in answering two questions: (1) In what ways do peoples of varying cultures resemble and differ from one another? and (2) How did they come to be as they are?

When I studied the various schools of psychology during my elementary education, I concluded that the developmental schema presented by psychoanalysts within the framework of the structural hypothesis and ego psychology was the one most likely to help me answer my second question. My hope that I could answer the first in my psychiatric and psychoanalytic practice in a metropolitan area populated by peoples of many national and racial backgrounds was soon dashed, and it became clear that only field work would help me answer the first. Consequently I was gratified when I was presented with the opportunity to do collaborative work with anthropologists and particularly when the nature of the major portion of my research was to be clinical. In that clinical situation, I learned that the transferential responses of my patient-informants were basically identical to those of whites from lower-middle-class and lower-class economic origins and that they responded in essentially the same ways to interpretive therapy, whatever their nosological categories.

Those who came to me suffered from anxiety states, phobias, hysteria, psychosomatic conditions, hallucinosis and acute paranoid reactions which were secondary to alcohol intoxication, and borderline personality disorders. Those troubled by the last-named condition were sometimes seen during the transient psychotic states which are common to those disorders. Among these Apaches, such psychotic states regularly resembled acute schizophrenic reactions. Although chronic depression was a fairly regular attribute of whatever psychopathological reaction or condition was evinced, obsessive-compulsive neuroses were not observed. It is of particular relevance to the present work that it soon became clear that their uses of fantasies, dreams, hallucinations, folklore and symbols were identical to those of my private patients, despite their cultural coloring.

The research team discussed their findings pertaining to social structure, child-rearing practices and the clinical interviews at length, four or five nights weekly; one evening was spent in the anthropologists' teaching me about their theories and investigative methods, and another in my discussing with them psychoanalytic points of view. It soon became eminently clear that the psychoanalytic developmental schema is equally applicable to the growing Apache children as to their white counterparts.

Following the lengthy period of continuous field work which occurred in 1959 and 1960, I had other interactions with anthropologists and folklorists which proved to be valuable to them and to me and further supported my conviction that cross-disciplinary collaboration holds great promise. Those interactions led to my helping graduate students with their doctoral dissertations and lasting collaborative research projects, some of which included field work among Northern Athabascans and Eskimos in Alaska, and to joint publications.

For the past eleven years, Ruth Boyer and I have participated in a colloquium named "Psychoanalytic Questions and Methods in Anthropological Fieldwork." The colloquium has been held annually as a function of the Fall Meeting of the American Psychoanalytic Association. For the past seven years I have had the honor of chairing the colloquium, which has been limited to some twenty-five members consisting of approximately equal numbers of anthropologists and psychoanalysts, and the occasional participation of folklorists. Initially, the colloquium occupied three hours of one day and the nature of our interactions was tentative. Within a few years, a regular core of participants was established, involving members who came at their own expense from such distances as Alaska, Europe and South America. The stimulation afforded by the exchange of ideas was such that we communally decided that the colloquium was the highlight of our scientific year and it became necessary to meet for five or more hours on each of two successive days. As a result of the colloquium, the level of sophistication of many of us has been enhanced and a number of collaborative research projects are underway. Our testing of the value of psychoanalytic thinking to anthropologists' understanding of the relationships among socialization processes, personality development and expressive culture has obviously been highly rewarding to us, as to psychoanalysts has been the opportunity not only to test their hypotheses, but also to look for areas where they might be modified.

The growing interest in applying psychoanalytic ideas and modified methodology to culture and personality studies is apparent in two recent developments. In 1974, a panel of anthropologists and psychoanalysts was convened in Mexico City as a function of the Annual Meeting of the American Anthropological Association. An audience of some 600 gave rapt attention during the morning session, and many more people sat through to the end of the afternoon meeting. For many years there was only one publication devoted to the psychological study of culture. Originally entitled *Psychoanalysis and the Social Sciences*, after the death of its original editor, Géza Róheim, it was renamed *The Psychoanalytic Study of Society*. ~~Three~~ Four others have appeared since its inception: *Transcultural Psychiatric Research, Ethos* ~~and, more recently,~~ and *The Journal of Psychological Anthropology* and fourth, *Ethnopsychiatrica*. The editorial orientation of the first, and third, journals is psychoanalytic.

Let us return to the value of this book. In my opinion, based on more than thirty years of clinical practice and twenty years of collaborative field work, it has worth for social science in general. It demonstrates beyond question that the psychoanalytic developmental schema within the framework of ego psychology and the uses of expressive culture, exemplified by folklore and its symbols, are as valid for these Apaches as they have been repeatedly shown to be for individuals of varying Western origins. No more is claimed, although our briefer collaborative field work among Alaskan Athabascans and Eskimos leads me to believe that the schema is also valid for them. While I believe that this conclusion will prove to be generally applicable, the validation of this view must await extensive research by others among the peoples of many other, widely divergent social backgrounds.

Much more work needs to be done before a universal theory of cognitive and emotional symbolism can be discussed with certainty. As a case in point, let us remember that our analyses of the bat stories indicated that their content closely reflected the commonly shared intrapsychic conflicts which are produced by Apache child-rearing experiences, even those of cradle days. We know that similar stories are to be found in cultures which do not include cradling in their socialization practices. The Brazilian Indians who share the tale variant described in Chapter VI do not use cradleboards. Their version of the rescue of the abandoned boy does not include a bag or a basket with its supporting filament, as was found in the version of the Indians of North America, who place their babies in some cradle variant. Our analysis of the bat stories indicate that the spider-web or horse-hair strand represents the umbilical cord or the thongs of the cradleboard, and reflect persistent ambivalent relations with the mother. Perhaps the Bororos and the tribes which are related to them and include in their oral literature "The Macaws and Their Nest" do not induce such pregenital ambivalence toward maternal figures by their puericultural customs, which may instead foment strong Oedipal ambivalence between fathers and sons and sibling rivalry. Sophisticated child-rearing studies have not been done among these Brazilian Indians, so we can but guess.

Let us leave aside the question of whether the theory of monogenesis and diffusion or that of polygenesis is the better to explain the widespread presence of nearly identical folklore content. According to modern psychoanalytic thinking, the themes and symbols of folklore must be suitable for assisting a culture's individuals to express and defend themselves against intrapsychic conflicts that have been produced by their puericultural practices and are common to the members of the group. Obviously, they must likewise be suitable to convey socialization lessons. If the folklore of another group is to be added to the indigenous stock of a culture, its themes and symbols must be adequate to serve substitutive or supplementary purposes. If it is to be substituted for already existent traditional literature, its representation of latent themes must be better disguised and thus more readily acceptable than those already present. Of course, the substitution may result from social conditions, such as those which obtain when one society is more powerful than another and imposes its lore upon the weaker group. Alternately, people in one group may envy those of another and emulate them through assumption of their cultural traits, including oral literature, as has occurred in the cargo cults. What is of particular importance here is that the answers to our questions concerning the reasons for the widespread distribution of folklore contents must include more research directed toward learning what problems are engendered by the child-rearing practices of the groups in which the traditional literature appears. Such research is also necessary to support or negate psychoanalytic explanations. Research will also test further the general applicability of psychoanalytic explanations about folklore contents. This volume shows unequivocally that they apply to the folklore of the Apaches.

This study is of value not only to social scientists in general, but specifically to psychiatrists and psychoanalysts who seek to understand

and treat patients whose cultural background differs from their own. It shows the immense utility of obtaining an intimate knowledge of the premises involved in their communications, knowledge which can only come about from cognizance of their social structure and child-rearing practices and especially their traditional literature. Surely no one who was ignorant of Apache lore and ritual could have comprehended the messages conveyed by the apparently bizarre utterances of Better To See You.

This book, then, is a beginning in rigidly structured psychoanalytic anthropology, a documentation of the close relationship between puericultural and expressive manifestations of the Chiricahua and Mescalero Apaches. It does not purport to answer all questions. It portrays in detail the in-depth emotional and cognitive responses of a few individuals and in some instances of the entire group, not only during the time of the field study but also to some extent in their historical past.

Perhaps this book can serve as a model to be followed or modified by future research teams in their quest to gain a better knowledge of many-faceted man. It indicates how the field work of the anthropologist supplies data which enhance the comprehension of the more sedentary psychoanalyst, and thereby his clinical efficacy. It illustrates also ways in which the unconscious elements of individuals, as made manifest to the psychoanalyst, provide a wealth of understanding which is usually unavailable to the anthropologist.

The success or failure of such a methodology hinges in large part on the quality of the socialization study which is one of its major components. That study requires intimate observations of the interactions among family members over a lengthy period. In the puericultural investigation of this project, seven families were carefully selected for investigation. Ruth Boyer spent eight or more hours daily in the home of a single family for a period of over six months before she felt she had acquired reliable data against which to compare information obtained from other families for shorter periods. The very presence in a household of an outsider, regardless of his or her empathic capacity, disrupts the customary behavior of its members towards one another. We are convinced that the success of the socialization study depends on the presence of a well-adjusted female investigator, and we recommend that she be a mature woman who has both had a successful personal psychoanalysis and reared children of her own. Our field experiences have convinced us that the presence in the household of a male investigator is much more disruptive of the usual interactions among family members.

FOOTNOTES

CHAPTER I

1. During a short period in 1957 and for most of the summer of 1958, the an-
    thropologists Drs. Ruth M. Boyer and David M. Schneider and the author engaged
    in a preliminary study of the Apaches of the Mescalero Indian Reservation, to deter-
    mine the feasibility of cross-disciplinary anthropological and psychoanalytic
    research among them. That work was supported by NIMH Grant M-2013. From
    1959 through 1965, the anthropologists Drs. Harry M. Basehart and Ruth M. Boyer
    and the author collaborated in a further study of the same Apaches, funded by
    NIMH Grant M-3088. The Boyers have spent more than two years in the field, the
    longest period consisting of almost fifteen months during 1959-1960, when they
    were accompanied for nine months by Basehart, co-director with the author of the
    project, and by the anthropologist Dr. Bruce B. MacLachlan during the entire field
    period. From 1959-1965 and for several subsequent years until his untimely death,
    Dr. Bruno Klopfer was the principal psychological consultant; at various periods he
    was assisted by Drs. Florence B. Brawer, Hayao Kawai and Suzanne B. Scheiner.
        Basehart and MacLachlan did standard ethnological studies directed primarily
    toward the study of social structure. Basehart's main work amplified his earlier in-
    vestigations pertaining to a land-claims study of the Chiricahua and Mescalero tribes
    (Basehart 1959, 1960). MacLachlan's studies eventually focused on traditional and
    modern legal philosophies and practices (MacLachlan 1962). While Ruth M. Boyer
    contributed much to the study of social structure (R. M. Boyer, 1964), her main in-
    vestigation pertained to socialization (1962). Her second major focus dealt with
    folklore, and has led to an individual publication (1972) and a series of articles writ-
    ten conjointly with the author (see Bibliography).
        The author had been introduced to the tribal Business Committee as a psychiatrist
    who was interested in learning how social structure and child-rearing processes in-
    fluenced personality development. The Apaches soon ascribed to him the status of
    white shaman. He was provided by the tribal Business Committee with an office,
    where from 1958 through 1960 he saw Apache informants in face-to-face
    psychoanalytically oriented psychotherapeutic interviews which focused primarily
    on studying the effects of transference and resistance interpretations. Approximate-
    ly one hundred Apaches of both sexes and ranging from four to over ninety years of
    age came of their own volition and were seen in hourly interviews. They included
    shamans who sought to compete in power struggles. A few informants appeared
    but once, while others came for varying periods, often five times weekly. One in-
    formant who had requested treatment of night terrors and phobias was seen 140
    times. The author also obtained over 300 Rorschach protocols.
        At the behest of the Business Committee, each informant was paid at the rate of
    $1.50 per interview with any investigator. It was clearly understood by the Business
    Committee and the informants that whatever information was obtained might be
    published.
        The several investigators' field observations were shared and discussed daily,

which enabled us to pursue leads immediately. This procedure was especially helpful in focusing socialization observations that might affirm or negate hypotheses which emerged from informants' interviews with the author.

Following 1960, the author no longer retained his office and changed his main focus of investigation to furthering the study of religiomedical practices and folklore. Although he never practiced shamanism, he was accorded the status of "family shaman" by two families, a position he still holds.

From 1960 through 1965, the Boyers spend about two months per year on the Reservation; Basehart was there for shorter periods. Then and subsequently, we have continued to meet once or twice a year for purposes of discussion of data and ideas and sharing of field notes.

Since 1965, the Boyers have spent weeks or months on the reservation every year but one. Our research has been supported in part by Faculty Grants to Ruth M. Boyer from the University of California at Berkeley, awarded during the years when she was Associate Professor of Decorative Arts in that institution. Following Dr. Klopfer's death some years ago, the psychologically sophisticated anthropologists Drs. George A. DeVos and Richard Day have served as psychological consultants.

2. A thorough comparison of the topographical or libido theory (sometimes known as id psychology) and the structural hypothesis, which led to the development of ego psychology, is to be found in Arlow and Brenner (1964) and Brenner (1974). Ego psychology takes into adequate account the influence of both innate givens and child-rearing practices on the formation of the individual's character structure, with its group commonalities and its idiosyncratic elements.

3. Folklorists are critical of Bettelheim's book *The Uses of Enchantment* because they deem it to lack scholarship. Psychoanalysts object to Bettelheim's having given the impression that most of the conclusions he presented were original with him, whereas they had been published elsewhere by other psychoanalysts whose works were not cited by Bettelheim.

4. It is beyond the scope of this book to spell out what is currently known about the conflictual differences experienced by boys and girls in their personality development, with the extent and meanings of castration themes in girls. Those who are interested are referred to Number 5 of Volume 24 of the Journal of the American Psychoanalytic Association, 1976, a special supplement on female psychology.

CHAPTER II

1. An aspect of the psychoanalytic theory of inherent maturational stages is the concept of phylogenetic influence on personality development. The biological effects of inbreeding and predisposition to personality configurations remain moot. If such a formulation is valid, it may well apply to these Apaches, although from the time when written records were first kept (Horgan 1954) cross-breeding with captives and intermarriage with members of the other Indian tribes have been very common. The observable socialization data alone would appear to adequately explain the growth of their personality structure. In 1962 the author published a record of the ethnic intermixtures of the tribal members (Boyer 1962, Appendix I), revealing much intermixture of tribal and racial backgrounds, particularly among the young. Subsequent data, including Griswold's (1977) recent compilation, indicate that there was yet a higher degree of intermixture.

2. Apaches do not develop "anal characters" (Freud 1908a), obsessive-compulsive neuroses or manic-depressive psychoses. Their psychotic reactions are uniformly schizophrenoid. In nineteen years, only one instance of severe depressive withdrawal has been noted. That occurred in a highly acculturated aged Chiricahua man who had developed a degree of object constancy which is somewhat unusual for these Apaches and who had recently lost his wife.

CHAPTER V

1.   Before the narrator told this personalized version of a standard Apache folktale, he had gone into detail about the shaman's need to sacrifice either his own life or that of another when he saved the life of a patient. Patients in therapy sometimes present their associations to a dream before giving its content. This informant had told me some days before that he planned to tell me, the next time we met, how his father acquired ga^nheh power.

2.   As mentioned previously, the clown of the ga^nheh is the personified representation of Coyote. The Apache name of Coyote is alternatively *bayeh* or *thlibayeh. Bayeh* also means wolf or monster. The prefix *thli* can be interpreted as tan or gray. Coyote will be discussed in Chapter VI. While he serves as a surrogate for *tubajíshchineh* the culture hero, he is also an evil figure, and the coyote is one of the cultural bogeys, as are all canines. It is of interest that all of the figures who confront the narrator's father in his quest of power in the cave are cultural bêtes noires. Only this informant and a few others presented 'this version of the acquisition of ga^nheh power. The narrator suggested that the origins of the bogeys themselves is depicted in his story. While his explanation is idiosyncratic, nevertheless his coming to that conclusion may be understandable in terms of the relationships among witches, ghosts and powers which were depicted in Chapter III.

3.   See also Hoijer (1938a: 171-181, 183-188) and Opler (1942: 1-20, 74-78). In other versions, the early people are destroyed by a flood, an idea doubtless attributable to Christian influences, and, in one version, White Painted Lady and Child Of The Water (*istsúneglezh* and *tubajíshchineh)* both survive the flood. That is, only the good-mother and her infant son remain, as is consonant with the symbiotic and Oedipal wishes of the youngster. According to some informants, before the old-time people are drowned or devoured, all of the animals talk Apache and are transformed into people. Here again we have the wishful removal of all rivals for the mother's attentions.

        In other myth narrations, different flesh-eating monsters appear, such as antelopes, bulls, eagles, snakes, etc. Their generic Apache name is *bayeh,* one of the words used for Coyote.

4.   In other renditions, a second culture hero, Killer Of Enemies, and White Painted Lady remain. Or *istsúneglezh* first bears Killer Of Enemies and later *tubajíshchineh,* or has several children before Child Of The Water, all of whom are eaten. Killer Of Enemies and Child Of The Water may also be twins.

        The position of Killer Of Enemies in Chiricahua and Mescalero mythology is unclear. He is the principal culture hero of the Navahos, Western Apaches, Lipans and Jicarillas (Opler 1942:3).

        In the versions in which the older children of White Painted Lady are killed, we have perhaps a reflection of the favoritism of Apaches for the youngest child. In the version in which Killer Of Enemies and Child Of The Water are twins and only latter survives, we have a reflection of the aboriginal killing of one twin. We see also the effects of the splitting mechanism of the infantile ego, but with a reversal of the good- and bad-mother introjects, now presented as bad and good babies.

CHAPTER VI

1.   This chapter was written in collaboration with Ruth M. Boyer.

2.   In this exposition of the uses which the Chiricahuas and Mescaleros make of the lore of the bat, we have presented all of their known oral literature in which Bat is a character and a small portion of the traditional literature of some other Southern Athabascan peoples. Those latter groups, like these Apaches, have common Nor-

thern Athabascan progenitors, and their socialization practices, basically similar to those of the Chiricahuas and Mescaleros, have created similar dominant intra-psychic conflicts with which they must cope. However, the reader who is not sophisticated in the study of folklore might get the erroneous impression that bat lore is specific to the Southern Athabascans and perhaps arose among them as a means to help them resolve the intrapsychic conflicts which Devereux (1956) called their ethnic unconscious. Cognate versions of the bat tales are widespread.

Each narrative detail mentioned in "Apache Lore of the Bat" is to be found in the oral literature of many other American Indian peoples and in much more of the folklore of the world (Dundes 1967a). Here we shall present but a small sample of the relevant literature.

The basic tale concerns an individual who is marooned through either having been carrried to an eagle's or a thunderbird's nest as food for the children of the big birds, or having been placed on or having voluntarily climbed onto a miraculously growing or rising rock. [Thompson (1955-1958) has given this motif the number B 31.1, Roc.] The unfortunate person or his equivalent is always rescued.

As we have seen, among the Chiricahuas and Mescaleros the equivalent of the marooned and rescued character is Coyote; among the Jicarillas it is the culture hero *jonayaiyin* (Russell 1898:257-258; Wherry 1968). In a "Mojave-Apache" version, "Little Baby Jesus" is the protagonist (Gould 1921). In a Ute story, the hero is Duck (Kroeber 1901:272-274), and in one from the Southern Utes he is Frost (Lowie 1924a:53-54). Among the Poncas, the protagonist is Rabbit (Dorsey 1890:30-31), and among the Winnebagos he is Hare (Radin 1948:94-95, 142-144).

As the protagonist varies, so does his rescuer. Thompson (1929:318, n.151) summarized the prototypical tale as follows: "The hero is carried to a cliff by a giant bird. Here, with the help of the young birds, he kills the giant bird. With the help of Bat he reaches the ground. This compound motif is common in the Southwest, on the plains, and the plateaus." He gave the motif number B 542.1.2 to the variant of the Roc story in which Bat is the rescuer, as he or she is among the "Mojave-Apaches," the Yavupa: (Gifford 1933:406-407), the Ute, the Zuni (Benedict 1935, 1:56-58), the Yokuts (Gayton and Newman 1940:75-78) and many other the first story, the "key-myth," of Levi-Strauss' (1964) *The Raw and The Cooked.* as a means of rescuing the protagonist, but in one Yokuts tale, after Measuring Worm and Lizard have failed in their efforts to save Eagle, Eagle calls on his maternal uncle, Bat, to try. "Bat demurred, but agreed to try. He folded his penis on himself and went. He reached Eagle, wrapped him in his penis, and safely brought him down" (Gayton and Newman 1940:77).

Among Central California Indian Groups, Measuring Worm and Lizard are sometimes the rescuers, and among the Zuni the ground squirrel stars (Stevenson 1894:47-48). But let us leave North America.

Dundes (1976a) finds one of the most astonishing parallels of all to the basic tale to be the narrative "The Macaws and Their Nest," of the Brazilian Bororo — which is the first story, the "key-myth," of Levi-Strauss' (1964) The Raw and The Cooked. In that version of the basic tale, the father orders his son to capture macaws which nest high on a cliff. He provides a pole, by means of which the son ascends and then he removes it, leaving the boy stranded. The son eventually avenges the wrong done him by donning false antlers and impaling his father on the horns (1964:35-37). To quote Dundes: "The son who originally rose on the erection of his father's 'pole,' that is, served as the victim of phallic aggression, succeeds in turning the tables by penetrating the father in the end! (pun intended)." In this key myth, the protagonist's rescuer is a jaguar, who commands the boy to jump and then catches him either in his paws or on his back.

CHAPTER VIII

1 .   Gill has recently considered the color of Navajo ritual symbolism and commented
      particularly on the methods of Reichard (1950), Wyman (1970), Lamphere (1969)
      and Turner (1966). Gill's (1975:362) last sentence warrants citation here: "Finally,
      upon this consideration of color symbolism, it is clear that the meaning of color,
      when found in the context of religious acts, cannot be fully understood if considered
      as an element in a complex system of human communication."

BIBLIOGRAPHY

Aarne, Antti 1913 Leitfaden der vergleichenden Marchenforschung. FF Communications No. 13 Hamina

Abraham, Karl 1909 Dreams and Myths. A Study in Folk Psychiatry. In: *Clinical papers and Essays on Psychoanalysis,* 2:149-209. New York: Basic Books, 1955.

Abraham, Karl 1912 Amenhotep IV: A Psychoanalytical Contribution Towards the Understanding of His Personality and of the Monotheistic Cult of Aton. In: *Clinical Essays and Papers on Psychoanalysis,* 2:262-290. New York: Basic Books, 1955.

Abraham, Karl 1922 The Spider as a Dream Symbol. *In: Selected Papers on Psychoanalysis,* pp. 326-332. London: Hogarth Press, 1948.

Abraham, Karl 1924 The Influence of Oral Eroticism on Character Formation. In: *Selected Papers on Psychoanalysis,* pp. 393-406. London: Hogarth Press, 1948.

Altman, Leon L. 1969 *The Dream in Psychoanalysis.* New York: International Universities Press.

Angulo, Jaime de 1973 *Coyote Man and Old Man Loon.* San Francisco: Turtle Island Foundation.

Arieti, Silvano 1948 Special Logic of Schizophrenia and Other Types of Autistic Thought. *Psychiatry,* 11:325-338.

Arlow, Jacob A. 1951 The Consecration of the Prophet. *Psychoanalytic Quarterly,* 20:374-397.

Arlow, Jacob A. 1961 Ego Psychology and the Study of Mythology. *Journal of The American Psychoanalytic Association,* 9:371-393.

Arlow, Jacob A. 1976 Contribution to "Psychoanalysis, Folklore and Socialization Processes," Panel Discussion, Annual Meeting of the American Psychoanalytic Association, Baltimore, May.

Arlow, Jacob A. and Brenner, Charles 1964 *Psychoanalytic Concepts and the Structural Theory.* New York: International Universities Press.

Atkinson, J. J. 1903 *Primal Law.* London: Longmans, Green.

Balint, Michael 1959 *Thrills and Regressions.* New York: International Universities Press.

Balter, Leon 1969 The Mother as Source of Power. A Psychoanalytic Study of Three Greek Myths. *Psychoanalytic Quarterly,* 38:217-274.

Barnouw, Victor 1949 The Phantasy World of a Chippewa Woman. *Psychiatry,* 12:67-76.

Barnouw, Victor 1955 A Psychological Interpretation of a Chippewa Origin Legend. *Journal of American Folklore,* 68:73-85, 211-223, 341-355.

Bascom, William 1953 Folklore and Anthropology. *Journal of American Folklore,* 66:283-290.

Bascom, William 1954 Four Functions of Folklore. *Journal of American Folklore,* 66:333-349.

Basehart, Harry W. 1959 *Chiricahua Apache Subsistence and Socio-Political Organization.* The University of New Mexico Mescalero-Chiricahua Land Project. Mimeographed.

Basehart, Harry W. 1960 *Mescalero Apache Subsistence Patterns and Socio-Political Organization.* University of New Mexico Mescalero-Chiricahua Land Claims Project. Mimeographed.

Benedict, Ruth 1935 *Zuni Mythology.* 2 vols. New York: Columbia University Press.

Benedict, Ruth 1949 Child Rearing in Certain European Countries. *American Journal of Orthopsychiatry,* 19:342-350.

Bettelheim, Bruno 1954 *Symbolic Wounds. Puberty Rites and the Envious Male.* Glencoe, Ill.: Free Press; London: Thames and Hudson.

Bettelheim, Bruno 1976 *The Uses of Enchantment. The Meanings and Importance of Fairy Tales.* New York: Knopf.

Bleuler, Eugene 1911 *Dementia Praecox, or the Group of Schizophrenias.* New York: International Universities Press, 1950.

Boas, Franz 1898 Introduction to Teit, James. *Traditions of the Thompson River Indians of British Columbia.* Memoirs of the American Folklore Society, Vol. 7.

Boas, Franz 1911 *Handbook of American Indian Languages.* Pt. 1. Washington: U.S. Government Printing Office.

Boas, Franz 1914 Mythology and Folk-tales of the North American Indians. In: *Race, Language and Culture,* pp. 451-490. New York: Macmillan, 1948.

Bourke, John G. 1890 Notes on Apache Mythology. *Journal of American Folklore,* 3:209-212.

Bourke, John G. 1892 *The Medicine-Men of the Apache.* Ninth Annual Report, Bureau of American Ethnology.

Boyer, L. Bryce 1956 On Maternal Overstimulation and Ego Defects. *The Psychoanalytic Study of the Child,* 11:236-256. Eds.: Eissler, Ruth S., Freud, Anna, Hartmann, Heinz and Kris, Ernst. New York: International Universities Press.

Boyer, L. Bryce 1961 Notes on the Personality Structure of a North American Indian Shaman. *Journal of the Hillside Hospital.,* 10:14-33.

Boyer, L. Bryce 1962 Remarks on the Personality of Shamans, with Special Reference to the Apaches of the Mescalero Indian Reservation. *The Psychoanalytic Study of Society,* 2:233-254. Eds.: Muensterberger, Warner and Axelrad, Sidney. New York: International Universities Press.

Boyer, L. Bryce 1964 An Example of Legend Distortion from the Apaches of the Mescalero Indian Reservation. *Journal of American Folklore,* 77:118-142.

Boyer, L. Bryce 1964a Psychological Problems of a Group of Apaches: Alcoholic Hallucinosis and Latent Homosexuality Among Typical Men. *The Psychoanalytic Study of Society,* 3:203-277. Eds.: Muensterberger, Warner and Axelrad, Sidney. New York: International Universities Press.

Boyer, L. Bryce 1975 The Man Who Turned into a Water Monster: A Psychoanalytic Contribution to Folklore. *The Psychoanalytic Study of Society,* 6:100-133. Eds.: Muensterberger, Warner and Esman, Aaron H. New York: International Universities Press.

Boyer, L. Bryce 1976 Anthropology and Psychoanalysis. *International Encyclopedia of Neurology, Psychiatry, Psychoanalysis and Psychology.* Ed.: Benjamin B. Wolman. New York: Van Nostrand Reinhold Co. and Aesculapius Publ.

Boyer, L. Bryce and Boyer, Ruth M. 1967 Some Influences of Acculturation on the Personality Traits of the Old People of the Mescalero and Chiricahua Apache. *The Psychoanalytic Study of Society,* 4:170-184. Eds.: Muensterberger, Warner and Axelrad, Sidney. New York: International Universities Press.

Boyer, L. Bryce and Boyer, Ruth M. 1967a A Combined Anthropological and Psychoanalytic Contribution to Folklore. *Psychopathologie Africaine,* 3:333-372.

Boyer, L. Bryce and Boyer Ruth M. 1972 Effects of Acculturation on the Vicissitudes of the Aggressive Drive among the Apaches of the Mescalero Indian Reservation. *The Psychoanalytic Study of Society,* 5:40-82. Eds.: Muensterberger, Warner and Esman, Aaron H. New York: International Universities Press.

Boyer, L. Bryce and Boyer Ruth M. 1976 Prolonged Adolescence and Early Identification: A Cross-Cultural Study. *The Psychoanalytic Study of Society,* 7:95-106. Eds.: Muensterberger, Werner, Esman, Aaron H. and Boyer, L. Bryce. New Haven and

London: Yale University Press.

Boyer, L. Bryce and Boyer, Ruth M. 1978 On the Roles of The Mountain Spirits and Their Sacred Clowns in Chiricahua and Mescalero Apache Ritual and Folklore. *Western Folklore*, in press.

Boyer, L. Bryce, Boyer, Ruth M. and Basehart, Harry W. 1973 Shamanism and Peyote Use among the Apaches of the Mescalero Indian Reservation. In: *Hallucinogens and Shamanism*, pp. 53-66. Ed.: Harner, Michael J. New York: Oxford University Press.

Boyer, L. Bryce, Boyer, Ruth M., Brawer, Florence B., Kawai, Hayao and Klopfer, Bruno 1964 Apache Age Groups. *Journal of Projective Techniques and Personality Assessment*, 28-397-402.

Boyer, L. Bryce, Boyer, Ruth M., Kawai, Hayao and Klopfer, Bruno 1967 Apache "Learners" and "Nonlearners." *Journal of Projective Techniques and Personality Assessment*, 31:22-29.

Boyer, L. Bryce, Boyer, Ruth M., Klopfer, Bruno and Scheiner, Suzanne B. 1968 Apache "Learners" and "Nonlearners." II Quantitative Signs of Influential Adults. *Journal of Projective Techniques and Personality Assessment*, 32:146-159.

Boyer, L. Bryce and Giovacchini, Peter L. 1967 *Psychoanalytic Treatment of Schizophrenic and Characterological Disorders.* New York: Science House Press.

Boyer, L. Bryce, Klopfer, Bruno Brawer, Florence B. and Kawai, Hayao 1964 Comparisons of the Shamans and Pseudoshamans of the Mescalero Indian Reservation: A Rorschach Study. *Journal of Projective Techniques and Personality Development Assessment*, 28:173-180.

Boyer, Ruth M. 1962 *Social Structure and Socialization Among the Apache of the Mescalero Indian Reservation.* Unpublished doctoral dissertation, University of California, Berkeley.

Boyer, Ruth M. 1964 The Matrifocal Family Among the Mescalero: Additional Data. *American Anthropologist*, 66:593-602.

Boyer, Ruth M. 1972 A Mescalero Apache Tale: The Bat and the Flood. *Western Folklore*, 31:189-197.

Boyer, Ruth M. and Gayton, Narcissus N. D. *Narcissus: A Chiricahua Woman.* Unpublished book.

Bradley, Noel 1965 The Vulture as a Mother-Symbol: A Note on Freud's *Leonardo. American Imago*, 22:47-56.

Bradley, Noel 1973 Notes on Theory-Making, on Scotoma of the Nipples and on the Bee as Nipple. *International Journal of Psycho-Analysis*, 54:301-314.

Brenner, Charles 1974 *An Elementary Textbook of Psychoanalysis.* Revised and expanded edition. New York: International Universities Press.

Breuer, Josef and Freud, Sigmund. 1895 Studies on Hysteria. *Standard Edition*, 1955, 2:1-305. London: Hogarth Press.

Briggs, Jean L. 1972 The Issues of Autonomy and Aggression in the Three-Year-Old: The Utku Eskimo Case. *Seminars in Psychiatry*, 4:317-329.

Briggs, Katherine M. 1970 *A Dictionary of British Folk Tales.* 4 vols. Bloomington: University of Indiana Press.

Brinton, Daniel G. 1868 *Myths of the New World.* New York. Cited by Bourke, John G. 1892 *The Medicine-Men of the Apache*, pp. 593-594. Ninth Annual Report, Bureau of American Ethnology.

Brinton, Daniel G. 1896 *An Ethnologist's View of History.* Philadelphia.

Brinton, Daniel G. 1899 *Religions of Primitive Peoples.* New York: G. P. Putnam's Sons.

Brody, Sylvia and Axelrad, Sidney 1970 *Anxiety and Ego Formation in Infancy.* New York: International Universities Press.

Brunvand, Jan Harold 1968 *The Study of American Folklore.* New York: Norton.

Burridge, Kenelm O. L. 1967 Levi-Strauss and Myth. In: *The Structural Study of Myth and*

Totemism, pp. 91-115. Ed.: Leach, Edmund R. London: Tavistock.

Campbell, Joseph 1959 *The Masks of God: Primitive Mythology.* New York: Viking.

Campbell, Joseph and Abadie, M. J. 1975 *The Mythic Image.* Princeton: Princeton University Press.

Carvalho-Neto, Paulo de 1956 *Folklore y Psicoanalysis.* Mexico City: Editorial Joaquin Mortiz.

Carvalho-Neto, Paulo de 1956 *Folklore y Psicoanalisis.* Mexico City: Editorial Joaquin 5:5-60.

Carvalho-Neto, Paulo de 1961 *Folklore del Paraguay. Sistemica, Analitica.* Quito: Editorial Universitaria.

Caudill, William 1949 Psychological Characteristics of Acculturated Objibwa Children. *American Anthropologist,* 51:409-427.

Chittenden, Hiram M. 1902 *A History of the American Fur Trade of the Far West,* Vol. 2. Stanford: Academic Reprints, 1954.

Chowning, Ann 1962 Raven Myths in Northwestern North America and Northeastern Asia. *Arctic Anthropology,* 1:1-5.

Clements, William W. and Mohr, Duane V. 1961 Chronic Subdural Hematomas in Infants. Paper presented before the Annual U.S. Public Health Service National Clinical Meeting, Lexington, Kentucky, April.

Cremony, J. O. 1968 The Apache Race. *Overland Monthly,* 1:201-209.

Darwin, Charles 1901 *The Descent of Man and Selection in Relation to Sex.* London: John L. Murray.

Davidson, Ronald H. and Day, Richard 1974 *Symbol and Realization: A Contribution to the Study of Magic and Healing.* Research Monograph No. 12. Center for South and Southeast Asian Studies. University of California, Berkeley.

Day, Richard, Boyer, L. Bryce and DeVos, George 1975 Two Styles of Ego Development: A Cross-Cultural, Longitudinal Comparison of Apache and Anglo School Children. *Ethos,* 3:345-379.

DeGubernatis, Angelo 1872. *Zoological Mythology.* London: Trubner.

deMause, Lloyd 1976 The Formation of the American Personality Through Psychospeciation. *The Journal of Psychohistory,* 4:1:30.

Dennis, Wayne and Dennis, Marsena G. 1940 The Effect of Cradling Practices upon the Onset of Walking in Hopi Children. *Journal of Genetic Psychology,* 56:77-86.

Deslongchamps, Loiseleur 1838 *Essai Sur Les Fables Indiennes.* Paris.

Devereux, George 1951 *Reality and Dream: Psychotherapy of a Plains Indian.* New York: International Universities Press.

Devereux, George 1953 Why Oedipus Killed Laius: A Note on the Complementary Oedipus Complex in Greek Drama. *International Journal of Psycho-Analysis,* 34:132-141.

Devereux, George 1955 A Counteroedipal Episode in Homer's *Iliad. Bulletin of the Philadelphia Association of Psychoanalysis,* 4:90-97.

Devereux, George 1956 Normal and Abnormal: The Key Problem of Psychiatric Anthropology. In: *Some Uses of Anthropology, Theoretical and Applied,* pp. 23-48. Washington. Anthropological Society of Washington.

Devereux, George and LaBarre Weston 1961 Art and Mythology. In: *Studying Personality Cross-Culturally,* pp. 361-403. Ed.: Kaplan, Bert. Evanston, Ill. and Elmsford, New York: Row, Peterson & Co.

DeVos, George A. 1961 Symbolic Analysis in the Cross-Cultural Study of Personality. In: *Studying Personality Cross-Culturally,* pp. 599-634. Ed.: Kaplan, Bert. Evanston, Ill. and Elmsford, New York: Row, Peterson & Co.

DeVos, George A. 1975 The Dangers of Pure Theory in Social Anthropology. *Ethos,* 3:77-91.

Dobzhansky, Theodosius A. 1962 *Mankind Evolving: The Evolution of Human Species.* New Haven and London: Yale University Press.

Dorsey, James O. 1890 *The Cegiha Language.* Contributions to North American Ethnology VI. Washington: U.S. Government Printing Office.

Dorson, Richard M. 1960 Theories of Myths and the Folklorist. *Daedalus,* 88:280-290.

Dorson, Richard M. 1963 Current Folklore Theories. *Current Anthropology,* 4:93-112.

Ducey, Charles 1977 The Shaman's Dream Journey: Psychoanalytic and Structural Complementarity in Myth Interpretation. *The Psychoanalytic Study of Society,* Vol. 8, in press. Eds.: Muensterberger, Werner, Esman, Aaron H., and Boyer, L. Bryce. New Haven and London: Yale University Press.

Dundes, Alan 1962 Earth-Diver: Creation of the Mythopoeic Male. *American Anthropologist,* 64:1032-1051.

Dundes, Alan (Ed.) 1965 *The Study of Folklore.* Englewood Cliffs, N.J.: Prentice-Hall.

Dundes, Alan 1967 North American Indian Folklore Studies. *Journal de la Societe des Americanistes,* 36:53-79.

Dundes, Alan 1976 A Psychoanalytic Study of the Bullroarer. *Man,* 11:220-238.

Dundes, Alan 1976a Contribution to "Psychoanalysis, Folklore and Socialization Processes," Panel Discussion, Annual Meeting of the American Psychoanalytic Association, Baltimore, May.

Durkheim, Emile 1915 *The Elementary Forms of the Religious Life, A Study in Religious Sociology.* London: Allen & Unwin; New York: Macmillan.

Durkheim, Emile 1927 *The Rules of Sociological Method.* Ed.: Catlin, G.E.G. Chicago University Press, 1938.

Eggan, Dorothy 1955 The Personal Use of Myth in Dreams. *Journal of American Folklore,* 68:445-453.

Eggan, Dorothy 1961 Dream Analysis. In: *Studying Personality Cross-Culturally,* pp. 551-578. Ed.: Kaplan, Bert. Evanston, Ill. and Elmsford, New York: Row, Peterson & Co.

Ekeh, Peter 1976 Benin and Thebes: Elementary Forms of Civilization. *The Psychoanalytic Study of Society,* 7:65-93. Eds.: Muensterberger, Werner, Esman, Aaron, and Boyer, L. Bryce. New Haven and London: Yale University Press.

Eliade, Mircea 1951 *Shamanism: Archaic Techniques of Ecstasy.* New York: Bollingen Foundation, 1964.

Emrich, Duncan 1946 "Folklore": William John Thoms. *California Folklore Quarterly,* 5:355-374.

Erikson, Erik H. 1939 Observations on Sioux Education. *Journal of Psychology,* 7:101-156.

Erikson, Erik H. 1943 Observations on the Yurok: Childhood and World Image. *University of California Publications in American Archaeology and Ethnology,* 35:257-301.

Erikson, Erik H. 1945 Childhood and Tradition in Two American Indian Tribes. *The Psychoanalytic Study of the Child,* 1:319-350. Ed.: Freud, Anna, Hartmann, Heinz and Kris, Ernst. New York: International Universities Press.

Erikson, Erik H. 1950 *Childhood and Society.* New York: Norton.

Erikson, Erik H. 1959 Identity and the Life Cycle. *Psychological Issues,* Vol. 1 New York: International Universities Press.

Erikson, Erik H. 1966 Ontogeny of Ritualization. In: *Psychoanalysis, A General Psychology. Essays in Honor of Heinz Hartmann,* pp. 601-621. Eds.: Loewenstein, Rudolph M., Newman, Lottie, Schur, Max and Solnit, Albert J. New York: International Universities Press.

Etkin, William (Ed.) 1964 *Social Behavior and Organization Among Vertebrates.* Chicago and London: University of Chicago Press.

Evans, John T. 1955 Case Report of an Amateur Artist: A Psycho-Pathological Report. *Journal of Nervous and Mental Diseases,* 121:480-485.

Fenichel, Otto 1927 Examples of Dream Analysis. In: *Collected Papers,* pp. 123-127. 1st series. London: Routledge & Kegan Paul, 1954.

Ferenczi, Sandor 1913 A Little Chanticleer. In: *Sex in Psychoanalysis,* pp. 240-252. New York: Basic Books, 1950.

Firth, Raymond 1934 The Meanings of Dreams in Tikopia, In: *Essays Presented to C. G. Seligman,* pp. 63-74. Evans-Pritchard, E. E., Firth, Raymond, Malinowski, Bruno and Schapera, Isaac. London: Kegan Paul, Trench, Trubner, Ltd.

Fischer, J. L. 1963 The Sociopsychological Analysis of Folktales. *Current Anthropology,* 4:239-295.

Fliess, Robert 1957 *Erotogeneity and Libido. Addenda to the Theory of the Psychosexual Development of the Human.* New York: International Universities Press.

Fortes, Meyer 1959 *Oedipus and Job in West African Religion.* London: Cambridge University Press.

Foulks, Edward F., Freeman, Daniel M.A. and Freeman, Patricia 1977 Pre-Oedipal Dynamics in a Case of Arctic Hysteria. *The Psychoanalytic Study of Society.* Vol. 8. Eds.: Muensterberger, Werner, Esman, Aaron H. and Boyer, L. Bryce. New Haven and London: Yale University Press.

Fox, Robin 1967 *Totem and Taboo* Reconsidered. In: *The Structural Study of Myth and Totemism,* pp. 161-178. Ed.: Leach, Edmund R. London: Tavistock.

Frazer, James 1894 *The Golden Bough.* New York: Macmillan Co., 2 vols.

Frazer, James 1910 *Totemism and Exogamy.* London: Macmillan, 4 vols.

Freeman, Daniel M.A. 1968 Adolescent Crises of the Kiowa-Apache Indian Male. In: *Minority Group Adolescents in the United States,* pp. 157-204. Ed.: Brody, Eugene B. Baltimore: Williams and Wilkins.

Freeman, Daniel M.A. 1976 Contribution to "Psychoanalysis, Folklore and Socialization Processes," Panel Discussion, Annual Meeting of the American Psychoanalytic Association, Baltimore, May.

Freeman, Daniel M.A. (Reporter) 1977 Panel Report: Psychoanalysis, Folklore and Processes of Socialization. *Journal of the American Psychoanalytic Association,* 25:235-252.

Freeman, Daniel M.A., Foulks, Edward F. and Freeman, Patricia 1976 Ghost Sickness and Superego Development in the Kiowa Apache Male. *The Psychoanalytic Study of Society,* 7:123-172. Eds., Muensterberger, Werner, Esman, Aaron H. and Boyer, L. Bryce. New Haven and London: Yale University Press.

Freeman, Derek 1967 *Totem and Taboo:* A Reappraisal. *The Psychoanalytic Study of Society,* 4:9-33. Eds.: Muensterberger, Warner and Esman, Aaron H. New York: International Universities Press.

Freeman, Derek 1968 Thunder, Blood and the Nicknaming of God's Creatures. *Psychoanalytic Quarterly,* 37:353-399.

Freeman, Lucy 1972 *The Story of Anna O.* New York: Walker and Company.

French, Thomas M. 1952 *The Interpretation of Behavior.* Vol. I. *Basic Postulates.* Chicago: University of Chicago Press.

Freud, Anna 1936 *The Ego and the Mechanisms of Defense.* New York: International Universities Press, 1946.

Freud, Anna 1965 *Normality and Pathology in Childhood.* New York: International Universities Press.

Freud, Sigmund 1900 The Interpretation of Dreams. *Standard Edition,* 1953. Vols. IV and V. London: Hogarth Press.

Freud, Sigmund 1908 Hysterical Phantasies and Their Relation to Bisexuality. *Standard Edition,* 1959, 9:159-166. London: Hogarth Press.

Freud, Sigmund 1908a Character and Anal Eroticism. *Standard Edition,* 1959, 9:167-176. London: Hogarth Press.

Freud, Sigmund 1909 Analysis of a Phobia in a Five-Year-Old Boy. *Standard Edition,* 1955, 10:5-147.

Freud, Sigmund 1911 Formulations of Two Principles of Mental Functioning. *Standard Edition,* 1958, 12:213-226. London: Hogarth Press.

Freud, Sigmund 1913 Totem and Taboo. *Standard Edition,* 1955, 13:1-161. London: Hogarth Press.

Freud, Sigmund 1913a The Occurrence in Dreams of Material from Fairy Tales. *Standard Edition,* 1958, 12:279-288.

Freud, Sigmund 1915 The Unconscious. *Standard Edition,* 1957, 14:159-215. London: Hogarth Press.

Freud, Sigmund 1916 A Connection between a Symbol and a Symptom. *Standard Edition,* 1957, 14:339-340. London: Hogarth Press.

Freud, Sigmund 1917 Mourning and Melancholia. *Standard Edition,* 1957, 14:237-258. London: Hogarth Press.

Freud, Sigmund 1920 Beyond the Pleasure Principle. *Standard Edition,* 1955, 18:7-66. London: Hogarth Press.

Freud, Sigmund 1923 The Ego and the Id. *Standard Edition,* 1961, 19:13-66. London: Hogarth Press.

Freud, Sigmund 1939 Moses and Monotheism. *Standard Edition,* 1964, 23:7-137. London: Hogarth Press.

Freud, Sigmund and Oppenheim, D.E. 1958 *Dreams in Folklore.* New York: International Universities Press.

Fromm, Erich 1951 *The Forgotten Language.* New York: Rhinehart.

Garza-Guerrero, A. Cesar 1974 Culture-Shock: Its Mourning and the Vicissitudes of Identity. *Journal of the American Psychoanalytic Association,* 22:408-429.

Gayton, A.H. and Newman, Stanley S. 1940 Yokuts and Western Mono Myths. *Anthropological Records,* 5:1-109.

Gifford, E. W. 1933 Northeastern and Western Yavapai Myths. *Journal of American Folklore,* 46:347-415.

Gill, Sam D. 1975 The Color of Navajo Ritual Symbolism: An Evaluation of Method. *Journal of Anthropological Research,* 31:350-363.

Goddard, Pliny E. 1916 The Masked Dancers of the Apache. In: *The Holmes Anniversary Volume,* pp. 132-136. Washington, D.C.

Bin Gorion, Mica J. (Ed.) 1913 *Die Sagen der Juden.* Frankfurt am Main: Rutter and Loening.

Gould, M.K. 1921 Two Legends of the Mojave-Apache. *Journal of American Folklore,* 34:319-320.

Graber, Gustav Hans 1925 Die Schwarze Spinne: Menschheitsentwicklung nach Jeremiah Gotthelfs gleichnamer Novelle, dargestellt unter besonderer Berucksichtigung der Rolle der Frau. *Imago,* 11:254-334.

Greenacre, Phyllis 1947 Vision, Headache and Halo. In: *Trauma, Growth and Personality,* pp. 132-148. New York: Norton, 1952.

Grimm, Jacob L.K. 1884 *Household Tales.* London.

Grimm, Jacob L.K. 1897 *German Household Tales.* Boston and New York.

Grimm, Whilhelm 1856 *Kinder- und Hausmarchen.* Leipzig: Reklam.

Griswold, Gillett 1977 The Fort Sill Apache. Their Vital Statistics, Tribal Origins, Antecedents. U.S. Army Field Artillery and Fort Sill Museum. Fort Sill, Oklahoma (mimeographed).

Grunberger, Bela 1962 L'antisemite devant l'Oedipe. *Revue Francaise de Psychanalyse,* 26:655-674.

Gunderson, John and Kolb, Jonathan E. 1978 Discriminating Features of Borderline tients. *American Journal of Psychiatry,* 135;792-796.

Hall, E.T., Jr. 1944 Recent Clues to Athabascan Prehistory in the Southwest. *American Anthropologist,* 46:98-106.

Hallowell, A. Irving 1936 Psychic Stress and Culture Patterns. *American Journal of Psychiatry,* 92:1291-1310.

Hallowell, A. Irving 1941 The Social Function of Anxiety in a Primitive Society. *American Sociological Review,* 7:869-881.

Harrington, M.R. 1912 The Devil Dance of the Apaches. *Museum Journal* (Philadelphia), 8:6-9.

Hartmann, Heinz 1939 *Ego Psychology and the Problem of Adaptation.* New York: International Universities Press, 1958.

Hartmann, Heinz 1950 Psychoanalysis and Developmental Psychology. *The Psychoanalytic Study of the Child,* 5:7-17. Eds.: Eissler, Ruth S., Freud, Anna, Hartmann, Heinz and Kris, Ernst. New York: International Universities Press.

Hartmann, Heinz 1951 Technical Implications of Ego Psychology. *Psychoanalytic Quarterly,* 20:31-43.

Hartmann, Heinz 1952 The Mutual Influences in the Development of Ego and Id. *The Psychoanalytic Study of the Child,* 7:9-30. Eds.: Eissler, Ruth S., Freud, Anna, Hartmann, Heinz and Kris, Ernst. New York: International Universities Press.

Hartmann, Heinz 1953 Contributions of the Metapsychology of Schizophrenia. *The Psychoanalytic Study of the Child,* 8:177-198. Eds.: Eissler, Ruth S., Freud, Anna, Hartmann, Heinz and Kris, Ernst. New York: International Universities Press.

Henry, Jules N.D. The Cult of Silas John. Unpublished manuscript.

Herskovitz, Melville 1934 Freudian Mechanisms in Primitive Negro Psychology. In: *Essays Presented to C.G. Seligman,* pp. 75-84. Eds.: Evans-Pritchard, E.E., Firth, Raymond, Malinowski, Bruno and Schapera, Issac. London: Kegan Paul, Trench, Trubner, Ltd.

Hippler, Arthur E., Boyer, L. Bryce and Boyer, Ruth M. 1975 The Psychocultural Significance of the Alaska Athabascan Potlatch Ceremony. *The Psychoanalytic Study of Society,* 6:204-234. Eds.: Muensterberger, Warner and Esman, Aaron H. New York: International Universities Press.

Hippler, Arthur E., Boyer, L. Bryce and Boyer, Ruth M. 1976 The Subarctic Athabascans of Alaska: The Ecological Grounding of Certain Cultural Personality Characteristics. *The Psychoanalytic Study of Society,* 7:293-329. Eds.: Muensterberger, Werner, Esman, Aaron H. and Boyer, L. Bryce. New Haven and London: Yale University Press.

Hippler, Arthur E., Boyer, L. Bryce, Boyer, Ruth M., Day, Richard and DeVos, George A. N.D. *A Psychoethnography of the Tanaina of Alaska.* Unpublished book.

Hippler, Arthur E., Boyer, L. Bryce, Boyer, Ruth M., Day, Richard and DeVos. George A. N.D.a *A Psychoethnography of the Upper Tanana of Alaska.* Unpublished book.

Hippler, Arthur E. and Conn, Stephen 1972 Traditional Athabascan Law Ways and their Relationship to Contemporary Problems of Bush Justice. *Occasional Publications.* Fairbanks: Institute of Social, Economic and Government Research.

Hippler, Arthur E. and Wood, John R. 1974 *The Subarctic Athabascans: A Selected Annotated Bibliography.* Fairbanks: Institute of Social, Economic and Government Research.

Hoffer, Willi 1949 Mouth, Hand and Ego Integration. *The Psychoanalytic Study of the Child,* 3-4:49-56. Eds.: Freud, Anna, Hartmann, Heinz and Kris, Ernst. New York International Universities Press.

Hoijer, Harry 1938 The Southern Athabascan Language. *American Anthropologist,* 40:75-87.

Hoijer, Harry 1938a *Chiricahua and Mescalero Texts.* Chicago: University of Chicago Press.

Honigmann, John 1961 The Interpretation of Dreams in Anthropological Fieldwork A Case Study. In: *Studying Personality Cross-Culturally*, pp. 579-586. Ed.: Kaplan, Bert. Evanston, Ill. and Elmsford, New York: Row, Peterson & Co.

Horgan, Paul 1954 *Great River. The Rio Grande in North American History.* New York: Holt, Rinehart, Winston, 1971.

Huscher, Harold A. and Huscher, Betty H. 1942 Athabascan Migration Via the Intramontane Region. *American Antiquity,* 8:80-88.

Ichon, Alain 1969 *La Religion des Totonaques de la Sierra.* Paris: Centre National de la Recherche Scientifique.

Jacob, Peyton, Jr. 1976 Contribution to "Psychoanalysis, Folklore and Socialization Processes," Panel Discussion, Annual Meeting of the American Psychoanalytic Association, Baltimore, May.

Jacobs, Melville 1952 Psychological Inferences from a Chinook Myth. *Journal of American Folklore,* 65:121-137.

Jacobs, Melville 1959 Folklore. In: *The Anthropology of Franz Boas,* pp. 119-138. Ed.: Walter Goldschmidt. *American Anthropologist* 61, No. 5, pt. 2, Memoirs of the American Anthropological Association, No. 89.

Jacobs, Melville 1960 *The People Are Coming Soon,* Seattle: University of Washington Press.

Johnson, Adelaide and Szurek, Stanley 1954 Etiology of Antisocial Behavior in Delinquents and Psychopaths. *Journal of the Americal Medical Association,* 154:814-817.

Johnson, Lusita B. and Proskauer, Stephen 1974 Psychosis in a Prepubescent Navajo Girl. *Journal of the American Academy of Child Psychiatry.* 13:1-19.

Jones, Ernest 1914 The Madonna's Conception Through the Ear. In: *Essays in Applied Psychoanalysis. Essays in Folklore, Anthropology and Religion,* 2:266-357. London: Hogarth Press, 1951.

Jones, Ernest 1924 Mother-Right and Sexual Ignorance of Savages. In: *Essays in Applied Psychoanalysis. Essays in Folklore, Anthropology and Religion,* 2:145-173. London: Hogarth Press.

Jones, Ernest 1953 *The Life and Work of Sigmund Freud. 1856-1900. The Formative Years and the Great Discoveries.* Chapter II. New York: Basic Books.

Jung, Carl G. 1916 *Psychology of the Unconscious.* London: Kegan Paul.

Jung, Carl G. 1935 *The Integration of the Personality.* New York and Toronto: Farrar and Rinehart, 1939.

Kaplan, Bert 1962 Psychological Themes in Zuni Mythology and Zuni TAT's. *The Psychoanalytic Study of Society,* 2:255-262. Eds.: Muensterberger, Warner and Axelrad, Sidney. New York: International Universities Press.

Kardiner, Abram 1939 *The Individual and His Society.* New York: Columbia University Press.

Kardiner, Abram, Linton, Ralph, Dubois, Cora and West, James 1945 *The Psychological Frontiers of Society.* New York: Columbia University Press.

Kernberg, Otto F. 1972 Critique of the Kleinian School. In: *Tactics and Techniques in Psychoanalytic Therapy,* 1:62-93. Ed.: Giovacchini, Peter L. New York: Science House Press.

Kernberg, Otto F. 1975 *Borderline Conditions and Pathological Narcissism.* New York: Jason Aronson; Inc.

Kestenberg, Judith S. 1956 On the Development of Maternal Feelings in Early Childhood: Observations and Reflections. *The Psychoanalytic Study of the Child,* 11:257-291. Eds.: Eissler, Ruth D., Freud, Anna, Hartmann, Heinz and Kris, Ernst. New York: International Universities Press.

Khan, Masud R. 1962 The Role of Polymorph-perverse Body-experiences and Object-relations in Ego-integration. *British Journal of Medical Psychology, 35:245-261.*

Kilborne, Benjamin 1977 *Symboles Oniriques et Modeles Culturels: Le Reve et Son Interpretation au Maroc.* Unpublished doctoral dissertation, Universite de Paris.

Kilborne, Benjamin 1977 *Les Interpretation des Reves au Maroc.* Paris: La Pensee Sauvage.

Kilborne, Benjamin 1977A Interpretation des reves et attitudes envers l'autorite au Maroc. *Psychopathologie Africaine,* 13:71-79.

Klein, Melanie 1957 *Envy and Gratitude. A Study of Unconscious Sources.* London: Tavistock Publishers, Ltd. and New York: Basic Books.

Klopfer, Bruno and Boyer, L. Bryce 1961 Notes on the Personality Structure of a North American Indian Shaman: Roschach Interpretation. *Journal of Projective Techniques,* 25:170-178.

Kluckhohn, Clyde 1944 The Influence of Psychiatry on Anthropology in America During the Past One Hundred Years. In: *One Hundred Years of American Psychiatry,* pp. 589-617. Eds.: Hall, J.K., Zilboorg, Gregory and Bunker, Henry A. New York: Columbia University Press.

Kracke, Waud 1978 Dreaming in Kagwahiv: Dream Beliefs and Their Psychic Base in an Amazonian Indian Culture. *The Psychoanalytic Study of Society,* Vol. 8, in press. Eds.: Muensterberger, Werner, Esman, Aaron H. and Boyer, L. Bryce. New Haven and London: Yale University Press.

Kris, Ernst 1956 The Personal Myth: A Problem in Psychoanalytic Technique. *Journal of the American Psychoanalytic Association,* 4:653-681.

Kroeber, Alfred L. 1901 Ute Tales. *Journal of American Folklore,* 14:252-285.

Kroeber, Alfred L. 1920 *Totem and Taboo:* An Ethnologic Analysis. *American Anthropologist,* 22:48-55.

Kroeber, Alfred L. 1935 *Totem and Taboo* in Retrospect. *American Journal of Sociology,* 45:446-451.

Kubie, Lawrence S. 1950 Psychoanalysis and Healing by Faith. In: *Practical and Theoretical Aspects of Psychoanalysis,* pp. 145-152. New York: International Universities Press.

Kuhn, Adalbert 1843 *Markische Sagen and Marchen, Nebst Einem Anhange Von Gebrauchen und Aberglauben.* Berlin: G. Renner.

Kuhn, Adalbert 1845 *Zur Altesten Geschichte der Indogermanischen Volker.* Berlin: Nauck.

Kuhn, Adalbert 1859 *Die Herabkunst des Feuers und des Gottertranks.* 2nd enlarged edition. Gutersloch: C. Bertelsmann, 1866.

Kunstadter, Peter 1960 *Culture Change, Social Structure and Health Behavior: A Quantitative Study of Clinic Use Among the Apaches of the Mescalero Indian Reservation.* Unpublished doctoral dissertation, University of Michigan.

LaBarre, Weston 1947 Primitive Psychotherapy: Peyotism and Confession. *Journal of Abnormal and Social Psychology,* 42:294-309.

LaBarre, Weston 1958 The Influence of Freud on Anthropology. *American Imago,* 15:275-328.

LaBarre, Weston 1970 *The Ghost Dance. The Origins of Religion.* New York: Dell Publishing Co., 1972.

Lamphere, Louise 1969 Symbolic Elements in Navajo Ritual. *Southwest Journal of Anthropology,* 25:279-305.

Lang, Andrew 1901 *Custom and Myth.* London (new impression).

Lantenari, Vittorio 1960 *The Religions of the Oppressed.* London: McGibbon and Kee, and New York: Knopf.

Lantenari, Vittorio 1975 Dreams as Charismatic Significants: Their Bearing in the Rise of New Religious Movements. In: *Psychological Anthropology,* pp. 221-235. Ed.: Williams, Thomas R. The Hague and Paris: Mouton.

Lantis, Margaret 1953 Nunivak Eskimo Personality as Revealed in the Mythology. *Anthropological Papers of the University of Alaska,* 2:109-174.

Leach, Edmund R. 1958 Magical Hair. *Journal of the Royal Anthropology Institute,* 88(2):147-164.

Leach, Edmund R. 1970 *Claude Levi-Strauss.* New York: Viking.

Leach, Maria (Ed.) 1949-1950 *Standard Dictionary of Folklore, Mythology and Legend.* New York: Funk and Wagnalls. Two Vols.

Leighton, Dorothy and Kluckhohn, Clyde 1948 *Children of the People.* Cambridge: Harvard University Press.

Lessa, William A. 1956 Oedipus-Type Tales in Oceania. *Journal of American Folklore,* 69:63-73.

Lessa, William A. 1961 *Tales from Ulithi Atoll.* Folklore Studies No. 13. Berkeley and Los Angeles: University of California Press.

Levi-Strauss, Claude 1949 L'Analyse structurale en linguistique et en anthropologie. *Word,* 1:35-53.

Levi-Strauss, Claude 1955 *Triste Tropique.* New York: Criterion Books, 1961.

Levi-Strauss, Claude 1958 The Structural Study of Myth. In: *Myth: A Symposium.* Ed.: Seboek, T.A. Bloomington: University of Indiana Press.

Levi-Strauss, Claude 1962 *The Savage Mind.* Chicago: University of Chicago Press, 1966.

Levi-Strauss, Claude 1964 *The Raw and the Cooked. Introduction to a Science of Mythology.* New York: Harper Torchbooks, 1969.

Levi-Strauss, Claude 1967 *Structural Anthropology.* New York: Doubleday & Co.

Lewin, Bertram D. 1950 *The Psychoanalysis of Elation.* New York: Norton.

Lincoln, Jackson S. 1935 *The Dream in Primitive Cultures.* London: The Cresset Press.

Lommel, Andreas 1967 *Shamanism: The Beginnings of Art.* New York: McGraw-Hill Book Co.

Lowie, Robert H. 1924 *Primitive Religion.* New York: Liveright, 1952.

Lowie, Robert H. 1924a Shoshonean Tales. *Journal of American Folklore,* 37:1-242.

Lubart, Joseph M. 1970 *Psychodynamic Problems of Adaptation: Mackenzie Delta Eskimos.* Ottaw: Queen's Printer for Canada.

Lubart, Joseph M. 1976 The Mackenzie Delta Eskimos: Problems of Adaptation to Changing Social and Economic Conditions. *The Psychoanalytic Study of Society,* 7:331-357. Eds.: Muensterberger, Werner, Esman, Aaron H. and Boyer, L. Bryce. New Haven and London: Yale University Press.

MacLachlan, Bruce B. 1962 *The Mescalero Tribal Court: A Study of the Manifestation of a Concrete Judicial Institution.* Unpublished doctoral dissertation, University of Chicago.

Maeder, Alphonse E. 1909 Die Symbolik in Den Legenden, Marchen, Gerbrauchen und Traumen. Psychiatrisch-Neurologische Wochenschrift, Vol. 10, Reviewed by Jung, Carl G., *Jahrbuch fur Psychoanalytische und Psychopathologische Forschungen,* 1910, 2:376.

Mahler, Margaret S. 1968 *On Human Symbiosis and the Vicissitudes of Individation. Infantile Psychosis.* New York: International Universities Press.

Mahler, Margaret S., Pine, Fred and Bergman, Anni 1975 *The Psychological Birth of the Infant. Symbiosis and Individuation.* New York: Basic Books.

Mails, Thomas E. 1974 *The People Called Apache.* Englewood Cliffs, N.J.: Prentice-Hall.

Makarius, L. 1969 Le Mythe du "Trickster." *Revue de L'histoire des Religions,* 175:17-46.

Malinowski, Bruno 1927 *Sex and Repression in Savage Society.* London: Routledge and and Kegan Paul, 1953.

Malinowski, Bruno 1929 *The Sexual Lives of Savages.* London: Routledge and Kegan Paul, 1953.

Malinowski, Bruno 1935 *Coral Gardens and Their Magic.* New York: American Book Co.

Manheim, Ralph 1977 *Grimm's Tales for Young and Old. The Complete Stories.* Newly Translated. Garden City, N.Y.: Doubleday and Company, Inc.

Marmor, Judd 1953 Orality in the Hysterical Personality. *Journal of the American*

Psychoanalytic Association, 1:656-671.

Mason, Otis T. 1889 Cradles of the American Aborigines. Report of the U.S. National Museum, Smithsonian Institution, Washington: U.S. Government Printing Office.

McKinnon, Roger A. and Michels, Robert 1971 *The Clinical Interview in Clinical Practice.* Philadelphia, London, Toronto: W. B. Sanders Company.

Mead, Margaret 1930 An Ethnologist's Footnote to *Totem and Taboo. Psychoanalytic Review,* 17:297-304.

Mead, Margaret 1932 *Changing Culture of an Indian Tribe.* New York: Columbia University Press.

Mead, Margaret 1949 *Male and Female. A Study of the Sexes in a Changing World.* New York: Mentor Books, 1955.

Mead, Margaret 1954 The Swaddling Hypothesis: Its Reception. *American Anthropologist,* 56:395-409.

Mead, Margaret 1963 *Totem and Taboo* Reconsidered with Respect. *Bulletin of the Menninger Clinic,* 27:185-199.

Meissner, W.W. 1975 *The Paranoid Process.* New York: Jason Aronson, Inc.

Meissner, W.W. 1976 The Question of Consensus. *Contemporary Psychoanalysis,* 12:81-89.

Mellaart, J. 1963 Excavations at Catal Huyuk: Second Preliminary Report. *Anatolian Studies,* Vol. 13.

Merton, Ambrose 1846 Folklore. In: *The Study of Folklore,* pp. 4-5. Ed.: Dundes, Alan. Englewood Cliffs, N.J.: Prentice-Hall, 1965.

Middleton, John (Ed.) 1967 *Myth and Cosmos. Readings in Mythology and Symbolism.* Garden City, N.Y.: The Natural History Press.

Middleton, John (Ed.) 1967a *Magic, Witchcraft and Curing.* Garden City, N.Y.: The Natural History Press.

Middleton, John (Ed.) 1967b *Gods and Rituals. Reading in Religious Beliefs and Practices.* Garden City, N.Y.: The Natural History Press.

Moore, William T. 1958 Concern about a Bee-Sting in the Analysis of an Eleven Year Old Boy. *Bulletin of the Philadelphia Association of Psychoanalysis,* 8:9-15.

Muensterberger, Warner 1950 Oral Trauma: A Psychoanalytic Study of an Indonesian Tribe. *Psychoanalysis and the Social Sciences,* 2:129-172. Ed.: Roheim, Geza. New York: International Universities Press.

Mullahy, Patrick 1948 *Oedipus: Myth and Complex. A Review of Psychoanalytic Theory.* New York: Grove Press, 1955.

Muller, Friedrich Max 1885 The Savage. *Nineteenth Century,* 17:109-132.

Muller, Friedrich Max 1988 *Biographies of Words, and the Home of the Aryans.* London, New York: Longsmans, Green.

Muller, Friedrich Max 1897 *Contributions of the Science of Mythology.* London, New York, Bombay: Longmans, Green.

Muller, Friedrich Max 1909 *Comparative Mythology.* London: Routledge & Sons.

Mundkur, Balaji 1976 The Cult of the Serpent in the Americas: Its Asian Background. *Comtemporary Anthropology,* 17:249-255.

Murphy, Yolanda and Murphy, Robert F. 1974 *Women of the Forest.* New York: Columbia University Press.

Newcomb, Franc Johnson 1970 *Navajo Bird Tales Told by Hosteen Clah Chee.* Wheaton, Ill., Madras and London: The Theosophical Publishing House.

Nicholas, Dan 1939 The Mescalero Apache Girls' Puberty Ceremony. *El Palacio,* 15:110-115.

Niederland, William G. 1964 Some Ontogenetic Determinants in Symbol Formation. *The Psychoanalytic Study of Society,* 3:98-110. Eds.: Muensterberger, Warner and Axelrad, Sidney. New York: International Universities Press.

Opler, Marvin K. 1959 Dream Analysis in Ute Indian Therapy. In: *Culture and Mental*

Health, pp. 97-117. New York: Macmillan.

Opler, Morris E. 1933 *An Analysis of Mescalero and Chiricahua Apache Social Organization in the Light of Their Systems of Relationship.* Chicago: University of Chicago Press, 1936.

Opler, Morris E. 1935 The Concept of Supernatural Power Among Chiricahua and Mescalero Apaches. *American Anthropologist,* 37:65-70.

Opler, Morris E. 1936 The Influence of Aboriginal Pattern and White Contact on a Recently Introduced Ceremony, the Mescalero Peyote Rite. *Journal of American Folklore,* 49:143-166.

Opler, Morris E. 1936a Some Points of Comparison and Contrast between the Treatment of Functional Disorders by Apache Shamans and Modern Psychiatric Practice. *American Journal of Psychiatry,* 92:1371-1387.

Opler, Morris E. 1938 *Myths and Tales of the Jicarilla Apaches.* Memoirs of the American Folklore Society, Vol. 31.

Opler, Morris E. 1940 *Myths and Legends of the Lipan Apache Indians.* Memoirs of the American Folklore Society, Vol. 36.

Opler, Morris E. 1941 *An Apache Life-way.* Chicago: University of Chicago Press.

Opler, Morris E. 1941a Three Types of Variation and Their Relation to Culture Change. In: *Language, Culture and Personality,* pp. 146-157. Eds.: Spier, Leslie, Hallowell, A. Irving and Newman, Stanley S. Menosha, Wis.: Sapir Memorial Fund.

Opler, Morris E. 1942 *Myths and Legends of the Chiricahua Apache Indians.* Memoirs of the American Folklore Society, Vol. 37.

Opler, Morris E. 1946 The Mountain Spirits of the Chiricahua Apache. *The Masterkey,* 20:125-131.

Opler, Morris E. 1947 Notes on Chiricahua Apache Culture. 1. Supernatural Power and the Shaman. *Primitive Man,* 2:1-14.

Opler, Morris E. 1969 *Apache Odyssey. A Journey Between Two Worlds.* New York: Holt, Rinehart & Winston.

Opler, Morris E. and Hoijer, Harry 1940 The Raid and Warpath Language of the Chircahua Apache. *American Anthropologist,* 42:127-134.

Oppenheim, A. Leo 1956 *The Interpretation of Dreams in the Ancient Near East.* Transactions of the American Philosophical Society, New Series, Vol. 46, Pt. 3.

Parsons, Anne 1964 Is the Oedipus Complex Universal? The Jones-Malinowski Debate Revisited and a South Italian "Nuclear Complex." *The Psychoanalytic Study of Society,* 3:278-355. Eds.: Muensterberger, Warner and Axelrad, Sidney. New York: International Universities Press.

Piaget, Jean 1926 *The Language and Thought of the Child.* New York: Humanities Press, 1952.

Posinsky, S.H. 1954 *Yurok Ritual.* Unpublished doctoral dissertation, Columbia University.

Posinsky, S.H. 1956 Yurok Shell Money and "Pains," a Freudian Interpretation. *Psychiatric Quarterly,* 30:598-632.

Posinsky, S.H. 1957 The Problem of Yurok Anality. *American Imago,* 14:3-31.

Pumpian-Mindlin, Eugene 1965 Omnipotentiality, Youth and Commitment. *Journal of the American Academy of Child Psychiatry,* 4:1-18.

Radcliffe-Brown, Alfred R. 1922 *The Andaman Islanders.* Glencoe, Ill.: The Free Press, 1948.

Radin, Paul 1909 *The Trickster: A Study in American Indian Mythology.* New York: Greenwood Press, 1956.

Radin, Paul 1915 *Literary Aspects of North American Mythology.* Ottawa: Anthropoligical Series, Canada Geological Survey, No. 6, Museum Bulletin, No. 16.

Radin, Paul 1927 *Primitive Man as Philosopher.* New York: Dover, 1957.

Radin, Paul 1948 *Winnebago Hero Cycles: A Study in Aboriginal Literature.* Memoir 1 of the International Journal of American Linguistics. Baltimore: Waverly Press.

Radin, Paul 1954-1956 *The Evolution of an American Indian Prose Epic: A Study in Comparative Literature.* Basel: Ethnological Museum.

Rangell, Leo 1954 The Role of the Parent in the Oedipus Complex. *Bulletin of the Menninger Clinic, 19:9-15.*

Rank, Otto 1909 *The Myth of the Birth of the Hero: A Psychological Interpretation of Mythology.* New York: Brunner, 1952.

Rank, Otto 1912 *Das Incest-Motif in Dichtung und Sage. Grundzuge Einer Psychologie des Dichterischen Schaffens.* Leipzig: Deutike.

Rank, Otto 1922 *Psychoanalytische Beitrage Zur Mythenforschung: Gesammelte Studien aus den Jahren* 1912 BIS 1914. 2nd ed. Leipzig, Vienna, Zurich: Internationaler psychoanalytische Verlag.

Rascovsky, Arnaldo and Rascovsky, Matilde W. de 1980 La Matanza de los hijos. In: *La Matanza de los Hijos y Otros Esayos,* pp. 9-38. Ed.: Rascovsky, Arnaldo. Buenos Aires: Ediciones Kargieman.

Rascovsky, Arnaldo, Rascovsky, Matilde W. de, Aray, Julio, Kalina, Eduardo, Kizer, Manuel and Szpilka, Jaime 1971 *Niveles Profundos des Psiquismo.* Buenos Aires: Editorial Sudamericana.

Reay, Marie 1957 Sweet Witchcraft. Paper presented at the Ninth Pacific Congress, Bangkok, November.

Reichard, Gladys A. 1934 *Spider Woman. A Story of Navaho Weavers and Chanters.* Glorieta, N.M.: Rio Grande Press, 1968.

Reichard, Gladys A. 1950 *Navaho Religion: A Study of Symbolism.* Princeton: Princeton University Press.

Reider, Norman 1960 Medieval Oedipal Legends about Judas. *Psychoanalytic Quarterly,* 29:515-527.

Reik, Theodore 1923 *Der Eigene und der Fremde Gott,* pp. 17-34, 75-99, 100-132. Leipzig: Internationaler psychoanalytische Verlag.

Richardson, William J. 1976 Discussion of Shands, Harley C., Myth or Illness: On the Function of Consensus. *Contemporary Psychoanalysis,* 19:75-350.

Ricketts, M.L. 1966 The North American Indian Trickster. *History of Religions,* 5:327-350.

Ricklin, Franz 1908 Wishfulfillment and Symbolism in Fairy Tales. *Psychoanalytic Review,* 1913, 1:94-107.

Ritvo, Samuel and Solnit, Albert J. 1958 Influence of Early Mother-Child Interaction on Identification Processes. *The Psychoanalytic Study of the Child,* 13:64-85. Eds.: Eissler, Ruth S., Freud, Anna, Hartmann, Heinz and Kris, Marianne. New York: International Universities Press.

Robertson-Smith, W. 1914 *Lectures on the Religion of the Semites.* London: A. & C. Black.

Roheim, Geza 1924 Die Sedna-Sage. *Imago,* 10:159-177.

Roheim, Geza 1925 *Australian Totemism: A Psychoanalytic Study in Anthropology.* London: Allen & Unwin.

Roheim, Geza 1941 Myth and Folktales. *American Imago,* 2:266-279.

Roheim, Geza 1941a Play and Analysis with Normanby Island Children. *American Journal of Orthopsychiatry,* 11:524-530.

Roheim, Geza 1945 *The Eternal Ones of the Dream. A Psychoanalytic Interpretation of Australian Myth and Ritual.* New York: International Universities Press.

Roheim, Geza 1947 Dream Analysis and Field Work in Anthropology. *Psychoanalysis and the Social Sciences,* 1:87-130. Ed.: Roheim, Geza. New York: International Universities press.

Roheim, Geza 1951 Hungarian Shamanism. *Psychoanalysis and the Social Sciences,* 3:131-169. Ed.: Roheim, Geza. New York: International Universities Press.

Roheim, Geza 1952 The Evil Eye. *American Imago,* 9:351-363.

Roheim, Geza 1952a Culture Hero and Trickster in North American Mythology. In: *Indian Tribes of Aboriginal America,* 3:190-194. Ed.: Tax, Sol. Chicago: University of Chicago Press.

Roheim, Geza 1953 *The Gates of the Dream.* New York: International Universities Press.

Rooth, Anna Birgitta 1957 The Creation Myths of the North American Indians. *Anthropos,* 52:497-508.

Rooth, Anna Birgitta 1962 *The Raven and the Carcass.* Helsinki: Academia Scientiarum Fennica.

Roose, H. J. 1928 *A Handbook of Greek Mythology Including Its Extension Into Rome.* London: Methuen & Co., Ltd. (fifth impression), 1953.

Rudofsky, Bernard 1974 *The Unfashionable Human Body.* Garden City, New York: Anchor Press/Doubleday.

Russell, Frank 1898 Myths of the Jicarrilla Apaches. *Journal of American Folklore,* 11:253-271.

Sachs, Hans 1942 The Community of Daydreams. In: *The Creative Unconscious: Studies in the Psychoanalysis of Art.* Cambridge: Sci-Art Publishers.

Sarnoff, Charles 1976 *Latency.* New York: Jason Aronson, Inc.

Savage, T.S. and Wyman, J. 1847 Notice of the External Characters and Habits of *Troglodytes gorilla,* a New Species of Orang from the Gaboon River; Osteology of Same. *Boston Journal of National History,* 5:417-443.

Schaller, George B. 1963 *The Mountain Gorilla: Ecology and Behavior.* Chicago: University of Chicago Press.

Schroeder, Albert H. 1974 *A Study of the Apache Indians.* New York: Garland Publishers, Inc. 2 vols.

Schwatka, Frederick 1887 Among the Apaches. *Century Magazine,* 12:41-52.

Seward, Georgene (Ed.) 1958 *Clinical Studies in Culture Conflict.* New York: The Ronald Press Co.

Shepardson, Mary T. 1961 *Developing Political Processes Among Navaho Indians.* Unpublished doctoral dissertation, University of California, Berkeley.

Silberer, Herbert 1910 Phantasie und Mythos. *Jahrbuch Fur Psychoanalytische und Psychopathologische Forschungen,* 2:541-552.

Singer, Milton 1961 A Survey of Culture and Personality Theory and Research. In: *Studying Personality Cross-Culturally,* pp. 9-90. Ed.: Kaplan, Bert. Evanston, Ill. and Elmsford, New York: Row Peterson & Co.

Sjoberg, Andree G. 1953 Lipan Apache Culture in Historical Perspective. *Southwestern Journal of Anthropology,* 9:76-98.

Skeels, Dell 1954 The Function of Humor in Three Nez Perce Indian Myths. *American Imago,* 11:249-261.

Slater, Philip E. 1968 *The Glory of Hera: Mythology and the Greek Family.* Boston: Beacon Press.

Sperling, Melitta 1961 A Note on Some Symbols and the Significance of Their Change During Psychoanalysis. *Journal of the Hillside Hospital,* 10:261-266.

Spindler, Louise S. and Spindler, George D. 1958 Male and Female Adaptations in Culture Change. *American Anthropologist,* 60:217-233.

Spiro, Melford E. 1952 Ghosts, Ifaluk and Teleological Functioning. *American Anthropologist,* 54:497-503.

Spiro, Melford E. 1953 Ghosts: An Anthropological Inquiry Into Learning and Perception. *Journal of Abnormal and Social Psychology,* 48:376-382.

Spiro, Melford E. 1974 Remarks Made in the Symposium on Psychoanalysis and Anthropology, Annual Meeting of the American Anthropological Association, Mexico City, November.

Spiro, Melford E. and D'Andrade, Roy 1958 A Cross-Cultural Study of Some Supernatural Beliefs. *American Anthropologist*, 60:456-466.

Spitz, Rene A. 1959 *A Genetic Field Theory of Ego Formation*. New York: International Universities Press.

Steinthal, Haymann 1856 *Gesammelte Sprachwissenschaftliche Abhandlungen*. Berlin: H. Dummler.

Steinthal, Heymann 1860 *Charakteristik der Hauptsachlichtsten Typen des Sprachbaues*. Berlin: Ferd.

Steinthal, Heymann 1862 Die prometheussage in ihrer ursprunglichen Gestalt. *Zeitschrift fur Volkerpsychologische Sprachwissen*, Vol. 2. Cited by Abraham, Karl 1909 Dreams and Myths. A Study in Folk Psychology. *Clinical Papers and Essays on Psychoanalysis*, p. 173. New York: Basic Books, 1955.

Steinthal, Heymann 1871 *Eintleitung in die Psychologie und Sprachwissenschaft*. Berlin: H. Dummler.

Stekel, Wilhelm 1935 *The Interpretation of Dreams*. New York: Liveright.

Stephens, William N, 1962 *The Oedipus Complex. Cross-Cultural Evidence*. Glencoe, Ill.: The Free Press.

Stevenson, Matilde Coxe 1894 *The Sia.* Annual Report of the Bureau of Ethnology, 11. Washington, D.C.: U.S. Government Printing Office.

Storfer, Adolf J. 1912 Zwei Typen der Marchenerotik. *Sexual-Probleme*, 8:257-262.

Taylor, Archer 1948 Folklore in the Study of Literature. *The Pacific Spectator*, 2:216-233.

Thompson, Stith 1929 *Tales of the North American Indians* Cambridge: Harvard University Press.

Thompson, Stith 1955-1958 *Motif-Index of Folk-Literature*. 6 vols. Bloomington: University of Indiana Press.

Ticho, Gertrude 1971 Cultural Aspects of Transference and Countertransference. *Bulletin of the Menninger Clinic*, 35:313-334.

Torres, Mauro 1960 *El Irracionalismo en Erich Fromm*. Mexico City: Editorial Paz Mexico.

Tsuchiyama, Tamie 1947 *A Comparison of the Folklore of the Northern, Southern and Pacific Athabaskans: A Study in Stability of Folklore Within a Linguistic Stock*. Unpublished doctoral dissertation, University of California, Berkeley.

Turner, Victor W. 1966 Colour Classification in Ndembu Ritual. In: *Anthropological Approaches to the Study of Religion,* pp. 47-84. Ed.: Banton, Michael. New York: Praeger.

Utley, Francis L. 1961 Folk Literature: An Operational Definition. In: *The Study of Folklore,* pp. 7-24. Ed.: Dundes, Alan. Englewood Cliffs, N.J.: Prentice-Hall.

Utley, Francis L. 1974 The Migration of Folktales: Four Channels to the Americas. *Current Anthropology*, 15:5-27.

Valory, Dale K. 1972 *Yurok Doctors and Devils: A Study in Identity, Anxiety and Deviance*. Unpublished doctoral dissertation, University of California, Berkeley.

Vigotsky, L.S. 1939 Thought and Speech Psychiatry. *Journal of Biological and Pathological Interpersonal Relations,* Vol. 2, No. 1.

Volkan, Vamik D. 1975 *Primitive Internalized Object Relations. A Clinical Study of Schizophrenic, Borderline, and Narcissistic Patients*. New York: International Universities Press.

Von Domarus, E. 1944 The Specific Laws of Logic and Schizophrenia. In: *Language and Thought in Schizophrenia,* pp. 104-114. Ed.: Kasanin, Jacob. Berkeley: University of California Press.

Waldhorn, Herbert F. and Fine, Bernard D. (Eds.) 1974 *Trauma and Symbolism*. New York: International Universities Press.

Waley, Arthur 1947 The Chinese Cinderella Story. *Folk-Lore*, 58:226-238.

Wallace, Anthony F.C. 1958 Dreams and Wishes of the Soul: A Type of Psychoanalytic

BIBLIOGRAPHY 195

Theory Among the Seventeenth Century Iroquois. *American Anthropologist,* 60:234-248.
Weidman, Hazel H. 1968 Anthropological Theory and the Psychological Function of Belief in Witchcraft. In: *Essays on Medical Anthropology,* pp. 23-35. Ed.: Weaver, T. Athens: University of George Press.
Weigert-Vowinckel, Edith 1938 The Cult and Mythology of the Magna Mater from the Standpoint of Psychoanalysis. *Psychiatry,* 1:347-378.
Wherry, J.H. 1968 *Indian Masks and Myths of the West.* New York: Bonanza Books.
Whiting, Beatrice B. 1963 *Six Cultures. Studies of Child Rearing.* New York: John Wiley & Sons.
Whiting, John W.M. 1959 Sorcery, Sin and the Superego. In: *Symposium on Motivation,* pp. 174-195. Ed.: Jones, M.R. Lincoln: University of Nebraska Press.
Whiting, John W.M. and Child, Irving L. 1953 *Child Training and Personality.* New Haven: Yale University Press.
Wilke 1914 *Geburt und Misgeburt in Mythus und Kunst.* Leipzig: Kroner.
Wilson, C. Philip 1967 Stone as a Symbol of Teeth. *Psychoanalytic Quarterly,* 36:418-425.
Winnicott, D.W. 1961 Ego Integration in Child Development. In: *The Maturational Processes and the Facilitating Environment,* pp. 56-63. New York: International Universities Press.
Worcester, D. E. 1942 *Early History of the Navajo Indians.* Unpublished doctoral dissertation, University of California, Berkeley.
Wulff, M. 1912 Beitrage zur infantilen Sexualitat. *Zentralblatt fur Psychoanalyse und Psychotherapie,* 2:6-17.
Wycoco, Remedios S. 1951 *The Types of North-American Indian Tales.* Unpublished doctoral dissertation, Indiana University.
Wyman, Leland Co. 1970 *Sandpaintings of the Navajo Shootingway and the Walcott Collection.* Washington: Smithsonian Institution Press.
Zbinden, Ernst A. 1960 Nordliche und sudliche Elemente in Kulturheroenmythus der Sudathapaskan. *Anthropos,* 55:689-733.
Zetzel, Elizabeth R. 1956 An Approach to the Relation Between Concept and Content in Psychoanalytic Theory (with Special Reference to the Work of Melanie Klein and Her Followers). *The Psychoanalytic Study of the Child,* 11:99-121. Eds.: Eissler, Ruth S., Freud, Anna, Hartmann, Heinz, and Kris, Ernst. New York: International Universities Press.

INDEX

DATE DUE

2/16/81			
AUG 2 3 198			